Abι

Abundance

On the Experience of Living in a World of Information Plenty

PABLO J. BOCZKOWSKI

OXFORD
UNIVERSITY PRESS

OXFORD
UNIVERSITY PRESS

Oxford University Press is a department of the University of Oxford. It furthers
the University's objective of excellence in research, scholarship, and education
by publishing worldwide. Oxford is a registered trade mark of Oxford University
Press in the UK and certain other countries.

Published in the United States of America by Oxford University Press
198 Madison Avenue, New York, NY 10016, United States of America.

Library of Congress Cataloging-in-Publication Data
Names: Boczkowski, Pablo J., author.
Title: Abundance : on the experience of living in a world
of information plenty / Pablo J. Boczkowski.
Description: New York, NY : Oxford University Press, [2021] |
Includes bibliographical references and index.
Identifiers: LCCN 2020056387 (print) | LCCN 2020056388 (ebook) |
ISBN 9780197565742 (hardback) | ISBN 9780197565759 (paperback) |
ISBN 9780197565773 (epub)
Subjects: LCSH: Information society. | Information technology—Social
aspects—Argentina. | Mass media—Social aspects—Argentina. |
Information behavior—Argentina. | Media literacy—Argentina.
Classification: LCC HN270.Z9 I44 2021 (print) |
LCC HN270.Z9 (ebook) | DDC 302.230982—dc23
LC record available at https://lccn.loc.gov/2020056387
LC ebook record available at https://lccn.loc.gov/2020056388

DOI: 10.1093/oso/9780197565742.001.0001

1 3 5 7 9 8 6 4 2

Paperback printed by Marquis, Canada
Hardback printed by Bridgeport National Bindery, Inc., United States of America

To Emma and Sofia, for the abundance of our love

Alguien dijo una vez
Que yo me fui de mi barrio,
Cuando?. . . pero cuando?
Si siempre estoy llegando!

Aníbal Troilo (1969), "Nocturno a mi barrio"

Aunque me fuercen
Yo nunca voy a decir
Que todo tiempo por pasado fue mejor
¡Mañana es mejor!

Luis Alberto Spinetta (1973), "Cantata de los puentes amarillos"

Contents

List of Figures

Preface

Poets and beggars, musicians and prophets, warriors and scoundrels, all creatures of that unbridled reality, we have had to ask but little of imagination, for our crucial problem has been a lack of conventional means to render our lives believable. This, my friends, is the crux of our solitude.

Gabriel García Márquez[1]

One evening in late June 2018, I was walking down Avenida Corrientes toward Plaza de Mayo, in the heart of the City of Buenos Aires. Research for this book had ended half a year before, and I was in the thick of data analysis. I had many ideas bubbling up and an intuition that they might connect, but had not yet found the theme to weave them together. I passed by my late father's office and shortly afterward by the Centro Cultural Ricardo Rojas—where three decades earlier I had taken an enthralling course about the works of Jorge Luis Borges with the writer and literary scholar Ricardo Piglia that forever changed my views of how to read. In the midst of this familiar territory, I saw a sadly common situation with a novel twist. It caught my attention, and subsequently led to the theme that made this book's argument coalesce.

There were two young people living on the street. They were seated next to each other on a couple of worn out chairs, facing the sidewalk, with a few possessions tucked away between their backs and the façade of a building. They had a large cardboard box turned upside-down in front of them, as an improvised dinner table, and were surrounded by smaller cardboard boxes piled up, feebly demarcating their semi-private space on the sidewalk. They were eating from a plastic container, with a can of Coke next to it. Their eyes were fixed on a screen from which emanated a dim light within an otherwise fairly dark setting. The screen in question belonged to a smartphone. The scene was a twenty-first-century, pauperized version of the iconic twentieth-century image of a family dining in front of the television set. In a situation of extreme material scarcity, these two people were nonetheless connected to an abundance of information.

The interpretations, emotions, and practices of dealing with this abundance in everyday life are the subject of this book. I ask: what is the experience of living in a world of information plenty? How do variations in macro-level structural factors such as age, socioeconomic status, and gender affect conditions of access to the array of technological and content options—from personal screens to social media platforms, and from news stories to serialized fiction—that embody this information plenty? Within these broad structural patterns, how do variations in meso-level cultural dynamics represented by the meanings individuals attribute to these technologies and content, and the routines enacted to engage with them, shape that experience in everyday life? Finally, what implications does this experience, and the various configurations of these structural factors and cultural dynamics, have for media, society, and politics?

The story of the homeless youth not only brings up the digital connection to a world of information abundance even in situations of material scarcity, but it also illustrates one of the three major findings of the present study: age—by itself and also as a proxy for being in a particular life stage—appears to be more important than socioeconomic status and gender in shaping the structural conditions within which people access technology and content. The structuring of information practices around age endows the contemporary moment with a high degree of dynamism since people grow older more frequently and predictably than they change socioeconomic status and gender identity—if at all—during the course of their lives. This dynamism, in turn, unsettles society since it ties to a destabilization of prevailing meanings and routines.

Within these structural formations, the meanings and routines of sociality are aspects of daily life in which this destabilization has been strongly felt. Cristian[2] is a forty-four-year-old employee at a small grocery store in a suburb of Buenos Aires, and father of three adolescent boys. He shares two related stories about this matter:

CRISTIAN: [At the dinner table] while the TV is on, there is a play in a [soccer] game that catches my attention. And I tell [my sons] "check it out." And they're like this [hunched over and immersed on their cell phones]. I don't like it.

INTERVIEWER: How do they reply when you say that?

CRISTIAN: They laugh [and] don't pay any attention to me [laughs] ... Nobody gets off their phones. I just had a mom and a daughter at the store. The mom asked the daughter, "one or two kilograms?" And the daughter was like that [makes a gesture of looking at the cell phone]. Three times the mom asked and the girl continued being like that. . . . I told the mom, "Send her a [message on] WhatsApp!" "Yes, we've done it more than once, even at home."

INTERVIEWER: Have you done something like this?

CRISTIAN: Of course! I shout to Gonzalo [son] for instance, "Can you check . . . ?" And he ignores me. So, I sent him a "Gonza" [over WhatsApp] and ask him for a pair of socks. He leaves his room, brings me the socks, and laughs. And I tell him: "Don't laugh at me, I have to send you a WhatsApp to get an answer." Otherwise he pretends I'm not there.

These two stories convey the deep imbrication of personal screens, social media, and messaging platforms in everyday communication. There has been a qualitative leap in the information that people routinely make available about their lives, and in their access to comparable content about the lives of others. This has been coupled with a remarkable level of attachment to the technologies that make this possible, and to the content accessed through them. The client's daughter and Cristian's sons are among many who find it increasingly difficult to detach from devices and platforms. What has emerged from these transformations is nothing short of an ongoing reconstitution of how we conceive and enact our sociality, and ultimately of what it means to be social beings. This is the second main finding of the inquiry summarized in this book.

Contemporary information abundance also affects how individuals look at traditional media. Like many other young people, Isabel, a twenty-four-year-old student from the province of La Pampa, some 400 miles southwest of the City of Buenos Aires, struggled to develop news consumption habits until she found a way to integrate them into her broader social media practices:

I don't sit in front of the television news because I don't like or enjoy [it]. . . . I asked myself: how can I stay updated? Because I'm also not prone to go to [the website of conservative newspaper] *Lanacion.com* and read [the news]. . . . It's not a habit that I have. . . . So, I took advantage of the fact that I do have social media incorporated [into my routines] and that I'm [connected] all the time. . . . I wake up and in the five minutes that it takes me to get up I [grab the phone and] check Twitter, Facebook. So, I told myself "let's read the headlines" [on social media]. Let's say it's like the way I found to . . . more or less stay updated. . . . I wouldn't say informed, because if you ask me, the truth is that I don't have any idea about what happened.

Isabel's derivative news consumption routines contrast with her audio-visual entertainment practices—even when they involve the same screen, the television set, that she so readily dismisses for learning about current affairs. She recalls that a few years prior to the interview she had become

a huge fan of a series called *One Tree Hill*. . . . I watched eight seasons in two weeks. . . . I had a final exam and failed it . . . [even though] I had passed the two midterms. . . . What normal person does watch eight seasons in two weeks? I hadn't even intended to watch [just] two episodes per day. But I [would wrap up] one day watching one and wake up [the next one] thinking "I have to keep watching."

Isabel is one of millions of viewers who intensely engage with serialized fiction on a daily basis, especially on streaming services. The contrast between her routines of news and entertainment consumption, and their respective roles in her everyday life, point to the divergent experiential valuation of these two types of traditional media content. Thus, the third key finding reported in this book is that while the uptake of news has devalued this type of content, the opposite has happened to the reception of serialized fiction.

This is an unsettled—and also unsettling—society, marked by the reconstitution of sociality, the depreciation of facts, and the appreciation of fictions. Welcome to the contemporary experience of information abundance, one that requires—paraphrasing Gabriel García Márquez—little of our imagination and lots of our observation once we stop taking for granted the unbridled reality of the society we have come to live in.

Four Distinct Features of This Book

In this book I analyze this experience in ways that set it apart from most existing research on the broad topic of how people, organizations, and societies deal with a massive surge in the information available. More precisely, there are four distinct features of this analysis.

The first one has to do with the overall framing of the project. As I will elaborate in detail in chapter 1, the vast majority of the relevant research has concentrated on how this surge affects the ways that both individual and collective actors process information, in particular for work-related purposes. By contrast, it is evident from both the questions asked and the vignettes presented in the previous section that I am interested in the meanings that people attribute to the technologies and content that embody this surge, how those meanings orient action, and how they are embedded in larger routines of everyday life undertaken for a range of instrumental, relational, and leisure purposes. One way to understand the difference between the prevailing research and the approach I have adopted is through media studies scholar James Carey's distinction between communication as transmission and communication as ritual.[3] For him, these "two alternative conceptions of communication have been alive in American culture since this term entered common discourse in the nineteenth century."[4] On the one hand, "the transmission view . . . is the commonest in our culture—perhaps in all industrial cultures—and dominates contemporary dictionary entries under the term. . . . [It views] communication [a]s a process whereby messages are transmitted and distributed in space for the control of distance and people."[5] On the other hand, the ritual view of communication "is directed not toward the extension of messages in space but toward the maintenance of society in time; not the act of imparting information but the representation of shared beliefs."[6] He adds that "if the archetypal case of communication under a transmission view is the extension of messages across geography for the purpose of control, the archetypal case under a ritual view is the sacred ceremony that draws persons together in fellowship and commonality."[7]

Carey argues that one reason for the dominance of the transmission over the ritual views is an "intellectual aversion to the idea of culture [which] derives in part from our obsessive individualism that makes psychological life the paramount reality."[8] Yet, as Jerome Bruner, one of the founders of cognitive psychology, argued in his seminal 1989 Harvard-Jerusalem lectures, "Our culturally adapted way of life depends upon shared meanings and shared concepts and depends as well upon shared modes of discourse for negotiating differences in meaning and interpretation."[9] Thus, to complement the individualistic tendencies of the research about what has commonly been labeled as "information overload," in this book I will offer an account that concentrates on meanings and routines, with a strong relational sensibility and an awareness of structural formations. This also goes against the grain of much scholarship on digital media, so often suffused with a fascination for big data and the counting prowess enabled by computational social scientific methods. Adding a novel twist to the old saying, I hope to show that while big data counts might be enlightening, small data accounts can be beautiful.

The second distinctive feature of the analysis undertaken in this book is in part tied to the first one. As stated above, the rise in the volume of information available has both technological and content dimensions. This can be clearly seen in the stories shared by Cristian and Isabel since they entangle screens and platforms with news and entertainment. By looking at shared meanings and broader routines, in this book I will complicate the neat division of labor in communication scholarship that has artificially separated the study of technology and content. This division has arisen from the historical tendency to separate the technological dimension of electronic, print, broadcast, and computational media from inquiries into the content dimension of interpersonal and mass communication.[10] In addition, scholars of the so-called new media have rarely incorporated insights from the work of their colleagues who have examined older media, and vice versa; and students of the news have rarely engaged with their counterparts focusing on entertainment, and vice versa. Moreover, as communication theorist Silvio Waisbord has perceptively noted, "During the past decades, intellectual fragmentation has become even more pronounced."[11]

Contrary to this division of labor dominant among the analysts—further reified in specialized journals, organizational units within learned societies, and sub-units within academic departments—the account offered in this book will be organized by the logic that emerges from, borrowing from science studies scholar Bruno Latour, following technology users/media audiences through society.[12] Because individuals use various kinds of technologies and consume diverse types of content not in isolation but in relation to each other, I will show that this strategy endows the resulting account with more realistic descriptions, greater explanatory power, and more grounded assessments of its societal implications. In other words, crossing subfields and integrating knowledge about objects of inquiry that are often kept separate sheds light on patterns that would have been lost had they not been analyzed in relation to the others.

The third distinct feature builds from the first two. In this book I not only integrate subfields and objects of inquiry that are often separate but also a meso-level cultural focus with a macro-level structural sensibility, and a contemporary foreground with a historical background. These two additional research strategies further differentiate the resulting text from the bulk of the comparable social and behavioral science examinations of the current rise in the volume of information available. I mix methods to integrate a cultural focus on the role played by meanings and routines with a structural sensibility that concentrates on variables such as socioeconomic status, age, and gender. I will provide details of the methodology in chapter 1 but, in a nutshell, I rely on data gathered through interviews with 158 individuals conducted in Argentina—primarily in the City of Buenos Aires and its adjacent suburbs—from March 2016 to December 2017. Then, I supplement the interview findings with data from a survey of 700 adults in Buenos Aires and its suburbs administered in October 2016, and designed to situate these findings within broader patterns of technology and media access and use. This research design will provide data about both fine-grained configurations of meanings and routines, and their embedding in broad patterns of technology adoption and content reception.

This is not the first time in history that members of a society find themselves in the midst of a significant rise in information relative to what they could access prior to that change. As I will discuss in chapter 1, people living in eras ranging from Antiquity to the Middle Ages, and from the Renaissance to the Enlightenment confronted various challenges arising from major transformations in technology and content. As is common during periods of historical discontinuity, this led them to talk about their assumptions, review prior practices, keep some of them, and develop new ones. While there is no preestablished threshold after which one can say that a historical discontinuity has taken place, a reading of both scholarly and popular analyses about the contemporary situation signals an information environment going through another significant historical shift. I take this situation as a transition that makes more visible patterns that are less visible during periods of greater stability, and whose study can yield knowledge useful to make sense not only of these patterns but also of more routine periods and future transitions—should the latter occur, as we might anticipate in light of the current pace of technological innovation. Thus, in the pages that follow I will draw from what we know from historical analyses to inform my assessment of contemporary dynamics.

Last, the fourth distinct feature of this account has to do with the location of the inquiry: Argentina, a relatively peripheral country in the worldwide circulation of economic, political, and cultural influence. To the best of my knowledge, as I will show in chapter 1 there have not been previous large-scale studies of the rise of information in countries outside of the Global North. Furthermore, as is often the case with scholarship in and about settings in the Global North, the vast majority of the relevant contemporary research has adopted a view from nowhere, furnishing findings and interpretations without much justification or self-reflexivity about the particularities of the conditions where the research has taken place. Against this backdrop of geographic concentration and lack of reflexivity, in this book I will present a self-aware tale originating at the very end of the world. While this novelty in itself amounts to a scholarly contribution, it turns out that Argentina has three key advantages for an inquiry of this kind, an issue I address in the concluding section of this preface.

On Argentina as a Site for This Inquiry

When I began the research that led to this book, as often happens with large-scale ethnographic projects, I only had an ill-defined focus in mind: the connection across the consumption of news, entertainment, and technology in the contemporary media environment. It was the sight of the homeless couple dining on the street while glancing at their smartphone that made me envision the topic of information abundance as the main thread tying together otherwise seemingly disparate trends that had emerged during fieldwork. I did not go on a walk down Corrientes Avenue to find that scene, nor did I set out to find the topic of information abundance. On the contrary, both the scene and, most important, the topic found me. The two prior years of research created the conditions of possibility that allowed me to be open to the topic—and receptive to the larger meaning of that scene. Buenos Aires in particular, and the Argentine context in general, were central to creating these conditions. As I have realized since then, there are three critical aspects that make Argentina a particularly conducive setting for the inquiry reported in these pages.

Usually known around the world for its red meat and hearty Malbec, political figures Juan Domingo Perón and Eva Perón, soccer superstars Diego Maradona and Lionel Messi, and religious leader Pope Francis, Argentina has been characterized over the past 100 years by what historian Luis Alberto Romero has called an "anguished and tumultuous national experience"[13] marked by a succession of military coups for the better part of the twentieth century and recurrent economic crises that remain to this day. One of the most salient indicators of these crises has been persistent high levels of inflation. According to data from the World Bank, the annual inflation rate of Argentina was 41% in 2016 and 26% in 2017, several orders of magnitude lower than the record-high 3,046% of 1989, but still much higher than the 1.1% and 1.9% annual inflation levels in the United States during 2016 and 2017, respectively.[14] As is often the case with endemic high levels of inflation, the socioeconomically disadvantaged strata of society have suffered it the most, further condemned to a life in structural poverty.

The devasting existence of structural poverty constitutes one of the three aspects that have turned Argentina into a fruitful setting for the study reported in this book. As I will show in chapter 1, the research on information abundance conducted in countries of the Global North has often taken for granted access to the technologies that both embody and connect to this information. By contrast, in a nation of the Global South like Argentina, it is more difficult to take this access for granted. Thus, a situation of greater material scarcity helps shed light on when, how, and why people might value information so much that they are willing to spend a sizable portion of their income on it. To illustrate these issues with some economic figures, the Argentine gross domestic product per capita—using the purchasing power parity comparison—was $20,308 in 2016 and $23,563 in 2017.[15] This was approximately three times less than the comparable figures in the United States. This relatively low level of average income is tied to a high level of inequality. At the time of this study, the top decile of income earners made almost twenty times more than the bottom decile.[16] Thus, the Organization for Economic Co-operation and Development's (OECD) "Multi-Dimensional Economic Survey" of Argentina for 2017 concluded that "the distribution of income . . . is currently very unequal and leaves one third of the population in poverty, and one out of five Argentinians at risk of falling into poverty."[17]

Putting these rather abstract figures more concretely, in order to not fall below the poverty line, a household required a monthly income of at least $909 during the second half of 2017.[18] In other words, a third of the population lived in households making less than $30 a day at the time of the study. An even more obscenely sad fact can be gleaned through what the Argentine government calls the "indigence line," which is essentially a measure of the most extreme poverty. During the second half of 2017 a household required a monthly income of at least $352, or almost $12 per day, to avoid being considered in indigence, a condition that applied to one in sixteen households then. The couple living in the streets that I mentioned at the start of this book are probably toward the bottom of this group since they do not appear to have a permanent dwelling. Purchasing a smartphone for them would entail several months of their entire—not just their disposable—income. The very fact that they possessed one, and likely connected to a world of information abundance through freely available Wi-Fi, is nothing short of a remarkable sociocultural event that signals how much individuals yearn for that connection.

This leads us into the second aspect that makes Argentina an especially fruitful setting for this inquiry. That connection afforded by personal screens and social media platforms is in no small measure a connection to others. There is a news and entertainment component, too—and I will get to that in a couple of paragraphs. But a major element of the recent rise in information availability has to do with the content that people contribute to the platforms they use and the reactions to the content contributed by their contacts, all of which are constantly and feverishly accessed by many through their ubiquitous smartphones. This content is mostly about sociality, and its spectacular growth is contributing to refashioning it. For the average Argentine, sociality has been a central element of everyday life and much more intensely so than in countries of the Global North. Thus, the Argentine context helps foreground and make visible the importance of a ritual view of communication that recedes into the background and loses some visibility in societies marked by more individualistic and utilitarian associational cultures.

In the second volume of their *Historia de la Vida Privada en Argentina—La Argentina Plural: 1870–1930*, Fernando Devoto and Marta Madero argue that "Argentine society is like a 'leopard skin': strategies of alliance, diverse forms of associative life, multiple uses of the same space, do not separate groups with systematic and differentiated strategies."[19] Strong and multifaceted associational bonds have marked the past couple of centuries of everyday life in the country. These bonds were in part born of relational practices that characterized settings such as the *café* and the *pulpería*—an all-purpose grocer's shop—in the nineteenth and early twentieth century,[20] and further deepened in the leisure, arts, and civic societies that blossomed in the first half of the twentieth century.[21] Cutting across these historical transformations has been the prominence of family life in everyday practices. The resulting centrality of strong associational bonds seems to have only intensified since then, as foreigners have often commented on visiting the country. For instance, Brian

Winter, editor-in-chief of *Americas Quarterly*, reflected about his experience in Argentina at the dawn of the twenty-first century as follows:

> I have lived in other Latin American countries in the years since, and social bonds are tight there, too. But—I insist—there's something special about Argentina. So much else has gone wrong over the years: the brutal dictatorship of the 1970s, the hyperinflation of the 1980s, and the devastating 2001–02 economic crisis, which I experienced firsthand—and eventually covered in my first reporting job. Why hasn't everybody just abandoned the country? Well, many did. But those Argentines who remained will almost universally tell you it was because of those bonds—family, yes, but also their crew from high school or college. The national talent for lifelong camaraderie is surely Argentina at its very best.[22]

Needless to say, not all Argentines who might have wanted to leave the country during one of its many recent crises had the monetary and social capital to be able to do so. But this "national talent" permeates all socioeconomic strata, and its embodiment in strong familial and friendship ties has historically often provided the most vulnerable sectors of society with an extra layer of social support to weather economic and political turmoil.

The third aspect that makes Argentina a useful setting for this study centers on issues of trust in mediated information. Periods of major technological developments have often been marked by moral media panics. A recent wave of this type of panic has emerged in the aftermath of the Brexit vote and United States presidential election, both in 2016. Trying to make sense of what to many were unforeseen—and unforeseeable—outcomes, media commentators and communication scholars zeroed in on the role of the very technologies and content that are at the core of this book. Social media turned into the nemesis of democracy, smartphones became addictive, and the news an endangered species that had to be protected. For instance, in *Antisocial Media: How Facebook Disconnects Us and Undermines Democracy*, media scholar Siva Vaidhyanathan has written one of the strongest indictments of the role of platforms in society, in which he states that

> if you wanted to build a machine that would distribute propaganda to millions of people, distract them from important issues, energize hatred and bigotry, erode social trust, undermine journalism, foster doubts about

science, and engage in massive surveillance all at once, you would make something a lot like Facebook.[23]

There is an assumption that users are devoid of agency and critical capacity in accounts of this kind. Thus, to Vaidhyanathan, "We have become data-producing farm animals, domesticated and dependent. We are the cows. Facebook clicks on us."[24] In order for individuals to be so passive and non-critical, they have to first trust the information they are exposed to. But, do they? Argentina provides a highly suitable environment to probe this question within the context of issues addressed in this book. For instance, the 2017 Digital News Report from the Reuters Institute for the Study of Journalism found that only 39% of respondents in Argentina agreed with the statement "Most of the time I trust the news overall."[25] This put the country in the bottom third of all nations included in that year's report. Furthermore, only 16% of respondents agreed with the notion that "the media is free from political/economic influence"—placing Argentina in the bottom fifth of those nations that year.[26] In other words, five out of six respondents saw journalistic organizations as chained to political and economic interests. These remarkably high levels of distrust in the news are not new. On the contrary, they have resulted from decades of perceiving even the most reputable media outlets not as objective but as presenting a slanted version of reality in relation to alleged political and economic gain. To cope with this situation, many Argentines have become highly skeptical and, as I will show later in this book, developed critical practices of reception and sociability to try to ascertain what they consider to be the real news behind the reported news. In a world in which, according to the 2020 Digital News Report, "overall levels of trust in the news [are] at their lowest point since we started to track these data,"[27] Argentina provides a sort of avant-garde to examine the character of agentic media reception and put in perspective the hypodermic needle nightmares commonly associated with contemporary information abundance—an abundance whose roots we start unpacking in chapter 1.

Acknowledgments

I worked on this book for almost five years and benefited tremendously from the contributions made by many people during the process.

I draw upon data that were gathered as part of a project jointly designed and led with Eugenia Mitchelstein under the auspices of the Center for the Study of Media and Society in Argentina (MESO). This is a joint initiative between Universidad de San Andrés in Argentina, and Northwestern University in the United States, that Eugenia and I co-founded in 2015. We are exceedingly grateful for the support provided by Carlos Rosenkrantz and Lucas Grosman, former and current rectors at Universidad de San Andrés, respectively, and Barbara O'Keefe, former dean of the School of Communication at Northwestern University, during the period the project was developed and undertaken.

The interviews were conducted by a team at the Center. It was coordinated by Mora Matassi, and included the research assistance of Victoria Andelsman, Tomás Bombau, Sofía Carcavallo, Paloma Etenberg, Rodrigo Gil Buetto, Camila Giuliano, Belén Guigue, Silvana Leiva, Inés Lovisolo, Mattia Panza, Jeanette Rodríguez, Celeste Wagner, and Marina Weinstein. The survey was undertaken by a third-party vendor led by Silvia Sánchez. I am truly grateful for the excellent data collection efforts regarding the interviews and the surveys.

Eugenia and I wrote a number of media articles and research papers based on findings from these data sets—one or more of them also co-authored with either Mora Matassi, Celeste Wagner, or Camila Giuliano. In addition to many wonderful conversations about the research project, Eugenia read earlier versions of many of the chapters and helped me with her always smart and no-nonsense advice during the review process. What started as a mentor-mentee relationship more than thirteen years ago has evolved into a wonderful intellectual partnership and a cherished friendship.

In addition to our jointly authored texts, Mora Matassi and Celeste Wagner also made major contributions to this book. As coordinator of research team, Mora played an integral role in the data collection process and was involved in many aspects of the initial analyses. She also read and gave feedback on earlier versions of several chapters of this book. Celeste commented on the entire manuscript before it went for the first round of peer review, advised on the revision process, and read the resulting final versions of key chapters.

Amy Ross Arguedas also read the entire manuscript in an earlier version and greatly improved it. She did triple duty by double-checking all the quotes from the interviews, copyediting the text and verifying the reference list, and providing feedback on the content. With the reviews at hand, I consulted Amy on revised versions of key chapters as well.

Other readers who provided most helpful comments on earlier versions of different chapters include Chris Anderson, Charlie Beckett, Claudio Benzecry, Ann Blair, Rachel Plotnick, Jane Singer, Facundo Suenzo, Fred Turner, and Silvio Waisbord.

Initial formulations of several ideas that I further developed for the book were published in single- and jointly-authored pieces—in the latter case with Eugenia Mitchelstein and Mora Matassi—written for *Revista Anfibia*. I learned hugely about making my work more accessible through the process of having the writing edited by Martín Alé, Sonia Budassi, Silvina Heguy, and Tomás Pérez Vizzón, and from conversations with Cristian Alarcón, María Mansilla, and Leila Mesyngier.

The heart of the conceptual argument emerged during a stay as Senior Research Fellow at the Weizenbaum Institute for the Networked Society in Berlin, Germany, during summer 2019. I thank Martin Emmer, Pablo Porten-Cheé, Lena Ulbricht, and Jeannette Hoffman for their hospitality and for providing ample time to pursue my own work, and the library staff at the WZB for their assistance with reference material. My experience was greatly enriched through discussions and outings with fellow visitors Sandra González-Bailón, Neta Kligler-Vilenchik, Dan Kreiss, and Mike Xenos. I had the great fortune that my visit to the Weizenbaum Institute coincided with Sheila Jasanoff's stay at the Robert Bosch Stiftung's Academy, which afforded many inspiring conversations reminiscent of past times in Ithaca, New York, and Cambridge, Massachusetts. Last but not least, neither my productivity nor my happiness would have been the same without the steady supply of cortados during long hours spent at Röststätte Berlin on Ackerstrasse, and the mango lassi sorbets at Rosa Canina adjacent to it.

A book like this is in no small measure the result of myriads of conversations, and a handful of them had a critical role in the process. An early chat with Claudia Greco made me realize the deep connection between the topic of abundance and facets of my personal life, which greatly energized the writing journey. Long discussions with Claudio Benzecry, Eugenia Mitchelstein and Silvio Waisbord helped me both made sense of key relevant traits of the Argentine context and, hopefully, properly convey them to readers not familiar with the country's history and everyday culture. As the book was coming to a close—and reminiscent to our exchanges around the same stage in the writing of my first book—Fred Turner encouraged me to not missing the forest for the trees.

The arguments I make in the book also gained by conversations about them with a large number of colleagues and practitioners, including Natalia Aruguete, Javier Auyero, Ingrid Bachmann, Christian Baden, Martín Becerra, Lance Bennett, Menahem Blondheim, Sandrine Boudana, Dominique Brossard, Michael Brüggemann, Julia Cage, Ernesto Calvo, Inés Capdevila, Dominique Cardon, John Carson, Lilie Chouliaraki, Iris Chyi, Akiba Cohen, Jean-Philippe Cointet, Jorge Coronado, James Curran, Michael Delli Carpini, Noshir Contractor, Nick Couldry, Guillermo Culell, Roei Davidson, Mark Deuze, Rafael Di Tella, Jamie Druckman, Brooke Duffy, Shira Dvir Gvirsman, Paul Edwards, Wendy Espeland, Elena Esposito, Martín Etchevers, Noah Feinstein, Patricia Ferrante, Richard Fletcher, Brenda Focás, Jean-Francois Fogel, Daniel Fridman, Paul Frosh, Marcela Fuentes, Sue Fussell, Julián Gallo, Karina Galperín, Dilip Gaonkar, Gerry Garbulsky, Víctor García Perdomo, Bernie Geogheghan, Homero Gil de Zúñiga, Gernot Grabher, Lucas Graves, Jonathan Gray, Shane Greenstein, Roberto Guareschi, Francisco Guerrero, Daniel Hadad, Daniel Halpern, Thomas Hanitzsch, Bob Hariman, Rod Hart, Kaori Hayashii, Gabrielle Hecht, Carol Heimer, Andreas Hepp, Mariana Heredia, César Hidalgo, Mei-Ling Hopgood, Phil Howard, and Lee Humphreys.

I also got valuable input from Belén Igarzábal, Steve Jackson, Sharon Jarvis, Nicholas John, E. Patrick Johnson, Candace Jones, Zohar Kampf, Elihu Katz, James Katz, Katharina Kleinen-von Königslöw, Rasmus Kleis Nielsen, Pablo Lapegna, Omar Lavieri, Bruce Lewenstein, David James Lick, Sonia Livingstone, Oren Livio, Wiebke Loosen, Amanda Lotz, Juan Manuel Lucero, Celia Lury, Mirca Madianou, Guillermo Mastrini, Gina Masullo, Lisa Merten, Gustavo Mesch, Oren Meyers, Norma Möllers, Fabian Muniesa, Gina Neff, Lilach Nir, José Nun, Barbara O'Keefe, Wanda Orlikowski, Marcos Peña, Trevor Pinch, Alison Powell, Woody Powell, Cornelius Puschmann, Eleonora Rabinovich, Jothie Rajah, Stephen Reese, Byron Reeves, Sue Robinson, Hugo Rodríguez Nicolat, Hernando Rojas, Alan Rusbridger, Dietram Scheufele, Annika Sehl, Julieta Shama, Limor Shifman, Susan Silbey, David Stark,

Nicolás Stier, Talia Stroud, Oren Tennenboim, Keren Tenenboim-Weinblatt, Yannis Theocharis, Neil Thurman, Benjamin Toff, Jeff Treem, Yariv Tsfati, Alejandra Uslenghi, Sebastián Valenzuela, Marc Ventresca, Mikko Villi, Judy Wajcman, Ellen Wartella, Steve Wengrowitz, Ariel Wilkis, Kate Wright, JoAnne Yates, Laura Zommer, and Ezra Zuckerman Sivan.

I also benefited from comments received during and after presentations of work-in-progress at the following venues: the American Bar Foundation, Boston University, Cornell University, Facebook, Facultad Latinoamericana de Ciencias Sociales, Festival de los Sentidos in Bogotá, Florida International University, the Hans-Bredow Institute, the Harvard Business School, the Hebrew University of Jerusalem, the London School of Economics and Political Science, Ludwig Maximilian University, the Metaksherim graduate student conference in Haifa, the Midwest Association for Public Opinion Research, the MIT Sloan School of Management, Northwestern University, Pontificia Universidad Católica de Chile, Sciences Po, TED en Español in New York City, TEDxRiodelaPlata, Tel Aviv University, Universidad de la Sabana, Universidad Nacional de Quilmes, Universidad Torcuato DiTella, the University of Bremen, the University of Edinburgh Business School, the University of Haifa, the University of Michigan-Ann Arbor, the University of Oxford, the University of Texas, Austin, the University of Warwick, the University of Wisconsin-Madison, the Weizenbaum Institute for the Networked Society, and the Women in the News Network. I also learned from feedback provided by conference attendees at the annual meetings of the Encuentro Nacional de Carreras de Comunicación of Argentina in 2016, the Hawaii International Conference on System Sciences in 2017, the International Communication Association in 2017, 2018, 2019, and 2020, the Midwest Association for Public Opinion Research in 2016, 2017, and 2019, and the National Communication Association in 2019.

Angela Chnapko at Oxford University Press has been a role model as editor. She has championed the project since our very first conversation about it, secured two most helpful peer reviews, provided excellent guidance during the revision process, and gave brilliant feedback on the final version of the manuscript by combining high-level insights with line-by-line edits. Alexcee Bechthold and the whole production team at Oxford University Press were a pleasure to work with. I also thank Gita Manaktala at MIT Press and Kyle Wagner at the University of Chicago Press. Sadly, a manuscript can only have one publisher, but I want to acknowledge their most valuable contributions. I am also very grateful for the criticisms and suggestions made by the reviewers commissioned by these three publishing houses. I do not know who you are, but please do know that I have taken your comments to heart—which has vastly improved the resulting text.

I moved from Argentina to the United States in 1994, yet part of my soul is—and will probably always be—in my homeland, especially in my beloved Buenos Aires. Working on this book has been a fabulous opportunity to maintain old friendships and develop new ones. As I argue in this book, friendship in Argentina is an art form, so my heartfelt appreciation goes to both old and new friends for blessing me with their company. There are a handful I would like to single out since they have made the journey that led to this book particularly meaningful: Gabo Charrúa, Inés Capdevila, Gerry Garbulsky, Claudia Greco, Martín Nemirovsky, Marcela Smetanka, the Thursday dinner group—Martín Agrest, Gabo Chaufán, Omar Lavieri, Javier Neumann, Lucho Poli, Ariel Schafer, and Javier Tabakman—and, as I mentioned above, Eugenia Mitchelstein and her husband Rubén Villán. Back in the States, friends such as Claudio Benzecry, Fabio Buda, Fabián Bustamante, Silvina Chmiel, Nosh Contractor, Shane Greenstein, Diego Kornberg, Rosa Lieberman, Stefano Mereu, Lony Mosner, Giuseppe Pina, and Ellen Wartella made the good moments during the research and writing process more enjoyable and the challenging ones more bearable. A couple of marvelous conversations with German Kral in Berlin and Munich infused my stay in Germany last year with a *porteño* air that made it seem as if time had for once magically stood still.

The almost five years that I spent working on this book coincided with the adolescence of my daughters, Sofia and Emma. There I was, a single dad with an Argentine perspective and a twentieth-century sensibility, trying to parent two teenage girls in the American heartland who epitomize a twenty-first-century outlook on life. Of all the positional and cultural differences that marked this process, our respective experiences of the world of information were one of the most daunting to me because of how much of their emotional and everyday lives is at stake in the digital environment. Listening to them and learning from their worldviews provided the foundation of a beautiful bridge that the three of us built to connect our perspectives and transformed us in the process. I am not the same person who started this journey in early 2016 and will be forever grateful for this opportunity to grow. I love you with all my heart, kiddos.

Evanston, Illinois, November 9, 2020

1

Abundance

The abundance of books is a distraction.

Seneca

No book is so bad as to not have something of use in some part of it.

Pliny

The experience of living in a world of information plenty is difficult to grasp, in no small measure since it is partly tied to developments in technology and partly connected to innovations in content. This is because, as information science scholar Leah Lievrouw and I contend, media and information technologies "are not only artifacts in the material sense but also the means for creating, circulating, and appropriating meaning. . . . In no other class of technologies—such as bicycles, missiles, bridges, and electrical grids—are material form and symbolic configurations so intimately tied and mutually constructed . . . [becoming] at once cultural material and material culture."[1] Thus, to understand how people experience the growth of information available in contemporary society it is essential to attend to both the technological and the content dimensions. Just a glimpse at a few indicators on each dimension gives an initial impression of the scale and scope of this growth over the past decades.

Personal screens have become the dominant devices through which we access information. More than 25 billion cellphones were sold worldwide between 1997 and 2019, including over 1.5 billion smartphones just in 2019.[2] When it comes to personal computers, almost 5.5 billion were sold globally between 1996 and 2019, with the last year accounting for 261 million of them.[3] That figure is almost 20% larger than the number of television sets sold worldwide that year.[4] In the past decade, social media have emerged as major drivers of the use of smartphones and computers. The Global Digital report from We Are Social and Hootsuite estimates that 3.5 billion people

Abundance. Pablo J. Boczkowski, Oxford University Press. © Oxford University Press 2021.
DOI: 10.1093/oso/9780197565742.003.0001

were on social media by the end of 2019—a stunning 45% of the world's population.[5] A significant portion of those who are on social media spend lots of time on their favorite platforms, and for many users the content they contribute, share, and encounter on them has acquired increasing importance in their lives.

There has also been a massive upswing in the amount of news and entertainment content readily available to the public. According to SimilarWeb, CNN.com was the top news site in the United States in August 2020: it had 755 million visits, and each visit accessed 2.03 pages on average, which means that the site served well over 1.5 billion pages that month.[6] By way of comparison, the same site rated Infobae.com as the top news site of Argentina that month, with 158 million visits, and each one accessing 3.67 pages on average, which amounted to almost 600 million pages served.[7] Moreover, unlike the case of televised news in which a person can view only a handful of stories per news segment, any of the users of CNN.com can access a massive archive of stories at any point in time. For instance, on this website on September 26, 2020, I conducted a search using the keyword "Trump" that yielded 97,607 articles. This is orders of magnitude more than what a patron could access via the print and microfilm collections typically available in a public library a mere quarter century ago—and accessible with much less hassle.

Regarding entertainment content, the streaming of movies and serialized fiction has upended the entertainment industry in the past decade, with Netflix becoming both the market leader and the emblem of this trend. As of April 2020, it had 193 million paying video-on-demand customers worldwide, and on July 10 of that year it "became the largest entertainment/media company by market cap" in the world.[8] During the first quarter of 2020, the United States became the country with the most subscribers on this streaming service with over 63 million, and Argentina ranked ninth globally with almost 5 million.[9] This expansion in the customer base has been paralleled by a tremendous increase in the content library, with one source estimating that Netflix had rights to almost 14,000 titles worldwide as of April 2020.[10]

But despite how remarkable these figures about the technology and content dimensions of the phenomenon might seem from today's vantage point, this is not the first time in history that members of a society have found themselves in the midst of a significant rise in information relative to what they could access prior to that change; the quotes by Seneca and Pliny from Ancient Rome that open this chapter suggest as much. Understanding this

history is helpful for putting contemporary matters in perspective, and identifying both recurrent patterns and potentially novel developments.

History

Historian Ann Blair contends that "the perception and complaints about
overload are not unique to our period. Ancient, medieval, and early modern
authors and authors working in non-Western contexts articulated similar
concerns."[11] Antiquity was an initial historical period when such concerns
were voiced, which subsequently led to then-novel media practices: "Scholars
in various ancient settings, such as Callimachus's Alexandria, Pliny's Rome,
and Eusebius's Caesarea, accumulated information on a large scale and
devised new methods for managing an abundance of books and of texts."[12]

The preoccupation with a significant increase in the information available
resurfaced with particular intensity during the Middle Ages due to a combination of discovery of new content—coupled with a rising interest in it—and
technological innovations. This triggered the development of new practices
to manage this phenomenon and an overall receptiveness toward gathering
and collecting information, some of which are both still present in the contemporary experience of print and digital media:

> By the middle of the thirteenth century, the principal ingredients both of
> a perception of overload and of solutions to it were in place. . . . An elite
> of scholars cultivated access to a vast and continuously increasing corpus
> of biblical, patristic, ancient, Arabic, and scholastic opinion and com-
> mentary. They devised new tools of text management, such as alphabet-
> ical indexing, systematic sorting, logical divisions of a text, and the visual
> cues for navigating them, and cultivated a new universalist ambition to
> accumulate material beyond the requirements of a particular profession.
> During the later Middle Ages a staggering growth in the production of
> manuscripts, facilitated by the use of paper, accompanied a great expansion
> of readers outside the monastic and scholastic contexts.[13]

These developments created a fertile cultural terrain for the amplification of the phenomenon during the Renaissance, in part in connection to
the invention of the printing press. This technological transformation did
not produce information overload—the latter's existence predated it and

the cultural conditions for its amplification originated prior to the adoption of the press—but nonetheless contributed to intensify it. Thus, Blair argues, "The Renaissance experienced information overload on an hitherto unprecedented scale, drawing a parallel with our experience today."[14] Prominent figures of this period voiced their concerns about a destabilization of prior information regimes tied to the increase in the availability of printed content. In the fifteenth century, pedagogue Juan Luis Vives reflected that "the number of books is now grown so immense . . . not a few are seized by terror, and a hatred of study, when they confront in every discipline the volumes requiring inexhaustible labor to read."[15] A century later, philosopher Erasmus of Rotterdam complained about the "swarms of books" and feared that profit-driven printers will flood society with texts that were "foolish, ignorant, malignant, libelous, made, impious and subversive."[16] Deep into the seventeenth century, polymath Gottfried Wilhem Leibniz struck an apocalyptic tone when he warned about the "horrible mass of books which keeps on growing. . . . For in the end the disorder will become nearly insurmountable."[17]

Concerns with massive growth in the volume of information carried over into the Enlightenment period, often sounding normative assertions similar to those voiced by academics, professionals, and journalists about the uses of digital media today. German studies researcher Chad Wellmon argues that "increased chatter about book plagues, floods, and the oversaturation of books in the last few decades of the eighteenth century was inseparable from worries about their deleterious effects on readers, who, critics like Henzmann claimed, had been infected by a reading addiction or madness."[18] According to literary scholar Katherine Ellison, these concerns were also present in some of the leading fiction writing of this period:

> The idea of overload is one consequence of the increasingly divergent concepts of information and knowledge during the eighteenth century. Characters are not overloaded by knowledge, but by information. . . . The citizens of [Daniel] Defoe's London break down when they receive messages that they cannot synthesize to create a broader understanding.[19]

There has been a renewed preoccupation in contemporary society with what has been perceived as yet another leap in the information environment. This preoccupation builds on centuries-old tropes, and adds a sense of ubiquity of content that invades even the most intimate settings and seemingly envelops everyday life. Speaking about the growth of media content during the second half of the twentieth century, sociologist Todd Gitlin claims that "the media flow into the home—not to mention outside—has swelled into a torrent of immense force and constancy, an accompaniment *to* life that has become a central experience *of* life."[20] This is because, according to media studies expert Mark Andrejevic,

> the amount of *mediated* information . . . has surely increased dramatically, thanks in no small part to the proliferation of portable, networked, interactive devices. Even before the advent of these devices, all we had to do was go to the library to feel overwhelmed by more than we could possibly absorb. Now this excess confronts us at every turn: in the devices we use to work, to communicate with one another, to entertain ourselves. [Glut] is no longer a "pull" phenomenon but a "push" one. We don't go to it, it comes to us.[21]

In sum, a glance at the historical record indicates that concerns with inhabiting a world replete with information are far from being unique to the twenty-first century. Furthermore, these concerns have often led to negative assessments by contemporaries, who at times even conveyed dystopian views regarding the implications for learning, working, socializing, and society at large. In part driven by these rather somber scenarios, people living in these different historical periods devised possible solutions to deal with these perceived problems, and some of these solutions are still in use today. Moreover, analysts of the trends over the past few decades have commented on a certain novelty relative to past comparable patterns; a sense of the ubiquity in the growth of information available seeps through our daily existence in a reticular fashion.

In light of both the deep historical roots and the current perception of novelty, it is not surprising that the growth of information available during the past several decades has triggered the curiosity of behavioral and social scientists. This has ushered in a stream of studies, usually under the rubric of information overload; other terms that have also been used include infobesity, information anxiety, communication overload, knowledge overload, information fatigue syndrome, cognitive overload, technology overload, and information explosion.[22] Despite the many differences among them, they have frequently shared what in the preface I called a transmission view of communication—focused on the movement of information across time and space, and the processes and effects of this movement. It is to the main findings from these studies that I turn next.

Transmission Views of Information Overload

Behavioral and social scientific scholarship on the consequences of the growth of information has ranged across multiple levels of analysis, from the personal to the societal. Some scholars have focused on the role of human cognition and its implications for team and group dynamics. This line of inquiry has usually either explicitly or implicitly built on the defining insight of a 1956 paper by psychologist James Miller about the limitations of individuals' information processing capabilities:

> There is a clear and definite limit to the accuracy with which we can identify absolutely the magnitude of a unidimensional stimulus variable. I would propose to call this limit *the span of absolute judgment*, and I maintain that for unidimensional judgments this span is usually somewhere in the neighborhood of seven.[23]

Therefore, if under normal circumstances a person can accurately process only seven—plus or minus two—units of information regarding a given variable at a particular point in time, then the presence of many more options naturally creates information processing challenges. Fifteen years later, economics Nobel Prize recipient Herbert Simon zeroed in on these challenges: "a wealth of information creates a poverty of attention, and a need to allocate that attention efficiently among the overabundance of information sources that might consume it."[24] This mode of thinking has permeated subsequent behavioral science research on information overload in a number of disciplines, including psychology,[25] marketing and consumer research,[26] library science,[27] and human-computer interaction.[28]

Another stream of scholarship has examined the effects of the growth of information in larger social systems, from organizations to cities to society as a whole. Georg Simmel is often credited with being the first social scientist to examine this matter in his 1903 essay "The Metropolis and Mental Life."[29] In Simmel's view, the overstimulation entailed by turn-of-the-century urban life was tied to the development of new attitudes and an overall blasé, callous stance toward social relationships. Subsequent studies have taken up this observation, including one by social psychologist Stanley Milgram, who began his 1970 article "The Experience of Living in the Cities" with a telling vignette:

> When I first came to New York it seemed like a nightmare. As soon as I got off the train at Grand Central I was caught up in pushing, shoving crowds on 42nd Street. Sometimes people bumped into me without apology; what really frightened me was to see two people literally engaged in combat for possession of a cab. Why were they so rushed? Even drunks on the street were bypassed without a glance. People didn't seem to care about each other at all.[30]

Milgram argued that the growth in the volume and complexity of sensory information involved in living in a large metropolis led to an "overload [that] characteristically deforms daily life on several levels, impinging on role performance, the evolution of social norms, cognitive functioning, and the use of facilities."[31] The notion that a significant growth in information has consequences for communication and social organization has since then been empirically examined by social scientists working in a number of fields, such as journalism and media studies,[32] management,[33] urban studies,[34] and political science.[35]

Underneath the diversity of intellectual traditions, levels of analysis, and domains of inquiry, there are six common patterns that characterize most of the behavioral and social scientific research on information overload—and associated concepts—undertaken during the past few decades: (1) an empirical focus on the instrumental uses of information, especially its role in decision-making; (2) an emphasis on decision-making for work-related purposes; (3) the notion that there is an optimum of the information instrumentally consumed to make decisions, after which a process of diminishing returns marks the start of the overload condition; (4) a discourse of deficit that foregrounds the negative implications of information overload for individuals and society; (5) the focus on countries in the Global North coupled with the adoption of a view from nowhere that takes the contextual characteristics of these settings for granted; and (6) the adoption of research designs that examine these phenomena from the vantage point of the analyst, and rely on quantitative methodologies to gather and process the data.

First, the prevailing lens has been on the use of particular units of information to inform certain decisions—to the detriment of other uses, especially entertainment, expressive, and relational ones. It is then not surprising that "the prior literature on information overload focuses on cognitive issues."[36] Second, often the decisions in question are work-related, made with finite time and resources, and have potentially high-stakes outcomes. Thus, communication scholar Eszter Hargittai and her colleagues claim that "only a handful of the studies dealt even marginally with typical media consumption outside of the work environment."[37] This is quite different from the dynamics of non-instrumental and non-work information consumption, especially for leisure, self-expression, and relationship building and maintenance—which arguably constitute a large portion of the ways and reasons that individuals consume information. The combination of these first two traits has been so prevalent that in their review of research on information overload, management scholars Martin Eppler and Jeanne Mengis argue that the dominant approach

is how the performance (in terms of adequate decision-making) of an individual varies with the amount of information he or she is exposed to. Researchers across various disciplines have found that the performance (i.e., the quality of decisions or reasoning in general) of an individual correlates positively with the amount of information he or she receives— up to a certain point. If further information is provided beyond this point, the performance of the individual will rapidly decline. . . . The information provided beyond this point will no longer be integrated into the decision-making process and information overload will be the result. . . . The burden of a heavy information load will confuse the individual, affect his or her ability to set priorities, and make prior information harder to recall.[38]

Eppler and Mengis point to the third common trait of most of the existing behavioral and social scientific study of information overload: the notion that there is an optimum amount of information necessary to best make decisions, after which the condition of overload kicks in and any subsequent increase leads to negative outcomes. This is evident in journalist David Shenk's account of the "data smog" that afflicts contemporary societies:

When it comes to information, it turns out that one can have too much of a good thing. At a certain level of input, the law of diminishing returns takes effect; the glut of information no longer adds to our quality of life, but instead begins to cultivate stress, confusion, and even ignorance. Information overload threatens our ability to educate ourselves, and leaves us more vulnerable as consumers and less cohesive as a society. For most of us, it actually diminishes our control over our own lives.[39]

This is tied to the imagery of an "inverted U shape" representing the sweet spot of an optimum at the apex that has pervaded behavioral and social scientific analyses of information overload, both inside and outside of the workplace. Thus, too little information is unhelpful, and too much of it is a burden. In the words of psychologist Barry Schwartz,

> When people have no choice, life is almost unbearable. As the number of available choices increases, as it has in our consumer culture, the autonomy, control, and liberation this variety brings are powerful and positive. But as the number of choices keeps growing, negative aspects of having a multitude of options begin to appear. As the number of choices grows further, the negatives escalate until we become overloaded. At this point, choice no longer liberates, but debilitates. It might even be said to tyrannize.[40]

The discourse of deficit of Shenk, Schwartz, and other contemporaries is the fourth common trait of behavioral and social scientific research on information overload. The assumption of overwhelmingly negative outcomes resonates with discourse prevalent among the actors in other historical periods, as was noted in the previous section of this chapter. The current conversation remains similarly filled with fairly dystopic assessments. In his Pulitzer Prize finalist book *The Shallows*, Nicholas Carr contends that "information overload has become a permanent affliction, and our attempts to cure it just make it worse."[41] Neuroscientist Daniel Levitin concurs: "The information explosion is taxing all of us, every day, as we struggle to come to grips with what we really need to know and what we don't."[42] To top it off, James Gleick, in his monumental treatise *The Information*, claims that "we have information fatigue, anxiety, and glut. We have met the Devil of Information Overload."[43]

The fifth and sixth common traits that are relevant for the purposes of this book have to do with methodological matters. To the best of my knowledge, the vast majority of the studies, and all of the large-scale ones, have not only been conducted in countries of the Global North but have also done this adopting a view from nowhere—a perspective that assumes that what happens in those countries is somehow universal. This overlooks how relevant contextual dynamics in those countries might affect how individual and collective actors deal with information overload. Finally, examining these phenomena from the perspective of the analyst and through quantitative methods is the sixth common trait. For instance, a recent review of research in the management field has found that only four of the 189 papers examined drew on qualitative methods.[44] This dominant approach has limitations in terms of exploring key dimensions of the phenomenon for which interviews, focus groups, and observations are better suited. Therefore, already fifteen years ago Eppler and Mengis suggested that

> a concerted effort needs to be made to employ research methods that can capture contextual factors . . . that are of critical importance for the occurrence of overload. In general, research that provides "deep context" is missing, as most information overload research is experimental, survey based, or purely conceptual.[45]

Despite its valuable contribution to knowledge, the scholarship summarized in this section has under-examined important aspects of the phenomena related to how people experience a world of information plenty. First, individual and collective actors take advantage of information not only to make decisions but also to use for goals related to enjoyment and expression, among others. Second, they draw on information not only for work but also for leisure, entertainment, and relationships. Third, while the assumption of optimality is reasonable for making decisions in the workplace, it quickly loses its purchase in other scenarios. How many text messages is it optimal to exchange with family members in the course of a day? How many minutes is it optimal to spend on a given social media platform? How many news stories is it optimal to read on a particular topic? How many episodes of one's favorite show is it optimal to watch on the day of the release of a new season? The answers to these questions are much more contextually dependent than those about the amount and quality of information required to make optimal instrumental decisions in organizational settings. This brings us to the fourth aspect: the assumption of deficit cannot do justice to the diversity of possibilities in the ways in which people experience the world of information. Contextually dependent issues are even heightened in the fifth under-examined aspect of the research reviewed in this section: the dominance of Global North settings for the conduct of that research and the lack of reflexivity about how the choice to focus on one geographic region might have shaped both the findings and the interpretations of them. This is related, in part, to the sixth aspect that has received limited attention, namely, the need for methodological approaches that foreground the perspective of the subjects and provide greater depth of context than what has been typically the case in most of the behavioral and social scientific scholarship on information overload. In the next section I build on the notion of a ritual view of communication introduced in the preface to develop a framework that helps illuminate these six aspects.

Toward a Ritual View of Information Abundance

Philosopher John Dewey argued more than one hundred years ago that individuals "live in a community in virtue of the things they have in common; and communication is the way in which they come to possess things in common."[46] The ritual view of communication draws on this notion to emphasize the role of joint meaning-making and what James Carey called "the construction and maintenance of an ordered, meaningful cultural world."[47] This empirical journey must then begin with the subjects' own accounts of their circumstances and what different technology and content alternatives mean to them. The ways various meanings both shape and are shaped by everyday routines are better elicited from personal stories than through either structured questions in a survey or preestablished scenarios in an experiment. Paraphrasing cognitive scientist Ed Hutchins, we need to understand the experience of living in a world of information plenty "in the wild"—and not only in the lab.[48]

To this end, in this book I rely on data gathered through interviews with 158 individuals to provide the "deep context" that Eppler and Mengis rightly identify as missing in the majority of the scholarship reviewed in the previous section. These interviews were conducted face to face in Argentina by a team of fourteen research assistants between March 2016 and December 2017.[49] The location of this research in a country of the Global South constitutes by itself an advancement from the existing overwhelming focus on Global North settings. In addition, as stated in the preface, to counter the view from nowhere that accompanies that focus, I reflect on how three salient and relevant features of contemporary Argentine society—material scarcity, primacy of strong associational cultures, and low credibility of news institutions coupled with high levels of critical reception of content—might facilitate data gathering and shape interpretation of the findings. Furthermore, the interviews covered a range of topics related to the connections across the consumption of technology, news, and entertainment in the contemporary information environment. This helps illuminate dynamics that cut across objects of inquiry artificially separated by the academic division of labor that has dominated scholarship in communication and media studies, as I also noted in this preface.

The initial goal of the research project was to conduct 100 interviews, with a balanced distribution in the following three categories: gender, age, and level of educational attainment—the last also as a proxy for socioeconomic status. But as the project unfolded a few groups within each category were over-sampled to explore more deeply then-emerging issues that were particularly prevalent among these groups. During data analysis I took into account this uneven distribution to avoid over-representing some groups in my interpretation of the findings due to the greater availability of data about them. Concerning gender, the goal of a 50–50 distribution was achieved for the first 100 interviews—the final set consisted of 89 female and 69 male interviewees. Regarding age, I aimed for at least 25 people in each of the following four age groups: 18–29, 30–44, 45–59, and 60 and older. This goal was also achieved, with a final count of 56, 37, 35, and 26 interviews for each one of these group, respectively—age information is missing about four interviewees. In terms of level of educational attainment, my objective was to have at least 33 interviewees in each of three groups: those with a high school degree at the most, those who were pursuing a tertiary education degree, and those who had obtained a tertiary degree or higher. This third objective was reached, too, with 39, 47, and 68 interviewees in each group—education information was also missing for four interviewees. Following Trost,[50] I also aimed for relatively balanced intra-category distributions. For instance, within each age bracket I achieved somewhat even distribution of gender and level of educational attainment. The same applied to the two other categories.

Thus, although not representative of the population of the entire country, the interview set constitutes a robust convenience sample of adults living in Argentina. A quick look at the wide range of occupations held by interviewees provides another perspective on the diversity of the sample: high school, community college, college, and graduate students; factory and construction workers; clerical employees in the private, public, and non-profit sectors; teachers in kindergarten, elementary, and high schools—there is no middle school in Argentina; models, athletes, interior designers, race car drivers, and film producers; blue-collar workers such as security guards, cooks, maids, waitresses, receptionists, butchers, handymen, doormen, and housekeepers; professionals such as attorneys, architects, psychoanalysts, accountants, financial analysts, graphic designers, speech therapists, computer programmers, astronomers, and management consultants; and retirees from a wide range of occupations.

Mindful that how people experience living in a world of information plenty is also shaped by structural formations, I supplemented the interview findings with data from a survey of 700 adults designed to situate these findings within broader patterns of technology and content access and use. It was administered in the city of Buenos Aires and its suburbs—where approximately 34% of the population of Argentina lives—in a face-to-face modality by a polling firm, during October 2016. The survey questionnaire was designed after approximately the first third of the fieldwork time had elapsed. It was informed by themes emerging from the then-ongoing and preliminary analyses of the interview data. A probabilistic multi-stage sample design was applied to select households. The response rate was 19%, and the selection followed quotas by gender and age. Furthermore, there was equal distribution in terms of both gender and age groups. There were 350 female and male participants. There were also 175 participants in each of the above-mentioned age groups.

Drawing on the data from the fieldwork primarily, and the survey secondarily, I expand the narrow instrumental gaze of most of the scholarship reviewed above by also looking at other reasons for information consumption, including entertainment, expressive, and relational ones. Consistent with a ritual view of communication, I enlarge the focus on cognitive matters to also include those of interpretation, affect, and practice. Inspired by Milgram's seminal 1970 treatment of information overload in urban life, I aim to capture this double expansion—from instrumental to multiple types of uses, and from cognitive to multiple dimensions of analysis—with a focus on the *experience* of living in a world of information plenty. As Wellmon suggests in his account of transformations in universities during the Enlightenment, "information overload refers to multiple projects, all of which were wrapped up with experiences of material conditions and technological change. 'Overload,' in my use, denotes experiences of excess."[51] The analytical purchase of the notion of experience for present purposes is also bolstered by Gitlin's insight that this excess has become particularly consequential in the contemporary information environment because "media are occasions for experiences—experiences that are themselves the main products, the main transactions, the main 'effects' of media."[52]

The ways in which individuals experience a situation marked by a massive growth in the volume and complexity of information is shaped in part by whether they care about this information. In turn, how information matters is influenced by structural and cultural factors. In other words, these factors mediate between the availability of information and the different experiences related to its uptake. Regarding structural factors, previous research has explored how a wide array of variables influences opportunities for access to technological goods and services, and news and entertainment content. In particular, as noted in the preface, I draw on scholarship that has paid particular attention to the relative contributions of three such variables—socioeconomic status, gender, and age—in this process.[53] Concerning cultural factors, and consistent with the focus on the role of meaning and routines outlined also in the preface, I drew on long-standing traditions of inquiry about the contextually dependent dynamics of technology use and media reception in science and technology studies,[54] and communication and media studies,[55] respectively. Although disparate in their objects of inquiry, both traditions have historically converged in highlighting the centrality of human agency in these processes.[56] To this end, I draw on sociologists Mustafa Emirbayer and Ann Mische in their understanding of agency as "the temporally constructed engagement by actors of different structural environments . . . which, through the interplay of habit, imagination, and judgment, both reproduces and transforms those structures in interactive responses to the problems posed by changing historical situations."[57] This centrality of agency provides the conceptual foundation for the shift—in the apt formulation provided by communication scholar James Webster—from the "what media do to people" perspective of the studies reviewed in the previous section, to the "what people do with media" stance that I adopt in this book.[58]

The historical record offers a powerful precedent about the role of cultural dynamics and sheds light on the current moment. As Blair shows, the emergence of what she calls an "info-lust"—"an attitude towards seeking out and stockpiling information"[59]—was a defining variable shaping the development of widespread societal perceptions of "information explosion" in the thirteenth century. This, in turn, led to associated practices of accumulation and the development of a series of information management techniques: "This new attitude more than any objective case of overload was the most important factor, I would argue, driving the appearance of the exhaustive and universalist ambitions of the largest reference books of the thirteenth century."[60] Furthermore, these cultural dynamics not only make possible the experience of information overload as a social fact, but also intensify it. The information lust of the thirteenth century led to reference books and compendia of various kinds, which then contributed to increase the scale and scope of information available. Similarly, our desire to not only know what others post on social media, for instance, but also our practices of liking, commenting, and sharing these posts, and adding our own posts, further exacerbates the feeling that we are inundated by information that is, nevertheless, relevant and worth attending to.

Cultural dynamics about information are partly the expression of prevailing notions about self and sociality: the information we value, seek out, comment on, and contribute to privately and publicly is an expression of who we are as individuals and collectives, and what we expect from the ties that bind us as communities of discourse. These attitudes about information, and notions about the self and sociality, are often mutually reinforcing. Therefore, understanding the experience of living in a world of information plenty requires being attentive to these attitudes and notions and the patterns that connect them. History also provides powerful examples of these issues. According to Wellmon, "Late eighteenth-century scholars described the problem of information overload as not just a managerial problem but also an ethical one that threatened the integrity of the person."[61] Therefore,

> The social unity of knowledge embodied in the university stood in for the desire to manage and manipulate a surfeit of knowledge, and the disciplinary self, the subject formed and cultivated in a community of like-minded individuals, provided a new figure of epistemic authority. They tied the legitimacy of a uniquely *scientific* knowledge to the character and virtue of the scholar, whose distinguishing feature was a capacity to discern unity and make connections in a modern media environment that seemed fractured and fragmented.[62]

Because of the connections cutting across cultural dynamics toward information and prevailing notions of the self and sociality, a significant rise in the scale and scope of the content available can destabilize prevailing expectations and practices about who we are and what we want from others. If this happens, it might lead to a certain unease about the character of knowledge—and knowledge-making—that was as characteristic of the Middle Ages and the Enlightenment as it seems to be of contemporary society. Thus, Blair notes that during the fifteenth century, "in a culture founded on the mastery of long-lived textual traditions, both in philosophy . . . and religion . . . the printing of new and newly recovered opinions posed with renewed intensity the difficult problem of reconciling conflicting authorities."[63] Similarly, Wellmon contends that three centuries later, "excess and overload confused the authority of knowledge. It confused what counted as real knowledge and thus threatened the capacity of humans to appeal to authoritative knowledge."[64] Andrejevic posits that in today's society—300 years after the Enlightenment,

> it is not just that there is more information available, but that this very surfeit has highlighted the incompleteness of any individual account. An era of information overload coincides, in other words, with the reflexive recognition of the constructed and partial nature of representation.[65]

This unease has most likely fueled the discourse of deficit in different periods. However, historical analyses suggest that the challenges of dealing with a massive growth of information have been met many times with innovations that have proven beneficial to society—some of them not only in the periods in which they were developed, but in subsequent eras as well. Thus, many of the information management techniques that were created in the Middle Ages are still in use today, and the disciplinary configuration of the research university that evolved in the Enlightenment has led to scientific and technological discoveries that have greatly increased the quality of life over the past three centuries. Furthermore, there is evidence of positive consequences in contemporary society, too. A survey conducted in 2016 by the Pew Research Center shows that

> the large majority of Americans do not feel that information overload is a problem for them. Some 20% say they feel overloaded by information, a decline from the 27% figure from a decade ago, while 77% say they like having so much information at their fingertips. Two-thirds (67%) say that having more information at their disposal actually helps to simplify their lives.[66]

Thus, informed by these historical and contemporary findings, I eschew the common discourse of deficit for a stance of emergent valuation. That is, whether particular experiences of living in a world of information plenty have positive or negative consequences should emerge from the process of inquiry rather than be assumed on the basis of normative ideals of optimality in information processing and social action. Furthermore, in consonance with this approach, I will switch from the notion of "overload"—suffused with negative connotation—to the more ambiguous one of "abundance"— which depending on context and goals can be either positive or negative. This ambiguity affords greater flexibility in both listening to the perspectives of subjects and assessing the consequences of their interpretations, emotions, and practices against a more pluralistic spectrum of notions of selfhood and sociality. This is because ultimately—and borrowing from Simmel's own conclusion in his 1903 foundational essay on this matter—"it is not our task either to accuse or to pardon, but only to understand."[67]

The approach adopted in this book contributes to the six aspects of the experience of living in a world of information plenty as follows: (1) it broadens the focus on decision-making to include issues of enjoyment and expression, among others; (2) it expands the instrumental goals to encompass leisure, entertainment, and relationships; (3) it moves away from the assumption of optimality; (4) it replaces the discourse of deficit for a stance of emergent valuation; (5) it counters the reliance on Global North settings undertaken with a view from nowhere with a reflexive attitude toward data from a country in the Global South; and (6) it complements survey and experimental methodologies centered on the perspective of the analyst with a research design that showcases the voices of its subjects.

This approach enables the book to achieve the four distinct features outlined in the preface: an emphasis on the role of meaning and routines; attentiveness to the technology and content dimensions to integrate objects of inquiry and fields of knowledge often separated; the blending of a meso-level cultural focus and a macro-level structural framework, as well as a contemporary foreground and historical background; and the broadening of the geographic scope accompanied with an awareness of the importance of location.

Outline of the Book

Undertaking the mandate "to understand" in Simmel's statement is never easy. A complicating factor in the present case is how rapidly the extraordinary character of information abundance has become part of the ordinary nature of our everyday lives. The commercialization of the web at the closing of the twentieth century, followed by the feverish uptake of social media platforms and mobile devices that have marked the beginning of the current one combined to usher in a qualitative leap in information available to the public. Novel technological and content possibilities have been woven into the daily fabric of our lives with outstanding speed and seeming naturalness. When growing up in the now-so-distant 1960s and 1970s, for instance, it would have been a matter of science fiction for me and my childhood friends to imagine living in a society where a majority of people carry small devices on which they can videoconference, get directions, perform commercial and financial transactions, look for romantic partners, read the news, watch videos, and find out what their friends, families, and co-workers are up to, among other popular activities. What was seemingly magical just a few decades ago has become mundane. Thus, the process of understanding must begin with seeing the magic in the mundane.[68]

Animated by this goal, I begin the empirical journey in chapter 2 with an examination of the contemporary looking-glass: personal screens. The analysis concentrates on mobile phones, personal computers, and television sets—three critical artifacts through which people currently connect and contribute to an environment of information abundance. The survey shows that age trumps socioeconomic status and gender as the main structural factor in who accesses which devices and how frequently they are used. For instance, whereas 95% of those aged 18–29 own a cell phone with internet access, only 29% of those 60 and older do so, which results in a difference of over 66 percentage points between the youngest and the oldest segments of the population. By contrast, the difference between the least and most disadvantaged is 27 percentage points—87% versus 60%—and between female and male is almost 12 percentage points—77% versus 65%. That the difference in owning an expensive device is almost one-and-a-half times larger between youngest and oldest than between wealthiest and poorest in a country with roughly a third of the population living below the poverty line is a remarkable structural indicator.

Until the 1980s, communication practices were relatively medium-specific: we called people on the phone, read the news in printed newspapers and magazines, sent written messages by mail and by telegram, and listened to music on the radio and the sound system. But contemporary personal screens have obliterated this medium-practice correspondence as their capabilities have become increasingly overlapping. Nowadays, we watch movies on smartphones, make calls via computers, go online on television sets, read and write messages on our smartwatches, and check the news on a stationary bike's screen. How do people manage the abundance of personal screens and decide to undertake certain types of information practices in one but not in others? The research reveals the centrality of the meanings interviewees attribute to their different devices and that orient their experiences of them. As sociologists William Isaac Thomas and Dorothy Swaine Thomas put it almost a century ago, when individuals "define situations as real, they are real in their consequences."[69] Thus, to many interviewees the mobile phone has become a prosthetic, an artificial body part with which they have a difficult time parting; the computer a tool they use primarily for work or study or both; and the television set a companion, often turned on but in the background. The phone's prosthetic quality is tied to the significant level of attachment people feel to the device. This attachment is particularly salient in its absence: whether one leaves work to fetch a phone forgotten at home, has difficulty turning it off in situations where it is not allowed, or feels high levels of anxiety when unable to use it, one feels as though an appendage has been lost momentarily.

The prosthetic quality of the mobile phone is in part related to how frequently it is used to connect to another major driver of information abundance: the content that we access, and contribute to, on social media. This is the subject of chapter 3. Similar to the case of personal screens, the survey also reveals the role of age over socioeconomic status and gender as the prime determinant of platform access and use. For example, in terms of who is on social media, the difference between the youngest and oldest groups is 58 percentage points—96% versus 28%—which is almost double the 30 percentage points between richest and poorest—86% versus 56%—and quintuple the 12 percentage points between female and male—77% versus 65%. This trend also affects a range of other outcomes, from access to specific platforms to frequency of access to self-perceptions about the indispensability of these platforms in daily life. To paraphrase an old saying, tell me your age and I will tell you how you live your social media life.

The five dominant platforms in Argentina at the time of the study were, in descending order, WhatsApp,[70] Facebook, Instagram, Twitter, and Snapchat, and the average user was active on three of them. From the vantage point of the users these platforms share a relatively similar portfolio of media, communication, and interactive features. However, the interviews show that, also as with personal screens, people attribute different meanings to each of them and act accordingly. In a nutshell, participants view WhatsApp as akin to a coffee place, a communication space affording a distinct public intimacy; Facebook as a mall characterized by its massive and generalist environment— a convenient yet unappealing venue; Twitter as a newsstand, an information-centered context marked by an informal and humorous tone; Instagram as a promenade, or a venue for an idealized and aestheticized visual presentation of the self; and Snapchat as a carnival, an equally visual but more ludic alternative. Thus, even though from a technical standpoint it is equally feasible to post a picture on all these platforms, a young user might post a meticulously staged and edited picture of an event like college graduation to Instagram then to be shared on Facebook for access by older relatives—and perhaps also circulated in family-oriented WhatsApp groups. However, the same photo will not make its way to either Twitter or Snapchat. Moreover, the coffee place, the mall, the newsstand, the promenade, and the carnival envelop life on social media—and often outside of it, too. Many interviewees experience remarkable attachment to the platforms they use, in the same way that they find it hard to disconnect from their phones. In the words of Romina, a college student who unsuccessfully tried to quit Facebook, "One always wants to fight against the system, but it's hard to live outside of it."

In addition to relational communication and everyday logistics, people use mobile phones and social media to consume news and entertainment. These are the topics of chapters 4 and 5, respectively. People already sought out news and entertainment via broadcast and print media, and desktop computers, but the number of ways of getting this content, the volume available, and the ability to get it anywhere and anytime magnifies the perception of information abundance. In today's media environment, it requires more effort to be uninformed or unentertained or both, than vice versa. How do people inform and entertain themselves? What are the dominant practices, interpretations, and emotions associated with their experience of both types of content?

Chapter 4 centers on news reception. The survey indicates that broadcast media remain the dominant source of information about current events, with digital counterparts as their main challengers. Print culture is on the way out—only 3% of the respondents said that print newspapers were their main source of news. Unlike the cases of screens and platforms, socioeconomic status is more important in predicting patterns of news consumption than age and gender. Television retains significant penetration in the population, but younger people use social media as their sources of news, and thus one can expect this medium to rise in prominence as time goes by. Moreover, and consistent with prior studies,[71] the reception of information about current affairs is highly routinized: 76% of the respondents agreed with the statement "I always consume the same media." However, the interviews show that the character of these routines is different in two important ways from those that marked the bulk of news consumption during the twentieth century. First, whereas in the past people had to seek out and obtain news content—for instance, by grabbing a newspaper or sitting in front of the television—people can now take advantage of the ambient character of news in an age of information abundance. Second, since news is "in the air," these routines are largely derivative, versus the primary ones that were dominant before. In other words, people often get the news as part of doing something else—being on social media, messaging, exercising, and so on—instead of as their main activity and focus of attention.

The ambient and derivative character of these routines connects with two other features of the news reception experience that were salient in the interviews. The first is a widespread assumption of intentionality in the reporting of current events—in part related to the high level of distrust in the political and economic independence of Argentine news organizations, as mentioned in the preface—and the perception that bias in the resulting stories is not the exception but the norm. By chance the fieldwork included a handful of interviews with people who had had a direct exposure to an event subsequently reported by the media. In all cases they were extremely dissatisfied with the coverage, which led to an intensification of the perception of systemic bias. As Carlota, a twenty-eight-year-old graphic designer reasoned, "If these things happen in [her small town], I imagine that at a greater scale it's all super manipulated." The second is the strongly negative affect that is tied to the experience of consuming news. In the words of Ester, a sixty-six-year-old maid, "There is much news that makes you feel badly. . . . So, I prefer not to see it." Thus, I conclude that the perception and practice of ambient content, the enactment of derivative routines, the management of what is viewed as systemic bias, and dominance of negative affect combine to generate an experiential devaluation of the news in everyday life.

In chapter 5 I switch the gaze from news to entertainment. The survey reveals that the top three entertainment activities among the respondents are watching television, listening to music, and being on social media, in that order. Ambiance and abundance cut across these activities: they can be enjoyed while doing something else and are directly affected by a massive increase of technological and content options. How do people manage the different options? As with screens, platforms, and news, age is the preeminent organizer of entertainment consumption. For instance, the oldest groups are 23 percentage points more likely to watch television than the youngest groups, but only nine percentage point separate the richest and poorest, and four separate female and male.

But a survey can reveal only so much about the ongoing reinvention of the routines tied to watching audiovisual content in the home. Contrary to the unidimensional image of the couch potato, what emerges from the interviews is the remarkable versatility of this experience. This versatility applies to how people access the content; the devices through which they watch it; with whom they do this; and the habits associated with this experience. Beneath this versatility lie patterns of entertainment consumption in an age of information abundance that shape not only practices within the household but also outside of it. This is particularly evident when contrasted with the perceived rigidity of going to the movies, the most direct counterpart in terms of content consumption. The need to travel to theaters—which have become increasingly concentrated in fewer neighborhoods—adapt to fixed schedules, and find companions and coordinate plans make this option a comparatively less desirable one than just a short decade ago—which is also evident in the parallel decrease of box office revenues for movie theaters in recent years. The affect related to consuming audiovisual entertainment within the household is overwhelmingly positive, as is the value assigned to the convenience and choice afforded by the abundance of information. Furthermore, there also appears to be a rising level of attachment to serialized content on streaming platforms, as was illustrated by the vignette from Isabel's interview in the preface. Altogether, the account shows an experiential appreciation of audiovisual entertainment content on television—which stands in stark contrast with the depreciation of news and also of other forms of entertainment outside of the household such as going to the movies.

In chapter 6 I take stock of the main findings from this empirical journey through the reception of screens, platforms, news, and entertainment and discuss their key conceptual and societal implications. To begin, the predominance of age as a structural organizer was all the more remarkable in a country where one-third of the population lived under the level of poverty at the time of the study and income inequality was rampant. This phenomenon is tied to a dynamism that seems to be unsettling to society. This is further exacerbated by the centrality of mobile phones and social media in daily life, both in the difficulty of relating to others without these technologies, and in the high level of attachment to both devices and content. This leads to an ongoing reconstitution of ideas and practices of sociality—something the historical centrality of strong associational bonds in Argentine everyday life makes particularly visible. This cuts across cohorts, but manifests differently across the age spectrum. For instance, both grandparents and grandchildren exchange and post pictures on social media. But while grandpas and grandmas often share images of their grandkids with their peers, the latter do not often reciprocate.

The reconstitution of sociality is connected with how much everyday communication practices and information management have become mediatized. As communication scholars Nick Couldry and Andreas Hepp put it in their reinterpretation of Peter Berger and Thomas Luckmann's classic *The Social Construction of Reality*,[72] "The more intense our social life feels, the greater its recursive dependence on technological media of communication."[73] This, in part, is also intertwined with the consumption of news and entertainment in an environment of information abundance. The analysis of the interviews suggests that the positive predisposition toward mobile and platform communication also applies to serialized fiction, but the opposite happens in the case of news. The thread that connects an unsettled society, a remaking of how we enact our sociality, and an experiential depreciation of facts and appreciation of fictions leads to an overarching sense that the ground is shifting. There is no clear end in sight for this transformation.

This appears to be akin to the crises in ways of knowing that characterized the experience of abundance in other historical periods. What seems to be a relative historical discontinuity, however, is the role of the desire to produce and share as much as to consume content. From an interactional standpoint, if the experience of abundance in the Middle Ages, the Renaissance, and the Enlightenment was marked primarily by the expansion of who got to be the recipients of information, in contemporary society abundance is marked by provision and recirculation of content. The "info-lust," to apply Ann Blair's apt phrase, that characterized the favorable predisposition toward the knowledge emanating from the elite seems to have expanded to all sectors of society. What we lust for nowadays is not so much the word of the expert but that of the common person, who shares everything from the banal to the original while watching the lives of others unfold on personal screens. This contributes not only to the growth in overall volume but also in the diversity of the voices that can be heard, which in turn fuels a certain loss of cultural authority of knowledge tied to the existence of this crisis.

The analysis also suggests that while the relevant technological conditions are the same for hard news and serialized entertainment, what explains the divergence in their respective experiences of reception is a combination of non-media ideas and practices, contextual factors, and affective states. On the one hand, the predominance of derivative routines of news consumption, the strong effect of ideological polarization in the perception of systemic bias, and the dominance of negative affect contribute to depreciate the value assigned to news reports in everyday life. On the other hand, the versatility of the habits enacted for entertainment consumption, the trend toward concentrating movie theaters in a few urban areas, and the presence of overwhelmingly positive affect aid in appreciating the worth of consuming audiovisual fiction within the household. Thus, my account suggests that non-technology and non-content variables play a major role in the experience of information abundance. Furthermore, this conclusion was enabled by challenging the common division of academic labor in studies of news, entertainment, and technology. This is not only a matter of descriptive fit but also of explanatory power: it is only by comparing the consumption of news and entertainment, for instance, that we can explain and assess their respective divergent configurations.

Chapter 6 ends on a note that eschews the discourse of deficit and enacts a stance of emergent valuation. Above all else, the ethos of the cultural dynamics of our time is an expression of the agency visible not only in the critical consumption of information—particularly salient in the Argentine context—but also in the willingness to produce and share content. This agency is the conceptual bedrock against the temptations to succumb to hypodermic needle narratives of misinformation tilting electoral processes, social media manipulations, and smartphone addictions, among other dystopic tropes that have gained remarkable currency in scholarly and media accounts during the past few years. This does not mean that technological innovations of various kinds—from algorithms to artificial intelligence—are not powerful, but that their ultimate societal consequences are filtered through structural formations and cultural dynamics. It is too soon to tell whether, returning to the quotes with which I opened this chapter, the balance will tilt either in favor of either Seneca's wariness or Pliny's hope.

However, if the historical record serves as a reliable predictor it will perhaps most be likely a mix of both. But it is not too early, as Simmel would have wanted, to begin the process of understanding. For that, the journey starts in the next chapter with an account of our fascination with the pixels on the screen.

2

Screens

[I have] my cell phone all the time. It's an extension of my hand.

Maria, twenty-two-years-old, college student

Cell phones, smartphones, desktop computers, laptop computers, liquid crystal display (LCD) monitors, television sets, tablets, electronic readers, smartwatches, virtual reality headsets, personal information trackers, and other personal screens have become ubiquitous elements of the contemporary landscape. From the office space to the living room, from the subway to the bar, and from the bedroom to the gym it is hard to think of a space where there would not be people interacting with personal screens. What better way to kill the boredom of indoor running than watching a few episodes of your favorite show on the built-in television screen of the treadmill? Even when there are collective screens present and our attention is supposed to be solely devoted to them, as in the movie theater, it has become increasingly difficult for some people to refrain from checking their mobile phones while watching the movie—much to the annoyance of the more restrained fellow spectators. In a scenario that experientially materializes anthropologist Donna Haraway's prescient work on cyborgs,[1] for many individuals like Maria, quoted above, it is very difficult to part with a digital limb that has become both the quintessential symbol of, and primary conduit to, a world of information plenty.

Not only have the types and ubiquity of personal screens available to the general public vastly proliferated in the last couple of decades, but also has their volume. Besides the global figures shared in chapter 1, there is ample evidence that their presence is also a fixture of the Argentine communication scene. Newer personal screens have been on the rise. For instance, there were over 21 million mobile phone internet users in the country in 2016, and that number grew to more than 25 million a year later, surpassing the 30-million mark in 2019, the latest year on record at the time of writing this

Abundance. Pablo J. Boczkowski, Oxford University Press. © Oxford University Press 2021.
DOI: 10.1093/oso/9780197565742.003.0002

manuscript.[2] In the meantime, older personal screens have remained om-nipresent. For instance, "as of 2019, household ownership of television sets in the country is 99%, with the majority of households usually having two sets."[3] Usage of these screens occupies a significant portion of people's time awake. Thus, by the end of 2017, 93.1% of the population had access to the internet,[4] and as of 2020 the daily average of time spent on it was 4 hours and 11 minutes; that of televised content—including via the internet—was one hour less than that.[5]

As the number of screens and the volume of activity have both grown in recent years, the boundaries across these screens have blurred due to their overlapping technological capabilities made possible in part by the rise of dig-itization. Nicholas Negroponte, founder of the Media Lab at Massachusetts Institute of Technology (MIT), argued a quarter century ago that "when all media is digital . . . bits commingle effortlessly."[6] Thus, in an expression of what media scholar Henry Jenkins aptly called "convergence culture,"[7] the smartphone has morphed into a small computer, the personal computer has turned into an entertainment center, and the television set has become the gateway to an array of interactive and communication options—some of which depend on integration with either the smartphone or the computer.

Even though the screens in question are personal, what we do with them is in no small measure relational—as has been the case with the use of tele-vision sets and other non-screen media in the past.[8] We call, email, and text others; watch television series on Netflix in part because others in our social circles have told us about them, and are also influenced by the suggestions of unknown others made available to us by recommender systems; and we go on social media to share events in our lives with others and learn about theirs as well, not only by seeing what they post but also by reacting and commenting to it, among other practices tied to personal screens. This re-lational dimension is at the basis of what digital culture specialist danah boyd has called "networked publics," which "are simultaneously (1) the space constructed through networked technologies and (2) the imagined commu-nity that emerges as a result of the intersection of people, technology, and practice."[9] This, in turn, poses increasing relational management demands on people's time and energy.

To examine how people deal with the proliferation of types, growth in volume, flurry of activity, overlapping capabilities, and relational demands associated with the personal screen dimension of information abundance, in this chapter I will concentrate on mobile phones, computers, and television sets. I have chosen to focus on these screens for three reasons. First, they are highly prevalent in the population studied for this book. Second, they represent three different kinds of personal screens in terms of their original profile: an entertainment center in the case of television, an information processing unit for the computer, and a mobile communication device when it comes to the cell phone. Finally, each of these personal screens has a different historical trajectory, marked in part by the period in which they became a popular consumer good: the era immediately after World War II for television, the 1970s for the personal computer, and the 1990s for the cell phone.

To start providing answers to the questions posed in the preface, in the next section I will examine the role that variables such as age, socioeconomic status, and gender have in affecting who accesses which personal screens and how frequently they are used. The following three sections will delve into the meanings that people attribute to the different personal screens and how those meanings shape various practices of use. Then I will address a key issue that has become increasingly relevant to the use of personal screens: the attachment to technology and content. The chapter ends with a section that will take stock of the main findings and their implications for the larger questions of this book.

The Landscape of Personal Screens

Consistent with the figures shared above, the television set is nearly universal among the people who participated in the survey: 99.14% of the households have at least one of them (Figure 2.1). The cell phone occupies a not-too-distant second place, with 91.57% of survey participants indicating that they owned one. Most of these cell phones—71% of them—have internet access and have surpassed the personal computer, which is present in 60% of households, in terms of digital usage. Finally, the tablet occupies a very distant fifth place, with 26.43% of the households owning at least one of them.

How does the prevalence of each of these personal screens relate to structural factors such as age, socioeconomic status, and gender? In light of the almost universal character of television, it is hardly surprising that there is virtually no variance by any of these factors (Figure 2.2).

There is more variance in cell phone usage, both by age and by socioeconomic status—and much less so by gender. Whereas 97.14% of the youngest survey participants owned one, that figure dropped to 76.57% among their

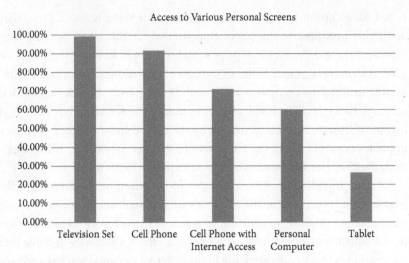

Figure 2.1. Access to various personal screens.

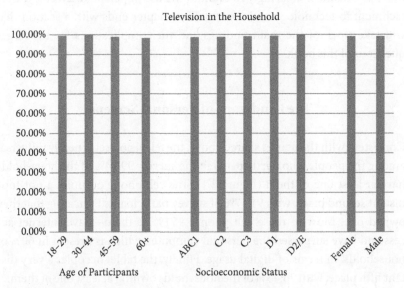

Figure 2.2. Presence of television set in the household.
ABC1: High; C2: Middle; C3: Lower Middle; D1: Low; D2/E: Extreme Low

oldest counterparts (Figure 2.3). Furthermore, while the rate of cell phone penetration was 98.73% among the wealthiest people included in the sample, it went down to 83.33% among their poorest counterparts. Thus, age appears to be more significant than socioeconomic status in determining cell phone

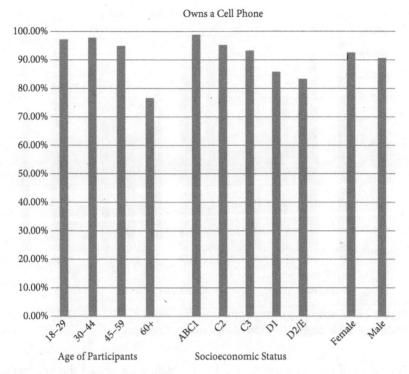

Figure 2.3. Ownership of a cell phone.
ABC1: High; C2: Middle; C3: Lower Middle; D1: Low; D2/E: Extreme Low

usage: 21 versus 15 percentage points, respectively. In addition, there is very little variation in terms of gender, with 92.57% of women and 90.57% of men owning a cell phone at the time of the survey.

This pattern substantively widens in the case of ownership of a cell phone with online access. While 95.43% of the youngest respondents had one, only 29.14% of their oldest counterparts did so (Figure 2.4). Moreover, 87.34% of those among the top socioeconomic bracket as opposed to 60.26% of those at the bottom owned a phone with internet access. This means that there was a 66 percentage-point gap between youngest and oldest, but only 27 percentage points between richest and poorest. Finally, gender played a greater role in terms of who owned phones that were not landlines: 77.14% of female respondents had one, but only 64.86% of men did. However, the difference by gender was smaller than by the two other factors.

The widening of the gap between age and socioeconomic status in the prevalence of these devices is related to a comparable disparity when it comes to who is online and how frequently they access it. On the one hand,

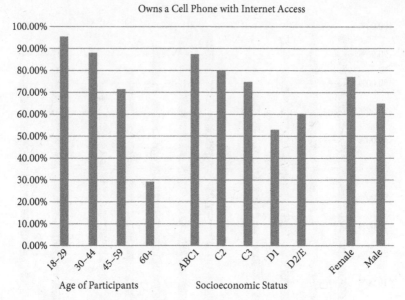

Figure 2.4. Ownership of a cell phone with internet access.
ABC1: High; C2: Middle; C3: Lower Middle; D1: Low; D2/E: Extreme Low

almost all of the youngest respondents—98.86%—accessed the internet at least once during the month before the survey, but only a third of their oldest counterparts did the same (Figure 2.5). On the other hand, while nine out of 10—89.87%—of the wealthiest respondents did this, the figure dropped to almost two-thirds among the most disadvantaged—62.82%. Thus, whereas the gap by age is 65 percentage points, the gap by socioeconomic status is 27 percentage points. Furthermore, women access the internet more than men, 80.29% versus 70.57%, a proportion that is consistent with the gender disparity in ownership of a cell phone with internet access.

Almost half—49.05%—of the people who access the online world do so "almost constantly," followed by 35.42% who do so "several times a day," 11.55% "approximately once a day," and a mere 3.98% "less than once a day" (Figure 2.6). Age differences are also greater than socioeconomic disparities in this case. On the one hand, 93.64% of the youngest respondents were online either almost constantly or several times a day, and 60.34% among their oldest counterparts had the same usage pattern (Figure 2.7). On the other hand, the figures were 92.96% of those at the top and 77.55% of those at the bottom of the income-earning pyramid, respectively. While the spread by age was 33 percentage points, by socioeconomic status it was 15 percentage points. There was virtually no difference by gender.

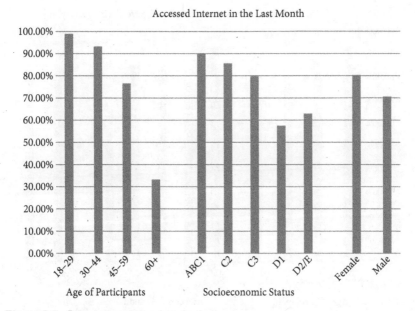

Figure 2.5. Internet access.
ABC1: High; C2: Middle; C3: Lower Middle; D1: Low; D2/E: Extreme Low

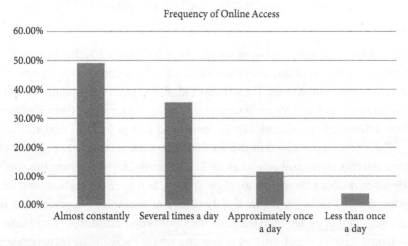

Figure 2.6. Frequency of online access.

Finally, the presence of a personal computer in the household was shaped more by socioeconomic status than by age, which is hardly surprising in light of the combination of the higher cost of this device and the fact that roughly three out of ten people in Argentina lived below poverty levels at the time of the survey. While 82.28% of the wealthiest participants had a personal computer at home,

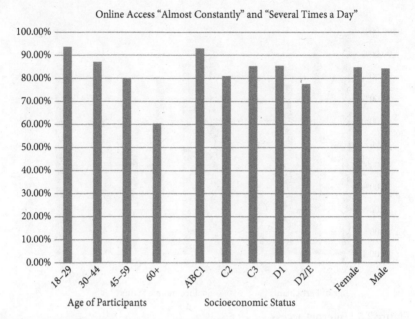

Figure 2.7. Frequency of "almost constantly" and "several times a day" online access, combined.

ABC1: High; C2: Middle; C3: Lower Middle; D1: Low; D2/E: Extreme Low

only 29.49% among their poorest counterparts did (Figure 2.8). By contrast, the level of penetration of this device was 70.29% for the youngest respondents and 32.57% for the oldest ones. Thus, the spread was 53 percentage points by socioeconomic status and 38 percentage points by age. Once again, there was very little difference by gender: 61.14% for female and 58.86% for male respondents.

The evidence presented in this section shows the primacy of age over socioeconomic status and gender as the key structural factor shaping the prevalence of mobile phones, personal computers, and television sets among the population. This helps situate the dynamics of technology access, but it is not sufficient to understand the meanings that people attribute to these three personal screens, which are tied to how and why the screens are incorporated into their daily lives. For that, it is necessary to listen to their own accounts, to which I turn in the following sections.

Cell Phones

The cell phone is ever present in both private and public places in contemporary Argentina. Lola, a seventy-seven-year-old retiree, says that she has it "at

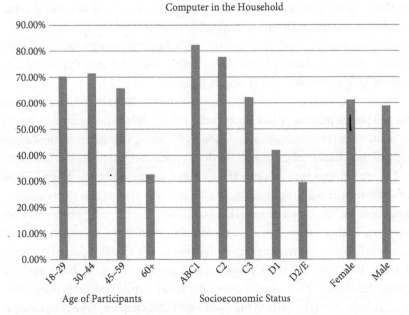

Figure 2.8. Presence of personal computer in the household.
ABC1: High; C2: Middle; C3: Lower Middle; D1: Low; D2/E: Extreme Low

hand all the time. If I'm alone [in the house], I take it with me [even when] I go to the bathroom. Because I'm concerned that something might happen to me and [that way] I can call somebody [for help]." This constant connection with the phone means sometimes that moments that would have previously been considered "dead time" become busy in relation to various practices of use. Marianela, a thirty-seven-year-old administrative employee, comments,

> It used to be the case that whenever I got in the bus I would fall asleep after a couple of blocks . . . [even] during a fifteen-block-journey. . . . Nowadays, I can go to the City of Buenos Aires (from her hometown of Beccar, in the suburbs) and I'm making phone calls, replying to WhatsApp [messages], jotting down notes about something I remembered while going to work. . . . These days [the journey] time is no longer lost.

The cell phone is not only used in a multiplicity of places but also at many times during the day. Carlos, a fifty-eight-year-old accountant, takes his phone with him from the bedroom to the office and never turns it off. "I sleep with my phone turned on, it's on my nightstand," he says. And adds, "I can't leave my house, my office or a meeting without it. . . . If I go to another office on the same floor for ten minutes, when I get back I check if something came in while I was away from my phone." Matias, a thirty-two-year-old community manager, is a bit more restrained in his smartphone use; he at least protects the peacefulness of his sleep: "Of the sixteen hours I'm awake, I'm seventeen of them with my cell phone [laughs]."

From the bathroom to the bedroom to the office, to many interviewees the cell phone feels more like a prosthetic device than a media artifact, partly in relation to this constant connection to it. Some, like Maria at the beginning of this chapter, elaborate about this connection. Santiago, a thirty-year-old manager, says that "it's practically a part of my body. . . . I don't know what I'd do without my phone." Lucas, an attorney who is also thirty years of age, concurs: "It's a part of me. That is, I don't have my cell phone and I get nervous." Pedro, a twenty-four-year old public-sector employee, uses similar words to describe his relationship to the phone: "It's a habit, a part of my body maybe." When interviewees become more specific about the body part the phone represents, they usually chose the hand. Isabel, another college student, echoes Maria's words at the opening of this chapter: "The cell phone is like an expansion of my hand."

Cell phones seem to have a prosthetic quality for different reasons among younger and older interviewees. On the one hand, for young adults the cell phone has a second nature–like quality, a device that they learned to use while coming of age in their communication, work, and leisure habits. On the other hand, for older adults the cell phone's prosthetic dimension appears to be more of an acquired taste, that is, a personal screen they found relatively late in life and whose permanent presence gives them a sense of personal safety at a time of their lives in which their fear of emergencies has grown. Lola, the seventy-seven-year-old retiree who takes the phone with her even to the bathroom, also carries it whenever she leaves her house: "I don't use it, but I have it for safety reasons, in case I need something. . . . That's why I'm telling you that it's about getting old." Marcela, a seventy-two-year-old clerical employee, also values the added sense of security related to having the cell phone with her all the time:

MARCELA: Last night, for instance, I went to dinner with my son, his wife, and their kids. We went to the city (she lives in the suburbs). They went on their own, and so did I. I came back at . . . midnight, and the cell phone is something interesting [to have] in case something happens to you, in case there is a problem with the car.

INTERVIEWER: Like an element of security or something like that?
MARCELA: Of course, totally.

Beyond differences related to practices and experiences of aging with technology, Lola's and Marcela's comments point to a key attribute of the mobile phone: it is the only personal screen that is with them all the time. Marisol, a thirty-one-year-old cook, says that "I have it always at hand, so it's more convenient to open than the computer, or the television, which I have to turn on and connect. . . . With this (pointing to the cell phone) I already have it and it's *always* connected" (emphasis in the original). Gabriel, a thirty-two-year-old insurance salesman, shares a similar sentiment: "I have the cell phone with me a lot, many hours of my day mainly because of my job. . . . Today it is possible not only to [check] messages and emails, but also issue a policy through the cell phone. . . . Without the phone I couldn't do my job nowadays."

These digital body parts are used variously for managing the stuff of everyday life, accomplishing work tasks, and fulfilling entertainment needs. Yet the first category of use is the most prevalent of the three. Jose, a forty-five-year-old clerical employee who is visually impaired, has a phone with "apps that guide you wherever you go . . . [like] *Lazarillo*, that [tracks] the bus route and tells you the street [the bus is driving on], the intersecting streets, [and] everything around, like an ATM machine, an ice cream shop, a pizza place, a subway station." Miriam, who is sixty-nine years of age and a Jehovah's Witness, says the many things she does with her phone include "also preach[ing]. . . . We have the presentations loaded, the videos to show people. . . . There are people who perhaps don't like hearing you but if you show them the videos you grab their attention. For instance, what is the Kingdom of God? The video explains it in 2 or 3 minutes . . . and from there they get the information on the biblical text."

Individual and group communication are key uses of the cell phone during everyday management and, as I will show at greater length in chapter 3, WhatsApp is central to this type of practice.[10] Alicia, a forty-two-year-old beautician, says that "I use [the phone] to be connected. Because of wasap [*sic*] it's fast to connect with my kids, send a picture rapidly, almost in real time. [I] send a picture about something from here to my sister who lives in France." Sonia, who is forty-six years of age and has an administrative job at a school, also stresses the centrality of WhatsApp in her everyday cell phone practices:

I always have [the phone] because of the kids, to be connected in case something happens to them or whatever. I also take it to see the news . . . maybe if I'm on the train or in the bus. But I use it most of all for the WhatsApp messages, the groups of third grade, sixth grade [parents]. . . . I realize that I use the cell phone more since WhatsApp showed up, before I didn't use it so much.

Work-related uses are widespread as well—especially among middle-age interviewees—and WhatsApp also plays an important role in this context. Rosario, a thirty-two-year-old Pilates instructor says, "I use [the cell phone] a lot for work, to organize the schedule of my . . . classes, especially WhatsApp." Gabriel, who is an insurance agent, also thirty-two, puts it bluntly: "My office is the cell phone nowadays." Dora, a fifty-five-year-old clerical employee, notes that she has to "have [the cell phone] always on because of work. . . . The emails come [and] . . . I have to reply to them. I use it mostly for communication [purposes], interviews, clients." For Marcos, who is forty-nine and works as a security guard, the connection between cell phone use and work practice is intense: "I'm with the phone all day, out and about with the phone . . . because of work. I have many clients, if one doesn't call me, the other does it, and all day like that. I have the cell phone turned on all day."

Young interviewees in particular also use their cell phones for entertainment purposes, albeit to a much lesser extent than for everyday management and work activities. A common entertainment use has to do with listening to music or podcasts. Sebastian, a twenty-four-year-old who works in marketing, comments, "I listen to a lot of music and touch the cell phone directly only once because I have the blue tooth headphones. . . . That's especially good to travel by train or bus because otherwise it gets complicated." Pedro, who is an employee in a public-sector office and is the same age as Sebastian, also listens to music as part of a broad portfolio of cell phone practices: "I use the cell phone in multiple ways: calls, messages, WhatsApp, Facebook, sometimes Netflix. I don't know, videos . . . music, I sometimes listen to the radio [on it], too."

The widespread use of cell phones triggered in many interviewees reflections about the broader impact of this type of personal screen. Some people also spoke about personal computers and television sets but much less than about cell phones. This might be because cell phones are more recent additions and—as I will show in a subsequent section—tend to be used more intensely than the former.

Some of the reflections have a positive tone and highlight novel communication possibilities. For instance, Marcela, the clerical employee, praised the efficiency of texting over the more cumbersome practice of talking on the phone:

If you make a call then you have to talk and [it's like] "how's this, how's that." You can't just say what you want to say, you see? For instance, I use WhatsApp a lot with my children. So, in the evening I ask my daughter, who has two kids, "how're they?" or "did you take them to the doctor yesterday?" . . . I think it's fascinating because at that time she's probably cooking dinner, feeding the kids, giving them a bath or putting them to sleep. And then she doesn't have to answer. Whereas if I called her . . . she would have to answer.

Yet the majority of the commentary centers on perceived negative implications. Celia and Silvia are, like Marcela, in their seventies and also have grandchildren. But unlike Marcela, they are bothered by phone-related family interactions. Celia "considers that we are over-communicated. . . . My grandchildren came [for dinner] . . . [and] got offended [by my request to] put their phones away." Silvia shares a similar family scene: "I have seven grandkids who're all day with that (referring to their cell phones). . . . They come to visit me but I observe that what's [on the screen] interests them more . . . or that they're laughing about something that the rest of the table doesn't understand. . . . It's like they laugh in secret, they laugh and maybe we're crying because my brother is sick." This type of complaint about co-located miscommunication related to cell phone use is not exclusive of intergenerational relationships. Kevin, a twenty-three-year-old college student, notes that "it happens to me many times that I'm in a gathering with friends and they're on their cell phones and I don't like that."

In some cases, interviewees reflect both positive and negative implications of cell phone use—though often giving more weight to the latter than to the former. Marta, a fifty-two-year-old psychoanalyst, confesses feeling "a bit prisoner (laughs) . . . because every time the cell phone beeps I have to answer the Wasap [sic], emails and the whole nine yards. . . . So I'm more alert [than before]. . . . The good thing is that . . . the other day was the birthday of my mother [who lives overseas] so my relatives sent me a video [of the celebration]. It was like being there, at a distance but [still] nice." Tatiana, a school librarian, notes that the extensive use of mobile phones "in a certain way makes [life] easier because maybe there would more miscommunication [otherwise]. But it is tremendous that you are always attentive to or knowing where the other person is, what she's doing. Sometimes not even [interested in that], but you're messing around, waiting and [then send a message] 'how're you, everything OK?'" Emanuel, who lives in Arequito, a small town of fewer than 7,000 inhabitants located over 300 miles away from the City of Buenos Aires, says,

> It's good that it informs you, but it also moves you away [from others]. There isn't a lot to do in Arequito's downtown, so before when we used to go out you would meet lots of people in the town square, and nowadays you don't find almost anybody. And, of course, what for? You can put together a group on WhatsApp and talk like that.

The overlapping capabilities of the different personal screens means that in addition to deciding for what purposes to use their cell phones, people also have to figure out whether to undertake those practices with the cell phone or with the other personal screens to which they have access. In the words of Juana, a twenty-year-old college student: "I could easily stop using the applications on the cell phone and use them in the computer. . . . I can transfer the activities I do on one to the other. But it's more convenient for me to do them on the phone. Or maybe I just got used to doing certain things on the phone, others on the computer, and others on the TV." Martin, who is also twenty years of age and goes to college, echoes Juana's sentiment when it comes to using the phone for entertainment purposes:

> I don't grab the computer for entertainment, I get the phone. It's more practical. . . . I really like to sit down on a couch which is in a room that is lit in a way different from the rest of the house [and] that makes me feel differently. And you don't sit there with the computer, you do it with the phone. Maybe people used to sit by the magazine holder and grabbed a magazine before. Nowadays, it's like you go with your phone.

Cell phones, television sets, and personal computers are interrelated in an ecosystem of personal screen use. The practices that connect cell phones and television sets are different from those that tie cell phones and computers. The first pair is often marked by concurrent use, whereas the second pair is usually characterized by non-simultaneous practices of either displacement or complementarity.

Agustin, the factory worker, says, "When I turn on the TV I'm also with my phone! And if I'm not with the TV I'm still with my phone. But, constantly!" Similarly, Jorge, a nineteen-year-old college student, comments that "whenever I'm with the television, I'm also with the phone by my side." He adds that there are no moments in which the content on the television set gets his full attention because "it's something I do in passing. Even if a soccer game is on, the most important thing is to listen to [what's going on] and I can do both things [at once]." In a country in which soccer is as close as it gets to a pagan religion, Jorge's practice of second screening is quite striking. However, people tie together the cell phone and the television set not only through second screening. Another typical way in which this connection is enacted is by having text messages prompt television viewing. Lucila, who is twenty-seven years of age and works in a media company, says that "many times my television consumption is highly mediated by WhatsApp. . . . Like [getting a message that says] 'check this out.' It's a notice. . . . For instance, yesterday there was [politician's name] on *Intratables* (a popular program) and [friends] sent me a WhatsApp [message that the politician was in the show]."

For some interviewees, cell phone use has displaced computer use. Jose, the administrative employee, states, "I don't pay much attention to the computer since I have everything on the cell phone." This is consistent with the experience of Sofia, a twenty-nine-year-old student and administrative assistant, who adds that "I even download and view on the cell phone the PowerPoint [slides] I have to study." Sara, another college student, shares a similar sentiment: "I have a computer, but I don't turn it on very much. . . . However, I'm all the time with my cell phone on." Marta, the psychoanalyst, concludes, "My relationship with the notebook has been practically substituted by [that with] the cell phone." Patricia, a fifty-one-year-old schoolteacher, states, "What happens with the computer is that nowadays I use the cell phone for everything. I replaced [the computer] a lot [for] doing research, using Google, checking mails, and of course everything that is chatting I do on the phone." Laura, who is in college and is twenty years of age, says that "you have all the computer stuff on the cell phone." Sonia, the school assistant, confesses,

I think I don't touch [the computer] . . . because everything I used to do with it you can now do with your phone. Because before to check Facebook you had to log in on the computer, but now you have it on the cell phone. You can also look at YouTube on the cell phone. And Google, which is what I use the most for the kids who need information at school, I also do it on the phone these days.

For other interviewees, however, their practices regarding the cell phone and the computer have a relationship of complementarity. Leon, a thirty-five-year-old lawyer, comments that "I use the computer for work and to watch series. And the cell phone to communicate, talk on the phone, access social media, read the news. . . . I think they're complementary." Luciana, a thirty-year-old accountant, agrees: "I have the cell phone mostly for social stuff; I use it for social networks like Facebook and LinkedIn, and in everyday life, maps and those kinds of things. And the computer for work." Consistent with what Leon and Luciana mention, Humberto, who is a businessman, and an attorney, zeroes in on a key aspect of how the computer is used and experienced by many interviewees by noting that "I can use it with Skype, as a work tool." The next section is devoted to unpacking this emerging meaning of the personal computer as a tool.

Personal Computers

The personal computer was the icon at the center of the notion of media convergence. Once upon a time it also sat at the top of the hierarchy of networked devices, and to some of our interviewees it still does. The ways in which Santiago, the manager, uses his computer illustrate this:

> I barely use the cell phone because I believe I might be the last person to have an old one [that can't] have WhatsApp, so people don't write to me anymore [laughs]. . . . I use the computer for everything. Since I don't have television or radio, it is through the computer that I listen to radio, watch TV, movies, play videogames, use social media, write . . . The computer is my life [laughs].

Santiago's comment also points to the perceived versatility of the personal computer, like that of the cell phone. This versatility is sometimes present in the discourse of interviewees. Fabian, who is forty-three-years-old and works as a doorman, states:

I use the computer to send emails . . . work with Excel and Word . . . [but] above all to send emails. I think it's much more convenient to send them from the computer than from the cell phone. [I also] watch videos on YouTube, maybe check Facebook, but very little [since] I use Facebook more on the cell phone. What else? Well, maybe once in a while I like to watch a movie . . . and connect [the computer] to the television [set].

What is particularly noteworthy about Fabian's personal computer practices is that even for a person who does not have a desk job and is not pursuing an education degree, the uses that first come to mind are of an instrumental kind like sending emails and working with software such as Excel and Word. This points to a broader pattern across interviews in which the primary use of the personal computer is work- and/or study-related—the latter in case of those pursuing a degree. Thus, Lucila stresses that she uses the computer "for work, not for silly things." Horacio, a fifty-one-year-old pharmaceutical sales representative, concurs: "The computer is for work: emails, bank account [stuff]." This also applies to Dora, an employee who is fifty-five years of age: "The computer is . . . not to play . . . [but] to work."

Many of the interviewees who are students express a similar prevalence of instrumental uses, in their case focused on school tasks. Martin states, "I can't think of a time that I grab the computer for something that is not school-related." Ana, who is working on her undergraduate thesis, agrees: "I use the computer almost exclusively to do things for school." Even those in college who enact a broader repertoire of computer practices stress out the dominance of instrumental ones. As Maribel, a twenty-one-year-old student, puts it, the computer is "mainly for school stuff, and maybe a bit to play music, or very rarely to check Facebook or Twitter."

The dominance of the computer's symbolic identity as a tool is complemented by its other types of uses, albeit in a much smaller proportion. Furthermore, these secondary uses tend to be more prevalent among middle-age and older interviewees than among their younger counterparts. Some of these secondary uses revolve around the information processing capabilities of personal computers. Nicolas, a fifty-five-year-old accountant, notes that he uses "the desktop [for] information consumption, emails, and . . . some stuff related to work." Another type of secondary use is more transactional, often tied to doing errands. Cecilia, who is a housewife and is forty-nine years of age says: "I do all the banking access via the Internet because of home-banking, so I have to open that daily during the work week because I make all of our utilities payments through that medium. And then I check the email, not every day, but once in a while." News and entertainment consumption are other purposes for which some of our interviewees use their computers. That is the case of Clara, a thirty-year-old psychologist, who "also use[s] the computer . . . to read the news, watch videos and series, and sometimes play videogames, too."

Because most interviewees think of their computers as tools, it is not surprising that they tend to use them most for work or study. To Juanita, a fifty-six-year-old school-teacher, "The computer is for work. It is from eight [in the morning] until four in the afternoon." Joaquin, who is a technician and twenty-eight years of age, shares a similar viewpoint: "I have the computer from work that I try not to open it unless I'm at work. . . . I try to avoid it outside of work hours." Therefore, many interviewees refrain from using the computer during non-work times and places. Along these lines, Lucas notes that "at home I don't use the computer . . . unless I have to work over the weekend." Marina, a twenty-two-year-old financial analyst, notes that "once upon a time I used the computer a lot. These days the truth is that I'm all day in front of a computer at work, [so] the last thing I want to do during my spare time is to use the computer."

Computer use in the home, instead of in the workplace, can sometimes also involve the television set. For example, one might project content obtained through their computer onto their television. Echoing Fabian's statements at the beginning of this section, Estanislao, a twenty-seven-year-old clerical employee, comments that "once in a while I watch a movie [on the computer] . . . and hook it up to the television set." Another way in which interviewees connect computer and television use in their daily lives is through a second screen practice—although this is less common than the use of the cell phone as the second screen. This is illustrated in the following excerpt of an interview with fifty-eight-year-old Matilde:

MATILDE: I work at night many times. I like it because I'm more at ease. During the day maybe I take a first pass at something and then I work on it [in the evening]. I like the night shift. And many times [I work] with the television on [and] in the background. And if I hear something that interests me, I turn around.
INTERVIEWER: Why do you have the television on and in the background?
MATILDE: Because sometimes it is a company in silence.

It is to this frequent companion in people's homes that I turn next.

Television Sets

If people use their cell phones primarily for the relational dimension of eve-ryday life and their computers mainly for work and study, the consumption of news and entertainment content is by far the main driver of television use. Agustin, a nineteen-year-old factory worker says, "The television set [is for] entertainment." Manuela, a housewife in her fifties, concurs, noting that the TV set is "for movies and series . . . and, well, the smart TV to watch Netflix [too]."

Matilde's comments about her concurrent use of the computer and the tel-evision set point to a strong pattern across many interviews: the sheer sound coming out of the artifact is an important aspect of television use. As Matilde puts it, for many people the TV is like a companion. Humberto, a forty-nine-year-old attorney and businessman, notes that "in general the TV is on as a form of companionship. . . . I have a four-year-old daughter and a two-year-old son who . . . are playing or wandering around [the apartment] and the tel-evision is always on with a kids' show, cartoons or something like that." Sara, the college student, expresses a similar experience when she is at home: "[The television set] is always on, like a companion. It's not that I'm attentive to it all the time, but it's like a company." Angeles, a seventy-nine-year-old re-tiree adds that for her, "the noise 'chin, chin, chin' is essential! I think that the same happened to me with the radio when I was younger, but not now. [Interviewer: Does the TV play that role?]. You know, that's right."

As Angeles's comment suggests, people also see the radio as a companion. For some interviewees, both media artifacts play that role in their lives, usu-ally at different times of the day. Graciela, a sixty-year-old public-sector em-ployee, comments that "I turn the radio on when I get here [workplace] at 7 am because it's a company. That whispering keeps my head free to work while at the same time being alert to the news. . . . When I get back home I turn the television on. . . . It has the same function that the radio has here." For others, the idea of the radio as a companion helps them frame how they use their tel-evision sets. Cristina, who is fifty-nine years of age, says that "normally [the TV] is on in some channel while I am out and about. . . . I use it like a radio." In a similar vein, Jazmin, a forty-four-year-old school assistant, says, "I don't use the radio a lot, but I do use [the TV] like that. . . . I used to listen to the radio a lot and slept with it turned on. But then I got tired of it. I now have the television on for sure because [otherwise] there is a lot of silence in the house."

Jazmin's reflection, like that of Matilde at the end of the last section, points to the idea that seeing the television as a companion is related to a certain discomfort with the experience of silence and that the sounds emanating from the television set act as a suitable palliative. Angeles, the retiree, comments that "in the morning I turn on the television because I don't like to be in silence. But I don't look at it. I live by myself and have to clean the house . . . and I hate, hate cleaning the house . . . so at least I listen to people talking. . . . Because I'm telling you, I don't like silence." Miriam, who's in her late sixties, shares a similar sentiment: "I sleep with the radio on . . . because I don't like silence, it bothers me." The discomfort regarding silence is not an exclusive province of the older interviewees. Isabel, who is in college, says that she "was living alone . . . and feeling badly [about it]. So [my parents] bought me a television set. Because I had told them 'mom, I need to hear [something], to have a background noise.' It was too much silence, it overwhelmed me."

Using the television set as a companion to alleviate silence is tied to a certain ambient disposition toward news and entertainment content—a topic to which I will return in chapters 4 and 5, respectively. Maribel, the college student, is "generally doing other things and [the TV] is in the background. I pay minimum attention [to it]. . . . That is, I generally don't sit down and only watch television. I'm always doing something else [too]." Hector, who is forty-seven years of age and manages a store, has a similar orientation to the radio which is "on at work, it sort of keeps me company . . . as noise, and whenever I can I listen to it, I prick up my ears (*paro la oreja*)." Matilde links this ambient disposition to "living so connectedly that we don't want to miss anything. . . . So, if I hear [something in the news that matters to me] then I stop what I'm doing, turn around, and watch the [program]."

I will address this sense of connectedness in the following section, but for now it is worth stressing that even though most interviewees relate their ambient disposition to information about current events, some others also experience it regarding entertainment content. Kevin says that he has the television set turned on "a lot. It's like normal people who when they wake up turn on the TV and leave the news in the background, well, I put a series on, one that I've already watched, and it's in the background so that it's there all day. . . . The same with Spotify. Spotify and Netflix are two things that I have there and use them as background, constantly."

Even though the ambient disposition applies to both news and entertainment, the affect associated with consuming these two types of content differs. On the one hand, watching news stories tends to be linked to negative affective states—an issue I will address more extensively in chapter 4. Gerardo, a fifty-two-year-old astronomer, relays a certain frustration with his parents' incessant watching of newscasts: "They watch television all day . . . and come and tell you 'you don't know about the girl who disappeared . . . ' as if it was something urgent and I don't have any idea, I was working all day. [They make it sound] as if it was something [very important]." On the other hand, entertainment content is more frequently, though not always, associated with neutral-to-positive affect—a topic that I will discuss at greater length in chapter 5. Paola, who is twenty-two years of age and works as a professional model, says that watching television series "is my moment. Tea, chocolate, and goodbye. Yes, my break. I disconnect a little bit from what's going on in this world and I immerse myself in the show, in that other world." As I will demonstrate in chapter 4, even for the interviewees who spend a lot of time following the news, it is uncommon that such an activity is described as something relaxing and fulfilling.

Attachment

Cristian's story introduced in the preface—about the interactions between a client and her daughter, and among him and his sons—reveals a pattern present in many interviews: the existence of a high level of attachment of people to the personal screens that populate their daily lives. It is not only that they use them a lot but that they also often feel subjectively tied to them and their social interactions. Thus, Martin confesses not "wanting to turn off the cell phone because it would make me feel a bit desperate, like I wouldn't know if my boyfriend got home. . . . I would get worried. So, I'm not calm turning it off." Along similar lines, Juliana, a forty-nine-year-old teacher, notes that she is "constantly attentive to" her cell phone.

These emotional states, such as being "not calm" or "constantly attentive" to personal screens, are sometimes tied to a parallel perception of a low level of connection with those nearby, as the stories relayed by Cristian illustrate. Carmela, a thirty-year-old mother of a toddler, shares her frustration about a recent visit by a friend who, upon arrival, began checking her phone repeatedly to follow a developing news story: "We couldn't interact between ourselves. And it reached a point that I [said] 'I'm done.' I had a terrible feeling since we hadn't talked all night because she decided to be on her phone. [My son] had fallen asleep and I felt it was in vain that she came to my place to talk." Along similar lines, Dalia, a twenty-seven-year-old foreign commerce employee, notes that "I feel that I immerse myself in the cell phone and I look at other people's lives. . . . It's like you isolate yourself, do you see? And you're very attentive to what others are doing and like you miss what's going on around you."

The actions of Carmela's friend, similar to what Martin, Juliana, and several other interviewees expressed, speak to a certain level of urgency to connect that binds them to their personal screens. This is an impulse that they do not like experiencing and that can be difficult for them to control at times. Romina, a nineteen-year-old student, comments, "I'm all the time looking at the phone, even if only to check out the time. . . . it's very bothersome." Humberto, a businessman and attorney in his forties, tells the interviewer that "it's overwhelming to see that I have a red dot [on my cell phone] and a notification I didn't answer." Roman, who is also in his fifties, conveys a similar stance toward notifications coming out of his phone: "The cell phone beeps . . . and you stop doing whatever you were doing to see what that message is about."

Roman's statement resonates with that of Marta, the psychoanalyst, in a previous section, who said she felt a "prisoner" to the notifications on her cell phone. This is why the combination of a heightened level of attentiveness and a sense of urgency are sometimes connected to a perceived loss of agency. That is, instead of being in control of their personal screens, some interviewees feel that they are controlled by them. In Romina's words:

I can try not to have a cell phone, but it is going to bring me more complications than having it. Do you get it? . . . One becomes used to having around all the time something that one thinks is a tool for oneself, but in the end, one becomes dominated [by it].

This combination of attentiveness, urgency, and perceived agency loss are not restricted to cell phone use—even though they are more common in relation to it. It also manifests in the increasingly popular practice of binge-watching streaming television content. In the introduction, I presented data from streaming television company Netflix about how rapidly the median viewer finishes a new season of a show. As I will address more extensively in chapter 5, within the lived experience of the subscribers this translates into, as Martin puts it, "that mania of having to watch one episode after the other.

I put an episode and at the end they link it up to the next. . . . And you're left [thinking] 'no, what's going to happen, holly s..t, I can't not know'. . . I'm willing to lose sleep just to watch several episodes." Norberto, a high school teacher, is aware of the pull of binge watching, especially of his favorite show *House of Cards*, but for him it "is not an addiction like for so many other people. I watch two or three episodes [and] stop. . . . I am hooked, but I don't have an addiction."

Norberto is not the only person who comments about being addicted to personal screens. On the contrary, several other interviewees express the same thing. The goal of the research reported in this book is not to make a diagnosis of whether one or more interviewees are addicted to their personal screens—and the methodology employed for the study is not adequate for making that diagnosis either. However, I treat the fact that interviewees use the metaphor of addiction as evidence of the pervasiveness with which they perceive a loss of agency and the negative connotation associated with it. Mora, a thirty-year-old graphic designer, uses her cell phone "all the time [and] everywhere. As a matter of fact, lately I've been feeling that I have a kind of addiction to it. It's like you don't know what to do [with your time] and use it I don't know what for." German, who is an attorney in his forties, also uses his cell phone all the time and everywhere, adding that "it's an addiction, you see? . . . It's the curiosity of seeing if I have a new email, a new WhatsApp, a message on LinkedIn, tweets to look at. . . . It's like a permanent journey (una recorrida permanente)." Humberto makes a telling comparison: "I smoke and sometimes I go to the balcony to do it. So, yes, I grab the phone and I'm looking [at it] but I'm not looking at anything. . . . I don't even know what I see, it's like you keep scrolling." Like with the cigarette, sometimes withdrawal can be difficult, as we learn from Isabel:

I'm from La Pampa. [During a visit to my parents] I left [the cell phone] charging until the last moment and I forgot it. I was two days without it and I felt that I was dying. . . . The television is, but couldn't be. The computer is, but couldn't be. The cell phone should be. Those two days I told myself "well, it can't be that bad that I don't have a cell phone, I'm not going to die." And I felt that I was dying. . . . And it wasn't even a week, just two days in which I felt all the time that I was forgetting something. . . . I was surprised at myself. I told [myself]: "how could it be that something let's say external was so necessary?"

Isabel's story illustrates how difficult it can be for some people to be away from their personal screens. Along these lines, Paola comments, "I couldn't be without the cell phone for a long time. [I would feel] that I'm missing something." Although these feelings are more prevalent with the cell phone than with the two other personal screens studied in this chapter, sometimes the feelings also apply to them. Agustina, a twenty-year-old student, said, "My computer broke down a week ago and I'm desperate because I realized that I can't live without it." The absence of personal screens can be hard to tolerate in everyday life, which is why some interviewees confess going the extra mile to fill that void whenever it occurs. Josefina, who is twenty-five and works in a public-sector office, recalls that "the other day I went to work, I realized I had forgotten [my cell phone at home] and I went back to look for it. . . . Why? Because I depend on it." Several other interviewees shared similar stories in which they left their office or a friend's house to look for a forgotten cell phone. Others discussed how awkward it is to be without their phones in social settings, like Tatiana, who said: "I remember that once I forgot the cell phone when I went to a party and everybody was with their phones I was like 'Hello!' Because I didn't know how to [interact with people] . . . It's like you feel the absence of the cell phone."

Because the level of attachment to personal screens is sometimes very high, a common pattern across interviews is the need to create screen-free moments and places. These moments function as sanctuaries in daily life, oases within the otherwise desert of personal screens. What these sanctuaries look like vary across interviewees. For Josefina, it is "when I go to mass." For Pedro, a twenty-four-year-old public-sector employee, it is "maybe when I walk two blocks to the kiosk." For Estela, who works in a non-profit and is in her twenties, it is when "I go to the therapist." In other cases, these sanctuaries do not mean parting ways with cell phones but turning off their connectivity. Thus, Humberto puts his cell phone on airplane mode "when I'm in a meeting," and Esteban, a forty-five-year-old administrator of a center for the visually impaired, comments, "When I go to the theater, movies, restaurant I turn my personal phone off, [but] not my work one." Other people create sanctuaries by protecting co-located social interactions. Thus, Carmela shares that her young child often "makes a gesture that I leave the phone on the table [to play with him]." Romina notes that "when I get together with my friends we have a no-phone rule . . . but it's really difficult," and Lucas says that "with my girlfriend, we have a tacit rule of not using [our phones]. . . . But when she starts doing something . . . I catch up with the phone." As Romina, Lucas, and others note, creating these sanctuaries in the midst of co-located interaction can be fraught with difficulties, a pattern that is illustrated in this tragic-comic anecdote of family life told by Susana, a seventy-seven-year-old retiree who is frustrated by her children's and grandchildren's constant screen use during their visits to her house:

> I have a friend who . . . when her family goes to her place she makes them put their cell phones in a breadbasket. . . . But I can't make it happen with my children. . . . If you invite them to lunch, they're all with their cell phones [at the table] and I don't like it. . . . And sometimes me too [laughs]! . . . One day they took a picture of me [during a family gathering] and I was with my phone [laughs]!

The main reason these sanctuaries are hard to implement appears to be less the pull of the personal screens per se than that of all the other non-colocated social interactions in which interviewees take part in their everyday lives. In other words, it is less a situation of personal screens competing with social interactions and more one of multiple domains of social interaction—most of them non-colocated—vying for people's attention. Sometimes these domains center around family life. Marcelo, a sixty-two-year-old owner of a small convenience store, "always" has his cell phone with him "to be in contact with all my children." Similarly, Jazmin, the elementary school employee, says that she has her cell phone "because of [my children]. They're teenagers, therefore it's mostly so that they feel comfortable sending me a message. . . . For instance, I have the phone at work because my children are not with me. . . . And if there is one [child] outside of the home, the cell phone is with me [too]."

Most frequently, cell phones enable participation in multiple domains of social interaction with non-family members and through social media platforms. Lucrecia, a twenty-three-year-old college student, confesses that she is "very addicted to the cell phone, [in which] I consume absolutely all the social networks: Facebook, Twitter, Instagram, every one that you can imagine, WhatsApp . . . I'm all the time attentive to my cell phone." Sofi, a forty-six-year-old substitute teacher, comments that on WhatsApp "there are two hundred thousand groups: parents' group, Sunday school group, friends' groups, siblings' groups. . . . There is always a message to read. And, well, I'm more attentive to the cell phone than before [I had] WhatsApp." I will return to the connections between cell phone use, social media practices, and the multiplication of interaction in chapter 3.

Concluding Remarks

Personal screens have emerged as the looking-glass of the contemporary experience of information abundance. They are often the principal entry to its products and services, becoming both windows into our sociality-in-the-making and also mirrors that reflect back a powerful image of some aspects of our collective identities and interests. What are the key patterns that emerge from the data about their reception presented in this chapter, and what are their main implications for the questions that animate this book and the approach adopted to answer them?

The survey findings indicate that structural factors variously shape differential rates of access and use. The analysis shows that age surpasses socioeconomic status and gender as the key driver of ownership and use of the main personal screens in everyday life. This pattern is consistent across both ownership of cell phones—with and without internet access—and frequency of online access. The one exception is ownership of a personal computer, which is not surprising if one takes into account the combination of the high level of expenditure for this device and the high level of poverty in the country. In light of the dominance of the cell phone as the preferred personal screen, the picture that emerges is one in which age has become the defining structural organizer of life in and on the personal screen. This picture is consistent with recent scholarship about access and use of personal computers, smartphones, and social media, which has highlighted the central role of age in these processes.[11] Thus, according to communication scholar Teresa Correa, "Age remains as the most consistent and enduring digital gap."[12] This pattern exists not only across age groups but also within them. For instance, in his examination of the "digital divide among seniors," media effects researcher Thomas Friemel concludes that "*age continues to have a differentiating effect, net of all other factors.*"[13]

The survey findings only tell part of the story, even when it comes to the role of structural variables such as age. The interviews reveal that while people from all age groups cherish the connectivity afforded by their smartphones, they do so for different reasons: young folks prioritize issues related to social life and entertainment, those in middle age place significant value in work and communication with both children and parents, and older adults appreciate relational and familial uses as well as the sense of security brought forth by the possibility of constant connection. The interviews also show that sometimes practices of use converge surprisingly across age groups, as when Silvia, frustrated by the lack of family communication, demands that their grandchildren leave their mobile phone aside at the weekly Sunday lunch gathering only to realize that she cannot part ways with her device either.

These various modes of use are partly shaped by the different meanings that people attribute to the three personal screens examined. Thus, the cell phone as a prosthetic, the computer as a tool, and the television set as a companion are symbolic constructions that become deeply intertwined with multiple dimensions of everyday life. These are dynamics that become visible when we complement models that express the transmission view of communication, with a lens embodying the ritual view of communication that animates this book through its emphasis on interpretation, emotion, and practice. Different meanings originate in social interaction and further coalesce with the spread of particular practices over time. Each of these meanings is tied to the affordances of each screen and the respective marketing strategies that the manufacturers deploy to sell them. Yet, these meanings cannot be derived from technological affordances and marketing strategies. For instance, even though the laptop has relatively similar affordances than the smartphone, and its mobility is also a centerpiece of its marketing, the prosthetic connotation was largely absent from the discourses and practices of the interviewees. Similarly, while a networked desktop computer can perform most of the same functions that a television does, it is hardly experienced as a warm, comforting companion like the television set is; instead, it has the cold, instrumental connotation of a tool.

This highlights the role of agency and attachment in the contemporary experience of information abundance. To begin, the combination of the overlapping capabilities of personal screens and divergent meanings attributed to them points to a significant degree of agency expressed in the different modalities of use. Furthermore, this also manifests in the creativity of the practices undertaken not to use them through the development of an array of everyday sanctuaries untouched by personal screens. This issue also connects to the high level of attachment many interviewees feel in relation to these personal screens, most notably in the case of their mobile phones, which reveals different kinds of connection to these devices and of attribution of roles in their daily lives. This far surpasses those of many other artifacts that populate our material landscape, from the faucet to the table, and from the chair to the mattress. The power of this level of attachment is seen not only through its visible presence but also, and as with the case of agency, through the reactions toward the absence of a particularly valuable personal screen. The sense of loss, even to the point of experiencing withdrawal- and death-like feelings, is as strong a sign as possible about the fundamental worth that these devices have acquired in contemporary context.

Overall, this analysis of the intertwined meaning, agency, and attachment shows the value of the ritual view of communication to illuminate at least four key dimensions of the experience of information abundance—and also underscores the concomitant limitations of prior research on information overload.

First, interviewees use personal screens not only to gather information to make decisions but also to variously express themselves and relate to others. On the one hand, of the three personal screens examined in this chapter, the mobile phone appears to be the one more directly tied to is-sues of self-expression and relationality. Yet interviewees gave numerous examples of resorting to it to gather information for decision-making. On the other hand, the personal computer was used more often for pro-cessing information related to making decisions than the two other per-sonal screens, but interviewees also variously resorted to it for tasks such as video-calling friends and family and connecting to social media. Thus, an exclusive focus on decision-making would have missed these other types of uses that add to the contemporary experience of information abundance.

Second, interviewees not only used personal screens instrumentally but also for leisure, news, entertainment, and relationship building and mainte-nance, among other purposes. Furthermore, these goals are distinct yet also interconnected; thus, understanding why the computer is seen mostly as a tool and used primarily for work helps shed light on the companionship role often attributed to the television set and the more varied practices typically enacted in relation to the mobile phone. Therefore, concentrating the an-alytical gaze on instrumental goals would have overlooked the panoply of purposes for which individuals engage with personal screens and the holistic experience that emanates from these practices.

Third, the wide diversity of modalities and purposes of use, partly tied to the even wider array of contextual circumstances in which the interviewees used personal screens, eschews any possibility of establishing a general optimum of information quality and quantity after which there are deleterious effects. Is it optimal to interact with and through the mobile phone the entirety of a public transportation journey—as Marianela does—or is it better to take a nap? Is it optimal to turn off the computer during off-work hours—as Juanita, Lucas, Joaquin, and Mariana do—or is it better to continue using it, even if only for non-work reasons, during that time? Is it optimal to have the television turned on many more hours than one is paying any attention to it—as Matilde, Humberto, Sara, and Angeles do—or is it better to save energy and deal in other ways with issues of silence and solitude? Regardless how tempting normative metrics of healthy personal screen use might be, once we move away from the narrow focus on decision-making for instrumental purposes, the notion of optimality becomes remarkably unfit to make sense of the range of positional and contextual dynamics that shape screen practice.

Fourth, rather than a blanket discourse of deficit, what results from the combination of agency and attachment dynamics is a mixed valuation of the experience of using personal screens from the vantage point of the interviewees. Concerning the mobile phone, for instance, on the one hand, Lola likes the sense of safety having it at all times gives her; Jose appreciates its capabilities for assisting him in street navigation given his visual impairment; Miriam enjoys its versatility for her evangelizing practice as a Jehovah's Witness; Marcela likes its efficiency in allowing her to communicate with her daughter about her grandson; and several interviewees comment about how its use makes them feel more connected to friends and family who are far away, among other positive valuations. On the other hand, Cecilia and Silvia feel that they are disconnected from their respective grandchildren even when they are in the same space; Marta does not appreciate feeling like a prisoner of the messages coming through the device; Emanuel and Tatiana dislike how their friends are more focused on the "elsewhere" rather than the "here and now" when they gather together; and several interviewees relay a sense of not being able to be fully in control of their mobile phone, among other negative valuations. These are some illustrations from the data of the juxtaposition of positive and negative valuations in the experiential tapestry of information abundance. It is not that living in a world of information plenty is always rosy, but that the black-or-white discourse of deficit often tied to the analyst's perspective—with its usually associated dystopic connotations—does not do justice to the spectrum of gray tonalities that emerge from the voices of the subjects.

The combination of agency and attachment also indicate a transformation in how people understand and enact their sociality. This transformation is an expression of a remarkable predisposition toward personal screens—in particular, mobile phones—and the information and connections accessed through them. This predisposition is akin to the "info-lust" that according to historian Ann Blair signaled thirteenth-century folks' positive valuation of information and subsequent accumulation of the resulting products. Yet, in the contemporary environment, the source of the information valued is less the natural world and more the lives of others. This also ties to what telecommunications specialist Christian Licoppe has termed "connected presence":

> a gradual shift in which communication technologies, instead of being used (however unsuccessfully) to compensate for the absence of our close ones, are exploited to provide a continuous pattern of mediated interactions that combine into "connected relationships," in which the boundaries between absence and presence eventually get blurred.[14]

The combination of the shift in the locus of the info-lust with notions of boyd's networked publics and Licoppe's connected presence provides the entry point to an ongoing reconstitution of sociality that marks the experience of information abundance. For instance, the role of WhatsApp as a major incentive for personal screen practices, in particular related to the cell phone, points to the centrality of social media platforms in enabling a sense of being able to participate in concurrent communication processes across time and space with an intensity not experienced before. This suggests that this reconstitution has been emerging at the intersection of personal screens and social media. Therefore, in order to make sense of it, it is first necessary to examine the uses—and sometimes abuses—of platforms in everyday life, to which I turn in the next chapter.

3

Platforms

Everything happens on WhatsApp.
Rosario, thirty-two years old, Pilates instructor

People have embraced social media with gusto since Sixdegrees.com was launched in 1997—and especially since MySpace and Facebook debuted in 2003 and 2004, respectively. Facebook's diffusion is so impressive that in just fourteen years of existence it managed to get adopted by 31% of the world's 7.7 billion population. Argentina has been no exception to this trend. As of 2017—the second year of fieldwork for this book—it had more than 29 million users, which amounted to two-thirds of the population of the country.[1] Combining all platforms, there were 34 million active social media users by the end of that year, a figure that represented a 10% increase from the previous year.[2] Consistent with the information presented in the previous chapter, 30 of those 34 million were active mobile social media users, a growth of 11% from the previous year.[3]

Not only are large numbers of people on social media, but they also are very active on the various platforms they use. For instance, 2.5 trillion posts were available on Facebook worldwide as of the third quarter of 2016.[4] A year earlier, the platform received on average likes on over 4 million posts per minute.[5] On WhatsApp, as of the second quarter of 2017, people exchanged 55 billion messages, 45 billion pictures, and 1 billion videos daily.[6] As I write these pages in October 2020, a free online application tells me that there are 9,172 new tweets to read, like, comment, and retweet every second I spend trying to put my thoughts on paper.[7] Assuming that this number stays constant by the time the book gets published and that it might take approximately an hour to read each chapter, reading the whole book will mean missing more than 231 million new tweets as they are posted.

This abundance of users and activity on social media are tied to the significant time devoted to the various platforms. According to the Digital 2018

Abundance. Pablo J. Boczkowski, Oxford University Press. © Oxford University Press 2021.
DOI: 10.1093/oso/9780197565742.003.0003

country report about Argentina produced by We Are Social and Hootsuite, the average daily time spent using social media on any device during 2017 was 3 hours and 19 minutes.[8] If the average person sleeps around 8.8 hours per day, this volume of usage amounts to 22% of their awake time spent on ways of interacting with information and people that did not exist a mere quarter century ago. To put things in a different perspective, this means that the average social media user in Argentina during the second year of research for this project spent one out of every five minutes of the time they were not sleeping on at least one platform—including during, and likely concurrent with, work and/or study. Given this intensity of usage, and given that many Argentines consider WhatsApp to be the most popular platform in the country, it is no wonder Rosario thinks that everything happens on it.

In light of the constitutive social component of social media—and, as I noted at the end chapter 2, the role of mobile devices in their practices of use—there has been a lot of consideration given in recent years to what the mixing of platforms and smartphones might mean for contemporary sociality. Claims about the adoption of novel communication technologies being intertwined with transformations in sociality long predate the contemporary setting.[9] However, concerns about this matter have resurfaced with a vengeance in relation to the growing popularity of mobile telephones[10] and social media.[11] Scholars have espoused different, and often conflicting, positions about this matter. For instance, whereas mobile communication scholar Rich Ling contends that "there is a continuance of sociation while at the same time there is also a new tool with which to enact the hopes and worries of this project,"[12] public opinion expert Lee Rainie and sociologist Barry Wellman identify a novel pattern of interaction that they call "networked individualism," in which "people function more as connected individuals and less as embedded group members."[13] To top things off, psychologist Sherry Turkle, who has been following the evolution of the incorporation of digital technology into people's lives since the 1980s, has recently warned that in the current moment "we came to ask less of each other. We settled for less empathy, less attention, less care from other human beings."[14]

In this chapter I will continue the analytical process started in the previous one to probe what the experience of information abundance means for the dynamics of contemporary sociality, among other topics. If personal screens are the looking glass of information abundance, social media platforms have emerged as its labyrinth: offering seductive pathways for expression and relationships, yet also a collective sense of not always knowing how to get out once we enter the connectivity maze. Aiming to reach a fruitful destination after traversing this empirical labyrinth, and consistent with the questions posed in the preface, in this chapter I will center on the roles of structural factors shaping access and attitudes toward the various technologies. I will also look at attributions of meaning orienting how and why the different platforms are and are not variously used given their relatively similar port-folio of capabilities—including multimedia content; reading, reacting, and commenting functionality; and various forms of interpersonal interaction. [15]

In the next section I summarize the findings from the survey about the varying roles of age, gender, and socioeconomic status on social media access and use. Then, in the following five sections I will examine the five most pop-ular platforms in Argentina at the time of this study—WhatsApp, Facebook, Instagram, Twitter, and Snapchat. Most users access multiple platforms, ei-ther sequentially or concurrently, and how they use one platform is often re-lated to how they use the others. However, for analytical clarity, I will address the practices, interpretations, and emotions related to each platform sepa-rately, yet do so informed by a relational sensibility. Moreover, I will resort to metaphors that aim to underscore the singularity of each platform as it is experienced by the interviewees. Each of these metaphors connects a social institution of everyday life in Argentina—and beyond, in several cases—in order to make comparisons more vivid. These metaphors were not directly expressed by the interviewees but emerged from the process of analysis, and they encapsulate what is most distinctive about the different meanings re-lated to each platform. Then, I will return to a central topic of the contempo-rary experience of information abundance that I examined in the previous chapter, in this case with a focus on platforms: the attachment to technology and content. Finally, I will wrap up the chapter by summarizing the main results of the inquiry, what they mean for the questions that animate this book, with special attention to the role that the combination of personal screens and social media platform use have for our sociality-in-the-making.

The Landscape of Social Media Use

According to the survey, 71% of those who were eighteen years of age or older used at least one social media platform as of fall 2016 (Figure 3.1).[16] This rate of penetration varied primarily by age, less by socioeconomic status, and even less by gender. First, whereas social media use was almost universal

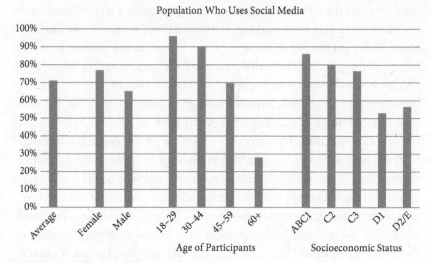

Figure 3.1. Use of social media.
Average: Average percentage of the surveyed population who uses social media.
ABC1: High; C2: Middle; C3: Lower Middle; D1: Low; D2/E: Extreme Low

among the youngest cohort (18–29) at 96%, it dropped precipitously to 28% among their oldest counterparts in the sample (60 or older). Second, whereas 86.08% of those with the highest level of socioeconomic status accessed social media, only 56.41% of their counterparts at the bottom of the socioeconomic ladder did so. Thus, the difference between youngest and oldest (58%) is almost double that between richest and poorest (29.33%). Finally, women (76.86%) are also more likely to use social media than men (65.14%).

Those who use social media access an average of three platforms (Figure 3.2). There is also greater variance by age than by socioeconomic status and gender regarding this matter. Whereas the youngest group uses an average of almost three-and-a-half platforms (3.49), the oldest one barely crosses the two-platform mark (2.19). By contrast, the wealthiest social media users access 3.39 platforms on average, while their most disadvantaged counterparts are just shy of the two-and-a-half mark (2.42). Therefore, the difference between young and old (1.3) is 34% larger than that between rich and poor (0.97). Finally, men use on average slightly more platforms (3.05) than women (2.94).

Most of the people who access social media find it to be critical to their everyday lives. When asked to state their level of agreement with the sentence "access to social media is indispensable to me," 55.43% of survey respondents on social media said that they agreed with it, and only 20.71% disagreed—the rest were neutral (Figure 3.3). Age plays a major role: whereas the proportion

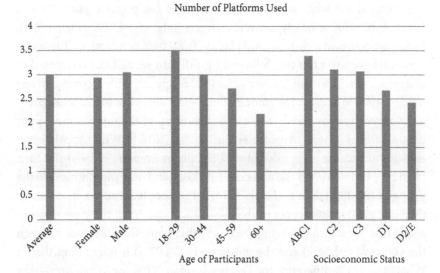

Figure 3.2. Average number of social media platforms used.

Average: Average number of platforms used.

ABC1: High; C2: Middle; C3: Lower Middle; D1: Low; D2/E: Extreme Low

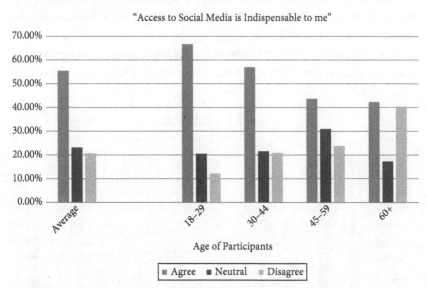

Figure 3.3. Percentage of users which agrees with the statement "access to social media is indispensable to me."

Average: Averages across age groups.

of agree-versus-disagree was 5:1 among the youngest respondents (66.66% versus 12.28%), it went down to parity among their oldest counterparts (42.31% versus 40.38%).

Among those who use social media, the most popular platform was WhatsApp, with a nearly universal access rate of 94.52% (Figure 3.4). Facebook comes at a close second place with 89.04% penetration. These two platforms occupy a top tier, followed by a distant second tier composed of Instagram (31.12%) and Twitter (25.44%). Snapchat, with a comparatively modest 10.57% prevalence among adults—but allegedly much more prevalent among tweens and teens—closes the group of the top five most popular platforms among Argentines during fall 2016.[17] WhatsApp led this elite group because it appealed almost equally to women (95.29%) and men (93.62%), and rich (94.37%) and poor (95.56%), and only slightly more to the youngest (97.08%) than to the oldest (87.04%) people surveyed. By contrast, there are greater differences in the use of Facebook in all these elements of social structure, with age being the most salient one: the difference between the youngest (94.74%) and the oldest users (74.07%) is larger than that of WhatsApp (21% difference for Facebook versus 10% for WhatsApp)—the rates of penetration among female and rich users are 6 percentage points higher than among men and poor users, respectively. Finally, Instagram is particularly prevalent among the youngest segment of the population who use social media, at 50.29%, and Twitter among those in the highest socioeconomic bracket, at 39.44%.

The frequency of use varies across the different social media platforms. There is a general pattern in which the most popular platforms are also those

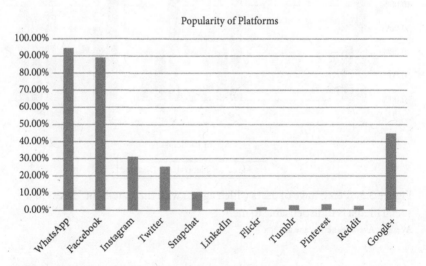

Figure 3.4. Popularity of the leading platforms.

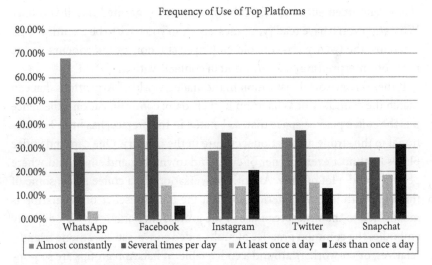

Figure 3.5. Frequency of use of the most popular platforms.

used more frequently. Thus, WhatsApp is not only accessed by 94.52% of the population, but 68.12% of those who do so use it "almost constantly," and none of them "less than once a day" (Figure 3.5). By contrast, 35.83% of those on Facebook use it "almost constantly," and 5.71% "less than once a day." At the bottom of the top five most used platforms, less than a quarter (24.03%) of Snapchat users access this platform "almost constantly" and almost a third of them (31.50%) "less than once a day." The picture that emerges from this analysis of the relative prevalence and frequency of use of the top platforms is that access to WhatsApp is not only almost universal but also nearly constant.

WhatsApp

It is evident from the data presented in the previous section that WhatsApp is omnipresent in the everyday lives of Argentines. Humberto, a forty-nine-year-old businessman and attorney, comments that he uses it "all day, for everything." Ricardo, a college student, concurs: "I'm attentive to WhatsApp all day . . . more than either Facebook or Instagram." Agustina, another college student, echoes Ricardo's sentiment by noting that "everybody uses it and it is super indispensable." She adds that there is an implicit assumption of reciprocity that is both an effect of the centrality of the platform and also a reinforcement of it: "Everybody takes it for granted that if you have WhatsApp you'll have read [your messages], so you have to be attentive to it." Estefanía, the twenty-six-year-old employee at a non-profit, concurs, to the point of "interpret[ing] it as my point of contact" with the world.

If there is one social institution in the analog world of Argentines that can match the centrality of WhatsApp in their daily communication experience it is the coffee place, a space that, as I stated in the preface, has been foundational to the strong associational culture in the country. One can find coffee places in almost every corner of cities and towns, big and small, and where people spend a lot of time. As with conversations in a coffee place, some of them are with just one interlocutor. But the omnipresence of WhatsApp is mostly tied to the widespread use of the group functionality, which digitally embodies the common practice of multi-sided conversations among friends, relatives, or co-workers around a coffee table. WhatsApp groups are so popular in many countries that as of February 2016 there were a billion of them in existence.[18] In addition to the dominance of group communication, other aspects of WhatsApp use that stand out from the interviews are the plurality of kinds of topics that are talked about on the platform, and the tension that sometimes arises because of this plurality; the versatility of using it for family, relational, and instrumental purposes; the practice of sharing news stories; the experience of being overwhelmed by the high levels of volume, and the temporal and logistical challenges of dealing with this; and the perception of having smaller publics and more intimate conversations than on other platforms.

Even though there are group capabilities on Facebook, their existence on WhatsApp is on a whole different level. Leila, a nineteen-year-old college student, comments that "there is a group for everything. . . . If someone has a birthday, [then, we create the group] 'birthday of . . .' [laughs]. I don't know, 'what presents do we buy?' I don't know, perhaps we can't decide what to do tonight, so 'what do we do tonight?'—another group!" This type of practice mimics coffee place interactions, but increases their frequency and reach exponentially. Carla, a forty-five-year-old attorney, puts it as follows:

> It can be exhausting. . . . I have a group on WhatsApp with my maternal family because they're all my maternal aunts and my female cousins. I'm not [available] at the time the majority is on that . . . [group] . . . There are twenty-five people [on it]. Then there is the [group] of the people from my children's school. I also have a pair of WhatsApps with friends from different

groups; the WhatsApp of those who belong to a museum committee; the WhatsApp from my law firm; and then the clients have also begun utilizing WhatsApp as a professional communication channel. So, I go to a meeting and when it's over I have 180 [new] messages. . . . Sometimes one spends the entire day answering WhatsApp messages and hasn't been able to start working.

In a country with a strong family-oriented culture, it is not surprising that WhatsApp is commonly used for family communication. Susana, a seventy-seven-year-old retiree, comments that she has a "beautiful group" with her children. "I used to have WhatsApp with each child separately, and one day I said 'no!' . . . We created a group and I write everybody at once and I find out everything about them. . . . [The group] is active every day, it's like saying 'good night' and restart the next day." Andrea, a thirty-one-year-old photographer, shares a similar experience: "I have groups with my families. With the family of my mom, with the family of my dad, with the family of my mom plus my uncles and grandparents, cousins; I have an extended-family group, a smaller one with my family, another even smaller with the family on my dad's side. . . . I use it a lot."

Another common use of this platform is for relational management. Lola, a seventy-seven-year-old retiree, and her husband routinely dance tango with several other couples in her age group. They created a WhatsApp group called "the *milongueros* swingers."[19] She is also active in another group of grandmothers "to talk about the grandchildren . . . the picture of my grandchild, also of my great-grandchild . . . 'Aw, he's so cute' 'Look, he went to school' 'Oops, he fell' . . . And if anyone had a problem, then it's 'how is it going,' 'what did the doctor say,' 'is she hospitalized?'" Rodrigo, a twenty-nine-year-old clerical employee, shares photos and videos on WhatsApp "all the time . . . because I want to interact with my friends. . . . It's a [form of connection] par excellence." Victor, a college student, does this also "to be close to people who are far away . . . to maintain contact" with them.

People also use this platform for instrumental purposes such as work and study. Carla commented that her firm has been fostering attorney-client interactions via WhatsApp. Physicians use it professionally too. Elsa, a sixty-six-year-old retired teacher and psychotherapist, noted that she recently "called a doctor to ask about something and what I get back is 'for that topic you have to communicate via WhatsApp to this number.'" Marcos, a forty-nine-year-old security guard, likes using this platform for work "because you communicate faster, it facilitates communication." Rosario, the Pilates instructor, is pursuing a degree and has a college group and "when there is a midterm or when we have to study we use WhatsApp a lot for sharing pictures of a book or videos . . . or voice notes."

Interviewees sometimes also share news stories on WhatsApp. Zoraida, a college student, notes that her friends are dispersed in various provinces so on "our WhatsApp group we share news about the [different] places . . . to be more or less updated of what is going on in the other place[s]." Marina, the financial analyst, says that "if there is a high impact story" it is shared on her friends' groups, "like, 'did you see what happened in this place?' or 'did you see what happened with this or that?' " Luciana, a thirty-year-old accountant, shares a similar practice, mostly focused on "funny news," like "a thief tried to enter [a house] to rob through the chimney but got stuck!"

There is an overall impression among the interviewees that the volume of activity and the importance of the communication has risen over the years and presents significant communication management challenges. Mariano, a thirty-five-year-old cook at an empanadas store, says that "sometimes I get up, leave my cell phone by the side for a bit, and then I look and there are 200 [new] messages." Cornelia, a sixty-three-year-old clerical employee, says that "generally I end [the day] at home at 2:00 a.m. answering WhatsApp [messages]." Ezequiel, a thirty-nine-year-old attorney, adds that this platform

has recently been mutating from what it was, a matter more of distraction or irrelevant communication, to issues that one could say are more important, that have to do with family matters, work matters, and so on. I would say that . . . the intensity of the part that is important to me has been growing.

The growth in frequency of use, volume of interactions, and perceived importance of the content is tied to a sense among many interviewees that WhatsApp, like a coffee place, affords a combination of smaller publics and more intimate conversations than other social media options. To Isabel, the college student, WhatsApp is "more private and more intimate." Victor, also a college student, concurs: "I feel that WhatsApp is more personal." Thus, daily routine interactions happen more often on this platform than on others. Luciana says that this type of interactions take place "on WhatsApp. We don't use Facebook with the people I see daily. Maybe I can see [their] pictures or if they went to a party, but not more than that." One instance in which this difference manifests quite clearly is in study groups. It is common among many interviewees in school that instructors create a Facebook group for a class at the beginning of the term. As the interactions among students unfold, those who develop friendships start their own separate groups, but on WhatsApp instead of Facebook. "There is a group on Facebook for [a class at her college] to which all students [taking that class belong]," comments Martina, a thirty-seven-year-old student and law firm clerk. But "with the girls with whom I hang out more, we have a WhatsApp group." Andrea sums up the comparatively unique experience of intimacy and smallness as follows:

It's not that [all] the people I have on WhatsApp are very close to me, but are people with whom I share some minimal relationship. Work, friendship, acquaintance, or a common need, "hey, let's get together to go somewhere" sometime [in the past]. . . . On Facebook I have all [the] people I know, but not that I necessarily talk to them. If a girl who went to high school with me requests to be friends on Facebook, of course I add her. Like, "let's see what's going on with her." . . . But it's not that I start talking with her or sending her a picture.

This does not happen on Facebook because, unlike the smallness and intimacy of the coffee place, many interviewees experience Facebook as a large and impersonal environment.

Facebook

Interviewees often talk about the massive scale and comprehensive membership on this platform. To Lucas, a thirty-year-old attorney, "Facebook is the social network par excellence because it's a mix of everything. . . . I have on my Facebook people from all age and social groups. . . . So, it seems the most comprehensive [platform]." Javier, a twenty-eight-year-old store employee, shares a similar perception: "I can't say that I see more of one thing on Facebook because it is extremely massive. . . . All ages, social classes, everybody is on Facebook." Patricio, a college student, echoes Javier's words: "On Facebook I have friends, family, college professors, classmates . . . that is, it's very broad." The kind of social atmosphere that transpires in this broad kind of platform is best represented by the mall, a large and convenient environment that is patronized routinely for shopping, dining, entertainment, or simply hanging out but that rarely elicits feelings of warmth or connection.

The perception that Facebook is like a mall is tied to a certain sense of impersonality and a lack of enthusiasm for participation on this platform. As Humberto puts it, "Facebook is a little bit [the platform] that represents all the other platforms; it makes you feel that you're in contact with somebody when you aren't in contact." Luis, a twenty-seven-year-old race car driver, does not comment on other people's posts on Facebook "with the exception of congratulating a friend for something they did. But I don't like to debate on Facebook . . . because it seems banal to me. The debate has to be around a coffee table." The contrast with the feelings of intimacy tied to WhatsApp is remarkable. Julian, a twenty-nine-year-old movie producer, resorts to a telling metaphor to convey the somewhat distant affect that several interviewees experience with respect to Facebook when he says that "it serves a purpose, it's ugly and you have to use it . . . because it's the form you have to communicate nowadays. But not because the network seems particularly interesting."

The common perception of comprehensive membership and massive scale shapes the kinds of practices undertaken on this platform. Adriana, a college student, compares how these matters affect what she does on Facebook versus Snapchat: "Snapchat is for something more fun, more spontaneous when you're bored. Whereas Facebook doesn't have this, you share more serious stuff. I'm not going to post a strange face on Facebook because anybody who's stalking me can see it." Along similar lines, Victor comments that he "has so many people on Facebook . . . that I don't like for them to see what I'm reading [and] what my interests are. . . . So I post silly stuff, mostly things related to soccer and posts like that, or maybe pictures with my friends if we're doing something [cool]."

Besides these perceptions of massive scale, comprehensive membership, and impersonality and disaffection, other salient characteristics of people's experience of Facebook are the slightly different ways in which the platform is used by different age groups; the prevalence of relational management, instrumental practices, and news consumption and sharing; and a certain sense of digital drift—of using the platform aimlessly and losing track of time—that is not so common on other platforms, such as WhatsApp.

As is evident from the survey results presented in a previous section, people from all age groups are on Facebook in relatively large numbers—although those who are sixty and older use it less. But how they use it varies somewhat by age groups, as is also the case of a mall. Several of the young interviewees share the notion that this platform has lost some of its coolness due to a combination of lack of novelty and multi-age membership. Maribel, who is twenty-one years old, says that Facebook "is less common for people of my age, it's being used less. . . . Facebook was the 'boom' at one point, now there are other things." Mora, a thirty-year-old industrial designer, concurs: "Facebook is getting a bit old. As a matter of fact, my younger cousins who were always there are not using it, they don't have it anymore. I'm in the middle generation so I keep logging in. But the Facebook stories are nonsense, and I don't have many people on Facebook who use them." Martina, the law firm clerk, who is seven years older than Mora, says that "I might put a picture of [my daughter] dancing, I don't know, some silly stuff. Once upon a time I was more active, but then I became more reserved. . . . I think it's because of my age, I don't know, you get older and you don't want to show that much." Other young people deliberately use Facebook to connect with people who are not of their generation. Jorge, a college student, comments that "there is a group I can't reach via Instagram . . . that could be family members or friends of family members . . . who are older [than me] and are more connected to Facebook, so I take advantage of that and share information on [this platform]."

At the other end of the age spectrum, Elsa, who is sixty-six and a retired school teacher and psychotherapist, confesses that she has "pictures of my grandchildren on my phone, but I don't like [to post them on Facebook]. . . . What comes here (referring to her cell phone) dies here. But there are people who spill that stuff all over and I don't like it to be in all places. You have people greeting you because they like how you greeted someone else. I don't follow all that." Marcela, a seventy-two-year-old clerical employee, shares Elsa's general sentiment, but goes one step further and refuses to be on Facebook—and social media more generally—because of that: "I don't have [Facebook] because I don't want to. It has to do with my age. To me, Facebook is pure gossip. I'm sorry, but I feel like that."

As with WhatsApp, relational management is also common on Facebook, in particular for friendships among people who are geographically distant. Estefanía says that her family moved a lot during her childhood and adolescence, so "I find a lot of utility in Facebook to connect with friends who live elsewhere, that to me is key. . . . I think I got a Facebook account a bit for that." This is also central to how Fabián, a forty-three-year-old doorman, experiences this platform:

Look, there are 117 cousins on my wife's side. And her cousins are my cousins, too. And they upload all kinds of stuff . . . so I use it mostly to gossip about what's going on with them. . . . We all have similar ages and are [focused on] kids' issues. Like if the boys play soccer . . . and for the girls, one goes to dance, and stuff like that.

Facebook is also used for instrumental purposes such as study and work. This type of use centers on information exchanges and logistical coordination. Carolina, a twenty-four-year-old college student, says that she uses Facebook "a lot for college. . . . Professors set up groups and we use the email in parallel." Maribel notes that "I use it mostly for the groups at college, not so much as a social network in the sense of friendships and publishing about friends' stuff." One of the interviewees who uses Facebook for work reasons is Julian, the media producer. He says that he has the Facebook "window open all day [on my computer] . . . because the postproduction coordinator reaches out to me on Facebook instead of calling me on the phone. So, I have it always open just to stay communicated." Claudia, a forty-one-year-old clinical psychologist, comments that on Facebook she has "colleagues from different continuing education courses, in the same profession, so we share conference and workshop updates, I get lots of information about classes, and that is information that is very useful to me. We share fragments of texts, of books . . . quite connected to what we do [professionally]."

The platform is also popular for consuming news. Sometimes this is deliberate, as in going on Facebook to look for information updates about current events. Other times it is incidental: encountering news while not intending to do so. Clara, a thirty-year-old psychologist, says she uses Facebook "a lot to see . . . news, too. I have many friends who share opinions or stories, so many times I end up finding out about important things that happen on Facebook." Laura, a twenty-year-old college student, goes one step further: "I believe what I use Facebook for the most is news." Lucila, who has a clerical job in a media organization, states that "many times I say 'wow, this major thing happened,' and it's because I saw lots of people talking about it on Facebook. So perhaps I saw it there before than in a newspaper." Using Facebook for news is sometimes a matter of convenience: "Everything is condensed in one place," as Adriana, a college student, puts it. Other times it is tied to the value assigned to one's contacts of being better editorial gatekeepers than media organizations and professionals. According to Agustina:

On Facebook it is not the media controlling the news in itself, but my friends sharing the news stories that interested them. And I think that's a nicer way of filtering the news. . . . [Because] on Facebook you're aware of which person is uploading the story, how that person thinks, and what political affiliations she has. So, you're more conscious that the news story comes with all that behind it.

Not all uses of Facebook are purposeful. On the contrary, many interviewees share stories about using this platform in a somewhat purposeless fashion. In Carmela's words, "I don't know if I go to look for something. I [just] like to look." Martin, a twenty-year-old engineering major, concurs: "Sometimes I realize that you open Facebook just because, and you don't really feel like opening it but you do it [anyway] and scroll down a bit. . . . I don't know, you lost fifteen minutes but, well, fifteen minutes of boredom passed, too." To Julieta, a thirty-six-year-old attorney:

In the end, Facebook is the same as channel surfing [on television]. . . . You do like this (makes the gesture of scrolling down the screen) searching for something that interests you, [but] that never really appears. It's the news that interests anybody. . . . And then you realize that you lost a couple of hours of doing that (repeats the gesture).

The equivalence between channel surfing on television and scrolling down on Facebook is due not only to the similarity between the massive amounts of varied content between the two but it is also linked to the number of advertisements on the social media platform. This is a deterrent to some interviewees but appealing to others. On the one side, Ernesto, a thirty-two-year-old education tutor, states:

I'm using Facebook less because it has too much propaganda, especially political propaganda, and I don't like that. For instance, there are many ads and groups of people selling and buying stuff. I do pay more attention to Instagram because it's more personal. I can add few people [to my contact list], only the ones I like and that's it. And I can post a picture with a brief caption and nothing else.

Daniela, who is twenty-eight years of age and works in an advertisement agency, says that "Facebook migrated to an older public, that is, forty-five [years of age] and above. By contrast, Instagram has this thing that is more about trends. . . . So, not everything that I share on Instagram I share on Facebook. . . . I have everything very divided, [like] two personas."

Instagram

Interviewees experience Instagram as the social media platform on which to see and be seen. Surely this also applies to a certain degree to Facebook, and to a much lesser extent to WhatsApp. But it is not the central attraction on these other platforms. On the contrary, monitoring how people look and providing the best visual representation of oneself are the dominant reasons that people use Instagram. Thus, if WhatsApp is akin to a coffee place and Facebook to a mall, Instagram is like a promenade: a well-kept walkway, placed in a somewhat scenic venue, that people visit to be part of the parade and enjoy the scenery leisurely—in this case made up of highly aestheticized pictures and videos of other platform members. That is, unlike an analog promenade, there is no environment surrounding it. Thus, Instagram users are not only subjects but also objects in a dual way: individually being the people others are watching, and collectively constituting the visual environment within which observation takes place—together with the advertisements that the company peppers in between posts. In comparison to the other main platforms, users experience Instagram as the most aestheticized alternative, which sometimes is tied to emotional pressure and negative self-evaluation; where people post less frequently, and more carefully edited, pictures and videos; where they follow celebrity accounts and share somewhat frivolous content. Overall, it is a more intimate space than Facebook—but less so than WhatsApp.

Instagram is also a platform for the young and, to a much lesser extent, the well-to-do. The difference in the likelihood of using this platform is sevenfold between the youngest and the oldest segments of those surveyed—50.29% versus 7.41%—and this difference decreases to almost double between richest and poorest—43.66% versus 24.44%. There is no significant difference with respect to gender. Thus, it is not surprising that the majority of the interviewees who had a strong connection to it were young adults, often with at least a college education, which is evident in the statements quoted in the paragraphs that follow.

Instagram users often feel a certain pressure to offer a pleasing visual impression of themselves, which can lead to negative emotional consequences. As Estefania, the employee at a non-profit, puts it:

Instagram has this thing that everything seems pretty, everything seems super cool. Like one has a perfect life through the eyes of Instagram. . . . I swear to you that this lowers your self-esteem. Well, not your self-esteem, but that you sort of say 'wow, what is this person doing well that I'm not?' [laughs] Because you say, "hey, that's the life." . . . It's always the case that another person's Instagram or the life of that other person seems really cool [on Instagram].

To some interviewees, the normative ideal that they perceive as orienting social practices on this platform might, on occasion, lead people to edit their pictures in such a way that the image on the screen is quite different from the image in person. Julieta, the attorney, says that there are

lots of people who you meet in person in 3D and they're different. I see pictures of those girls and if I met them I'd say "wow, what a goddess!" If my partner would give a "like" to a picture of that goddess I would get madly jealous. . . . And when I see that picture and [then] meet the person I say . . . "How are you not ashamed of posting a picture that you know it's favoring your looks infinitely to a way that is unreal?". . . "Do you want to be a blonde? Go to the hair stylist and dye your hair, and if you like it, take a picture and even for five minutes it was real.". . [But] there are many things that are . . . strange, half borderline deceptive.

Interviewees often use the platform to embellish their pictures and videos of themselves, trips, pets, food, material possessions, and any other objects about which they post. So much so that sometimes the platform is used predominantly for its visual editing software capabilities. For example, Rosario, the Pilates instructor, uses Instagram "more than anything, if I'm being honest with you . . . to put filters to the pictures! Have you seen that on Instagram you can put filters to the pictures or stitch together two pictures, [and] color them? I use it mostly for that, to make eye-catching pictures for my Pilates page." Because she has her Instagram and Facebook pages interlinked, she uses these photo editing capabilities to make sure "that the picture is prettier when it makes it to Facebook [too]."

This high level of aestheticization shapes how people use other platforms also, in particular Snapchat. Maribel notes that "to me since Snapchat emerged it took the daily stuff away from Instagram. Like nowadays you leave the prettiest pictures for Instagram. Maybe you took one on Snapchat that came out great and you shift it to Instagram." Maribel's comments point to how this aestheticization also relates to frequency and type of posting on Instagram: most users share milestones rather than more mundane occurrences, and they do so more sporadically than on other platforms like Snapchat. She adds that on Instagram she "posts something from a special moment, like [a] more important [one]." Along similar lines, Carolina says that "Instagram originated to share the moment and now people share pictures from five years ago." Estela, a twenty-six-year-old employee at a non-profit, states, "I'm going to say something that bothers me: people who post a picture every two minutes and they're about quotidian stuff. I give [Instagram] a value that I like the pictures that are the prettiest on it." To her, "the person who posts [a picture] eating a hot dog is making a bad use" of this platform.

The aestheticization of Instagram is related to the fact that users follow celebrity accounts in a way that is much less common on other platforms. Furthermore, this trend appears to be more prevalent among female interviewees than among their male counterparts. Marina, the financial analyst, says that on Instagram "maybe I don't read news about culture per se but, as I was mentioning before, I follow several famous [people]." She adds that "only on Instagram I follow famous [people], not on Facebook . . . [which] I use to see pictures that [ordinary] people post." Florencia, a college student, also says that on Instagram she follows "lots of famous [people]. . . . I enjoy following Selena Gomez, Justin Bieber." Luciana comments that on this platform she "follow[s] some artists, musicians, DJs." Sara shares a similar practice and rationale to Marina's, Florencia's, and Luciana's: "I follow famous [people] because I like to look at entertainment news." As it is often the case with interests in celebrity news in traditional media, following the accounts of famous people on Instagram can be a way of vicariously experiencing a sense of glamour that counters the perception that one's life is fairly ordinary. Thus, Isabel comments that on Instagram she "follows quite a few famous [people]. I enjoy seeing what's going on in the lives of the famous since my [own] life is quite routine."

This celebrity focus is tied to a shared understanding that frivolous or light content has a special home on Instagram. Ana says that she uses

"Instagram . . . as my most frivolous social network. I follow clothing brands and silly things like that. No way I would follow a news page!" Sabrina, a twenty-one-year-old college student, echoes Ana's words: "On Instagram I follow accounts that interest me, like clothing brands but also bloggers. I have fashion bloggers, food bloggers, travel bloggers, whatever you can think of." Leila, also a college student, sums it up by saying that Instagram is mostly "to consume in an entertainment mode, like videos." Agustina concurs: "I watch funny videos more than anything." Gabriel, a thirty-two-year-old insurance agent, shares a similar sentiment when he says that "only every so often I upload something [on Instagram] and it's mostly about entertainment."

This thematic concentration of the activity on Instagram is well suited for people whose occupations are in the field of entertainment—and therefore can help users monetize their activity on this platform. Thus, for Paola, the professional model, Instagram

> is a work tool because it's like a second book. . . . There are brands which see me on Instagram and contact me via Instagram. Even though I'm represented by a modeling agency, [these brands] talk to me first [via Instagram] anyway. . . . Every day I post, at least, one picture. . . . And I tend to it. I take care of the aesthetics [of these pictures] a lot.

Even though many interviewees follow a lot of celebrity and entertainment accounts, there is a common notion that, as far as their own followers go, Instagram is a much smaller space than other platforms. Ernesto, a private tutor, says that Instagram is "more personal, I can add a few people, only the ones that I want and nothing else. And I can post a picture with a brief caption and that's it. . . . I can choose very well whom to follow, whereas on Facebook even with the protections that it has now it's not so easy and I don't like it." He adds that "I like to be able to choose the people to whom I show things." From a technical standpoint, this is the case for all platforms studied in this chapter. However, as Ernesto's statement shows, people view different platforms as having different levels of intimacy, with Instagram appearing as a place for congregating smaller and more selective publics. This, in turn, shapes the kinds of content that people post on this platform, and the extent to which they make it available on others. Ramiro, a twenty-one-year-old architecture major, says that his parents and older family members are not on Instagram:

There are times in which I post stuff that is not for the girl whom I follow and who might not be interested in it, [but] I want for it to be seen by the people who might be interested. I posted a picture of a school project, a mock-up that came out really well . . . and I wanted the people who probably don't have Instagram to see it, then I shared it on Facebook and then I saw a comment from my aunt "Aw, Ramiro, how cute you are."

The entertainment- and celebrity-oriented, frivolous content that marks most people's experience of Instagram is a contrast with that of other platforms, in particular Twitter. As Lucrecia, a twenty-three-year-old student, puts it: "I use Instagram mostly to relax, but Twitter is more like information[centric]." Estanislao, who is twenty-seven years of age and works in an accounting firm, concurs: "I use Twitter mostly to inform myself of certain news stories, and Instagram is something that has more to do with my personal and social life."

Twitter

Newsstands abound in the streets of Buenos Aires and of many other cities in Argentina. They primarily sell newspapers and magazines but sometimes also offer other small goods. People often congregate there—perusing the latest issues of their preferred publications and maybe buying something else, too; on occasion, they also engage in casual conversation with the person running the establishment as well as fellow customers and passers-by. Interactions at this fixture of the urban landscape tend to be brief and information-centered, in which a few regulars mix with a larger cast of more transient people. Twitter is the social media equivalent of this institution of Argentine urban culture: a digital environment where interactions revolve around news and information, have an informal tone and often feature a funny angle, are recurrent but brief, and combine small groups of core habitual interlocutors with a much larger cast of interlopers. Access to Twitter skews in favor of the young and those at the top of the socioeconomic pyramid. The likelihood of being on this platform among those included in the survey triple from oldest to youngest—11.11% versus 35.67%—and poorest to richest—13.33% versus 39.44%. It is also slightly more prevalent among the male than the female respondents—27.23% versus 23.91%. As with the case of Instagram, these social structural patterns are visible in the quotes included in the remainder of this section.

Lucas, the attorney, says that "nowadays you find out everything sooner from Twitter than from newspapers." And he adds:

> I really use it to inform myself. For instance, the speeches of politicians, nowadays they use Twitter instead of press secretaries. And then you have news analyses. Something happens that is important and within five seconds you have the analysis from all the different viewpoints.

Bruno, an eighteen-year-old student, echoes Lucas's experience of Twitter: "It's more like my news center because whenever something happens with a controversial news story, everybody comments about it." In a language reminiscent of agenda-setting theory, Zoraida, also a student, comments that she "uses Twitter to know what is being talked about in the world . . . and what people are talking about." Thus, when there is a major political story, for instance, those who are on Twitter flock to the platform to follow the events. Estefania remarks that during the 2015 presidential elections in Argentina, "at one point the results were going to be announced and I was searching on Twitter. It makes you feel a bit like you're talking to a large group, that you're sharing opinions, or that somebody saw the same [news] that you saw because somebody [else] commented [about it]."

Many interviewees intentionally go on Twitter to access news. Ana, a twenty-one-year-old student, says that "I inform myself a lot through Twitter. The first thing I do in the morning is go on Twitter and look at the Trending Topics." Juana, also a student, shares a similar practice: "I wake up in the morning and the first thing I open is Twitter, not Facebook. The morning is the time [of the day] in which all of the newspapers post their news stories. Since I follow three or four different newspapers . . . the only thing I see on my feed is one news story after the other." But to some other interviewees, their news consumption on Twitter is less intentional and more incidental. That is, they go on Twitter not necessarily looking for news content, but find it anyway. "If I'm doing nothing I go [on Twitter] and start reading what other people write; if I see that they're talking about something that I don't know anything about, then I go [online] to see what's going on (laughs)."

An accelerated temporal cycle is a key characteristic of how interviewees experience Twitter. Victor uses Twitter a lot in part because "it's fast, it's like you have everything instantaneously. . . . [T]hat's the advantage that it has" over other platforms, in his view. But not all interviewees find this characteristic to be appealing. On the contrary, to some, the immediacy is a reason they do not use this platform. Lucila is a Twitter non-user. When asked why that was the case, she laughed and then replied by resorting to graphic metaphor, "Twitter seems like the devil to me. . . . The 140-character format is to vomit any thought that you have."

Beyond speed, Juana's prior comments point to a common distinction that several interviewees made concerning their primary motivations for visiting Twitter and Facebook: news and information on the former, and relationship management on the latter. Gabriel, a thirty-two-year-old insurance broker, puts it as follows: "The issue of checking out information every day happens on Twitter; and Facebook is to see what a family member [or] a friend are doing." This difference in content is tied to a difference in style, with discourse on Twitter registering a more informal and spontaneous tone, whereas that on Facebook takes a more formal and controlled one. Juana again: "[On Twitter] I see jokes. In addition to seeing news and retweeting serious stuff, I also retweet things about soccer, I don't know, Independiente [Football Club], jokes by friends . . . all those silly things. Facebook is more serious. It's a different style, less dispersed, then like I publish more pictures, pictures with filters." Sara concurs by saying that "the way I see others use [both platforms] is . . . that on Twitter they post the first thing that comes to their minds, whereas Facebook is maybe more reserved." Thus, Sabrina confesses that she "uses [Twitter] a lot to post things that occur to me and are funny." Jorge adds that in his experience, discourse on "Twitter is very ironic . . . has its own sense of humor." Reinforcing this idea, Martin notes that "Twitter is to have fun . . . to laugh my ass off. . . . Twitter is a space with lots of very funny people." This applies even to otherwise serious matters like presidential elections. Estefania, who as noted above, followed the 2015 election returns in Argentina on Twitter:

> What happens to me with Twitter is that it's very funny. For instance, during the [2015] elections, it was very funny to read the news, but with a comical angle. Because people are taking something that is serious, between inverted commas, and adding to it a bit of humor. That's what I like about Twitter.

But Twitter is not the only platform to which interviewees attribute a humorous tone. Snapchat is another one. Maria, a twenty-two-year-old college student, says that an advantage of Snapchat is that "to me it's super fun that [posts] disappear [after 24 hours]. I don't know, because it gives you a use that Twitter doesn't [give you]. Like I can post a picture that maybe is a bit silly, maybe doesn't make much sense. . . . I don't know . . . something more spontaneous that stops being [available]." Thus, while both Twitter and Snapchat are seen as platforms where humorous discourse prevails, the kinds of content that embody that humor differ. The news-centric textual material that characterizes Twitter gives way to visually oriented ludic posts that mark the experience on Snapchat, the social media carnival.

Snapchat

As evident from the survey findings, Snapchat is a platform of the young and the well-to-do—the typical user is generally a minor, and therefore below the age limit of the people included in this study. Its prevalence is 14.04% and 18.31% among the youngest and wealthiest groups in the survey, respectively, as opposed to 5.56% and 2.22% among their oldest and poorest counterparts, also respectively. Thus, it should come as no surprise that most of the interviewees who use Snapchat are younger than thirty years of age and are either college students or graduates. For them, Snapchat is like the digital enactment of Carnival, the traditional festivities that in Argentina are most notably celebrated in the city of Gualeguaychú, in the province of Entre Ríos, every February. As in Carnival, interactions on Snapchat are mostly playful, have a strong visual orientation but are less aestheticized and more creative than on Instagram, possess an episodic rhythm and a fairly spontaneous character, are considered to be ephemeral, and are often less inhibited than in other platforms. Thus, Snapchat has become a space where young people gather to socialize and enjoy themselves for short periods of time, and they do so predominantly through spontaneous interactions marked by the playful use of pictures and masks.

To Laura, "Snapchat is more to mess around with my girlfriends, like, 'I send you a picture' [and that's it]." Florencia concurs: "Snapchat [is] to have fun, to mess around." The centrality of playfulness on this platform is such that it led Patricio to stop following journalists on it:

It's all entertainment. I used to follow two journalists, but I stopped because it wasn't commensurate with how I used Snapchat, which was totally to send crazy pictures and nothing more than that. And to show . . . for instance, if I'm eating something. . . . I can show things that it wouldn't occur to me to show on other platforms. . . . Because in the other [platforms] they stay there forever unless I erase them, whereas Snapchat has another [kind of] use. People see it or not if they want, nothing gets any comments. And my followers also do [this].

Like the costumes in a Carnival, the filters on Snapchat add a playful layer to a visually centered interaction. Estela, a twenty-six-year-old non-profit employee, comments that she "takes pictures, adds funny filters . . . and you can create your story, share them or send them to one person." Laura reinforces the centrality of the visual aspect by noting that "those little faces that you can create are, nothing, to have fun." However, this visual component is different from that of Instagram, because it is less aestheticized and more mundane. In Agustina's words, "Snapchat is like Instagram, but allowing absolutely everything. . . . You're posting a lot of silly stuff and everybody else is posting a lot of silly stuff, so it's socially accepted that people post silly stuff."

Another difference is that whereas an episodic temporality guides posting frequency on Instagram, on which people focus on important milestones, a more continuous rhythm marks shared practices and expectations on Snapchat. Interviewees note that on Snapchat they privilege "the moment." According to Sabrina, "Snapchat is about what I'm doing right now, at this very moment." Maribel adds that this platform "is more spontaneous of the moment. . . . I use Snapchat for the daily stuff . . . like I'm studying something or what not; and I post on Instagram something from more special . . . more important [stuff]." This instantaneity is linked to fairly continuous uses, to "sharing moments all the time," as Adriana, a college student puts it. Patricio ties this matter to posting about banal activities: "I show more, for example, if I'm eating this or that . . . I can show things that I wouldn't share on another network." Therefore, many interviewees see Snapchat as, paradoxically, less time demanding, because, in Bruno's words, "I can log in for two seconds and then I go on with my life." In this sense Snapchat is perceived as akin to Twitter, as Juana says:

Snapchat is like for the daily stuff, you know? Like Twitter, you post a tweet about the moment . . . like you found your cat in a strange position, or a friend with pouty face, or you stepped on shit, I don't know, you're tired, a picture in bed, whatever. You post it, it lasts a day, nothing happens, nobody saves it or anything like that. There is no record [of it], that's also important.

Juana's comments underscore that ephemerality figures into the appeal that Snapchat has among young people. Most posts disappear after 24 hours, which is a stark contrast with the four other platforms analyzed in this chapter, where the default setting is that posts stay indefinitely unless they are manually removed by the account owner. In other words, it is not impossible to achieve that kind of ephemerality on Facebook, for instance, but it requires a level of effort and consistency that is already embedded within the technical architecture of Snapchat. Therefore, most users assume that posts will stay permanently on the other platforms. Agustina comments that on Snapchat "you have a day in which you're a jerk and [a post] disappears, whereas on Facebook it stays there. It happened to me the other day, on a Friday night, that [somebody asked me] 'have you seen the picture that [a common acquaintance] posted on Snapchat?' I was like 'no.' And they told me 'uh, no, you can't see it anymore because a whole day went by.'"

Most Snapchat users are keen on the ephemerality of this platform because it allows communication practices that are looser and less inhibited. Ramiro notes that "the good thing about Snapchat is that it's more ephemeral.... [A post] is floating around for 24 hours and then gets erased.... Like I upload some silly stuff, send it to my friends, we laugh, and it ends there." Agustina concurs: "It's like Friday evening and you were drunk and shared a picture scantily clothed and there is no record [of it]." She adds that these more relaxed posts provide an almost real-time window into others' lives: "I was just talking to some girlfriends who said that Snapchat was great because you can know what others are doing at all times.... You find what each one of your friends is doing, if they're in a bar or a party, because people film everything that they do.... It's like being with the other all the time."

This sense of being with the other all the time is linked to a perception that connections are more intimate on Snapchat than on other platforms. Magnolia, a twenty-two-year-old teacher assistant, "doesn't like to make things public [but] on Snapchat [posts] stay between one and the other." Maribel concurs: "Snapchat is more relaxed [than other social media options] ... more personal, belonging to the group of friends, people closer [to me]." Carolina adds that "maybe Snapchat doesn't have as many users as other networks." Thus, to Ramiro there is a sense of "public intimacy" on this platform: "I say, 'I tell you [something] for three seconds and that's it. I'm not going to send you anything intimate about myself, but I'll tell you something, it's [soon] forgotten and ends [quickly]. . . . I'm not going to be telling it to a million people.'"

As noted in the introduction to this section, the mix of playful, quotidian, less inhibited, and more intimate character of Snapchat is particularly appealing to the very young and much less appealing to those who are not so young. Middle-aged and older interviewees do not enjoy this platform. Moreover, even several young adults seemed either unaware of it or quite unattracted to it. Mora, a thirty-year-old industrial designer, is not a platform user: "I believe it is a generational issue, like the moment to use Snapchat is gone [for me]." Sofia, a twenty-nine-year-old, downloaded the Snapchat app, but "I don't use it; my little niece does. She plays with the little faces. . . . What happens is that Snapchat is for the youngest, who're publishing all the time what they've been doing. [On the contrary] what I do doesn't interest the whole world!"

Attachment

As I showed in chapter 2 with respect to personal screens, many interviewees feel a significant level of attachment to particular social media platforms. Time and again people noted that they feel more connected to the various platforms they use than they would ideally like to feel, and the urge to check them is difficult to resist. They also experience what they deem to be negative consequences from using them.

Bruno, the student, says that being on these platforms "consumes time [while] you're trying to do something productive." He adds that "it's like social networks are calling you. I don't know, like it's difficult to move away from them. . . . In general, when I go on [these platforms] they can consume one or two hours [of my time]." Jorge, also a college student, says that he checks social media "on average . . . 10 minutes per hour." And he then clarifies, "without counting when I'm sleeping." Given the amount of time her social media use takes up, Romina tried to quit Facebook for two months. "And then I realized that it was hard because there were people with whom if I didn't have my cell phone and I needed to talk to them [I couldn't], or if I wanted to find out about events . . . Things like that." On the basis of that experience, she went back on Facebook and concluded that "one always wants to fight against the system, but it's hard to live outside of it." Estefania reports experiences similar to those of Bruno, Jorge, and Romina, and notes that for her

> maybe it's something psychological [laughs]. I don't know, like you have to be up to date, you have to know what's going on because otherwise [I'd feel] that I'm missing out. . . . Have you seen that thing that is very fashionable these days? That in English it's called FOMO. It's like "fear of missing out," no? Well, I have FOMO!

The attachment to social media is not confined to one particular platform but applies to all of them. Marisol, the cook, confesses that she "used to be all the time looking at Facebook or WhatsApp . . . attentive to the response of other people." Juanita, the schoolteacher, states that she uses WhatsApp "a lot, to interact [with people]. The group I use the most is with my aunts, we share pictures. . . . Or with the other teachers, to share pictures of school. But, yes, I use it, I use it a lot." Romina, the student who switched from a regular cell phone to a smartphone just to be able to have WhatsApp, says that she is "aware that this isn't a very human practice, to be all the time glued [to the platform]." She adds that she has "a bit of an addiction. It's what I was telling you especially about Facebook, looking at all the s..t that everybody does. . . . Before, when I didn't have a smartphone, I was on the subway looking at people [on their phones] and I said to myself 'look at these people, oh my God.' " By contrast, for Estefania, Twitter is the platform from which she has a hard time disconnecting. She says that she has to be on Twitter "whenever I'm doing something else. For instance, if I'm watching television I also have to be on Twitter." The interview continued as follows:

ESTEFANIA: Twitter gave me this [habit].
INTERVIEWEE: What happens if you do just one thing?
ESTEFANIA: I feel that I have to grab something, that is, my cell phone, you see? I even made the movement (simulates the movement while talking). Where is my cell phone? (laughs)
INTERVIEWEE: I see. Why do you say that "Twitter gave me this"?
ESTEFANIA: I don't know, because . . . the first social network that grabbed my attention the most or that got me addicted was Twitter.

Yet, to others like Andrea, the photographer, Instagram is the Achilles heel. "I feel like I lose a lot of time every day of my life on social media. A lot. Then, I don't want to do it anymore." But she keeps going back, and illustrates it with a revealing family anecdote:

> I check [Instagram] automatically, which I think it's terrible, but that's what happens to me. I mean, all of a sudden I'm like this (makes a gesture of looking at the screen) and [my husband] tells me 'all set? No more pictures on Instagram?' 'Ouch, don't tell me you were here (referring to the bed), and I was here (referring to the platform).' . . . And I didn't realize that he was [next to me]. Maybe I was just looking at a message and since I was there . . . Terrible!

This high level of attachment to social media is often linked to the fact that people will look at a given platform as a way of filling empty time. In Zoraida's words: "One second that I'm doing absolutely nothing and I go on Twitter . . . same with WhatsApp. In this sense I use both platforms when I have a break, to see what's going on. Do you understand?" David, a twenty-four-year-old employee at a paint shop, says that he uses social media "mostly during an idle moment. I'm at home sitting on the couch and I begin to read Twitter." The aimless way that people use social media to fill time means many interviewees get lost within the maelstrom of posts and spend a lot more time than they would otherwise. Ramiro, the architecture student, puts it as follows:

> You get hooked on things that really don't interest you. You scroll down "wow, look, let's see, let's open this," or "ah, this interests me" and then I open it, and then you tell [yourself] "look, this also interests me." And a chain gets formed that makes me feel uncomfortable. It doesn't make me feel uncomfortable, but it bothers me. I mean, I'm losing time. I sat down at 4:00 pm, and it's 4:30 or 5:00 and I keep doing silly stuff, not things that interest me. . . . How is it that this which is nothing, that doesn't generate anything in me . . . keeps me scrolling down as if by chance I will find something that all of a sudden interests me? . . . It never happens, or very rarely happens that you find something that you really like and that interests you.

Another reason people become attached to social media is the expectation that messages, posts, and comments will be attended to and reciprocated. "There is little tolerance," says Marisol. "Many people become intolerant if you don't reply to their messages.... [And] everything has to be fast, everything has to be easy." She also notes that being constantly connected through social media might bring people closer together, but at the expense of paying less attention to what happens outside of the digital environment. "It brings you closer to the people you have far away, and in one way or the other it keeps you attentive to the phone all the time.... But in some other way it keeps you away from the people [you have nearby]." Cornelia concurs: "I spend a lot of time with very young people, godchildren of mine, and they really get isolated on social networks.... I see them as growing apart from society." Flavia, a forty-eight-year-old interior designer tells a story that vividly illustrates this dynamic:

Last night, [a group of female friends] were sitting at the table, chatting. And I had five [of them] around me while I was talking to one at the head of the table. Two of them were on this side and three on the other side, and they were in this position (hunched over, head facing a screen) looking at Facebook.... Ten in the evening, with food on the table, people chatting, shouting, and they were looking at Facebook on their phones, in another world, looking at the lives of others.... Absent, gone [from the physical space].

As with the attachment to personal screens, it is common for interviewees to have measures of self-control, practices that they put in place to free certain times and places from the presence of social media. "I really like Twitter and it's definitely [the platform] I use the most," says Victor. Therefore, "when I'm about to take an exam, I close my account [temporarily] to avoid getting hooked reading things and wasting my time." Along similar lines, Zoraida comments that she "loves going on Twitter, Facebook. . . . I don't have Facebook on the computer so I have to check it out on the cell phone. I put this limit because otherwise I'd log in like an idiot to do nothing." Moving from the personal to the relational, Sofia confesses that "with my boyfriend we aren't connected on Facebook. This way we survive [as a couple, and] ... we don't have to be attentive to what we published, the likes we gave. [Otherwise] it leads to conflict.... Because if you start searching it's terrible. If you search, you will find."

Concluding Remarks

What have we learned about the structure and culture of the experience of information abundance from this empirical journey through the social media labyrinth?

The analysis presented in this chapter shows that age has a greater influence as a structural factor than both socioeconomic status and gender in the uptake of social media. This pattern influences a number of issues, from who is on social media in general and on specific platforms to the average number of platforms used, and from the perception of indispensability of these communication technologies to the frequencies with which they are used. Furthermore, this pattern is consistent with what happens in the case of personal screens, as I showed in chapter 2. It is also in part related to it, since, for instance, the use of the smartphone is inextricably tied to being on social media. Thus, the appropriation of the technological infrastructure of information abundance is structured primarily around matters of age, and secondarily around those of socioeconomic status and gender.

In a country in which one-third of the population lived under the level of poverty at the time of this study—with one in every sixteen households below the indigence level—and with high levels of income inequality, the greater structuring power of age than socioeconomic status is particularly noteworthy. Research suggests that one reason age might play this role has to do with the greater centrality of digital innovation in the consumption of the tools that we use for socialization, self-expression, information, and entertainment. During most of the twentieth century, the main artifacts people resorted to for these goals—such as telephones, letters, newspapers, and radio and television sets—were fairly stable and simple to use after an initial period of introduction and adaptation. By contrast, the relentless pace and ever expanding breadth of technological change have made the experience of mediated interaction, news, and entertainment into one that is, borrowing from the apt notion coined by economic sociologists Gina Neff and David Stark, "permanently beta."[20] In this environment, the well-documented[21] greater interest of younger people in newer technologies—as well as their typical greater predisposition to tinker with them—leads to dynamics in which "children perceive themselves, and are perceived by their parents, as agents teaching their parents how to use digital media."[22] Drawing upon her work in Chile, Argentina's neighbor across the Andes mountains, Teresa Correa argues that these dynamics foster among low-income families a process she labels "bottom-up socialization" whereby "greater perceived influence by youths on computer adoption and learning reduced the SES [socioeconomic status] divide in their parents' computer use. Similarly, youths' perceived influence on Internet adoption closed the gap in their parents' Internet use."[23] It is possible that the cumulative effect of this type of socialization accounts for at least part of the reduction of the role of socioeconomic status as a structural factor and further raises the importance of age.

I have also shown that within these structural parameters people experience the abundance of content and interactions partly shaped by the meanings variously attributed to the different platforms by themselves and those in their social milieu. These meanings are tied to a series of norms and expectations of what each platform is most suitable for—and what it is not. These meanings, norms, and expectations orient people's actions regarding what to post where and when, how to react to the content available, and how to communicate with others on each platform.[24] Thus, commentary on a major, breaking news story will probably be posted primarily on Twitter—and maybe shared on Facebook and/or WhatsApp, secondarily—but it will not be featured on Instagram or Snapchat. What will show up in this latter platform, in all likelihood, is a stream of pictures documenting mundane interactions among a group of friends during a rainy Saturday afternoon, and most likely none of these pictures will make it to any of the other platforms—unless one of them came out particularly well, in which case it may be shared on Instagram to mark the occasion. None of these behaviors are determined by the technological capabilities of each of these platforms. Even though the default ephemerality of Snapchat is tied to lower levels of inhibition on this platform, this type of behavior seems more a social spillover than a technical necessity since users can erase posts on all platforms—in which case ephemerality would result from additional effort rather than from technical settings.

The various combinations of interpretation, affect, and practice highlight the role of agency in the use of platforms. This manifests in the plethora of practices undertaken to take advantage of certain capabilities regarding certain types of content and aimed at certain imagined audiences on one or more platforms but not on the others. This is also evident in the various strategies interviewees pursued—successfully and unsuccessfully—to disconnect from social media. This, in turn, connects to issues of attachment. As with personal screens, interviewees sensed at times that it was difficult to feel in control of their experience and to easily unplug. This in part had to do with the perception among many that there is very little of everyday life that happens outside of platforms, as Rosario's quote at the beginning of this chapter suggests with respect to WhatsApp. Therefore, unplugging from them also means unplugging from everyday life. In the words of Romina, "One always wants to fight against the system, but it is hard to live outside of it." All of which provides a unique window into an ongoing reconstitution of sociality that is evident in three interrelated but distinct processes.

First, being on social media enables individuals to partake in multiple interactions concurrently, blending co-located with non-colocated contexts.[25] This expansion in the potential scope of the social world has been met with a tremendous curiosity for the lives of others. As I noted in the preface and chapter one, if the information abundance during the Middle Ages was connected to what Ann Blair has called an info-lust about the natural world, the contemporary era of information abundance switches that register to the lives of others. Without this remarkable level of interest about the lives even of people an individual does not know personally—such as contacts of contacts on social media—this expansion in the scope of the social world would be technically possible but socially inconsequential. This is also tied to a certain acceleration of the expected response time, all of which seemed for many interviewees to take a respite only when they go to sleep. The combination of these patterns contributes to create the impression that is indeed possible to partake in an ever expanding number of social relations concurrently, that one's life also has to be reciprocally open and available to others, and that there is a speeding up in the rhythm of sociality.

Second, interviewees often felt that these mounting pressures challenged their abilities to control the flow of communication to their satisfaction.[26] This tension between self-perceptions of efficacy and inefficacy translated into experiencing the use of these technologies as both empowering and disempowering: the former in the sense of opening spaces for novel and valued forms of relating to others, and the latter of being unable to curtail both practices of use and connections with others. Thus, interviewees conveyed a certain sense of not being fully in control of their sociality, which led them to enact multiple practices of self-discipline in terms of when, how, with whom, and for what purposes they used each screen and platform. Complementing these dynamics there was also a certain tension among a subset of interviewees between a perception of information overstimulation on the one hand, and having difficulties contending with silence—or lack of information—on the other hand. For these interviewees, having the television or radio sets always on, or constantly checking their messages and social media feeds has contributed to making solitude a rare occurrence. All in all, these issues of self-efficacy, power, and control converge in shaping the dialectic between agency and attachment that is central to the contemporary experience of screens and platforms.

Third, the combination of quantitative increases in volume and qualitative challenges to the ability of being on top of the communication flow frequently intertwined with interviewees' own interpretations about the value of these ongoing changes in their sociality. These interpretations reflexively shaped what they did, and why they thought they did what they did. There was also a tension between positive and negative assessments of the impact of various ensembles of screens and platforms. On the one hand, a majority of survey respondents suggested that the use of social media is indispensable to their relational life. There was, however, a significant difference related to age—with this sentiment being much more prevalent among the youngest than the oldest groups of respondents. Furthermore, this was sometimes accompanied by reflections about the convenience and freedom afforded by new forms of sociality. But, on the other hand, many interviewees, especially those in the older age spectrum, expressed reservations and/or outright objections about ongoing changes in social practices and expectations in relation to the prevalent patterns of screen and platform use. These divergent assessments reinforce the worth of adopting a stance of emergent valuation about the consequences of information abundance that animates this book, since it eschews the simplistic discourse of deficit prevalent in the prior relevant scholarship. Instead, it favors one that makes sense of the combination of positive and negative aspects from the vantage point of the subjects rather than an abstract normative ideal that appears to be particularly ill-suited to deal with the sprawling multiplicity of positional and contextual circumstances of screen and platform use. These assessments also speak about the widespread perception of change in modes of sociality that are experienced as significant enough to generate a level of reflexivity that is absent during more routine periods.

Taken together, these three dimensions challenge the assertion by Rich Ling, presented in the introduction to this chapter, of a "continuance of sociation," and indicate the presence of significant discontinuities in perceptions, practices, and interpretations. These discontinuities, however, do not seem to be in the direction argued by Lee Rainie and Barry Wellman— of lower levels of embedding in groups. On the contrary, most of the growth in the volume of the interaction, and of the concerns with how to manage it, appeared to be lodged in preexistent groups, from immediate to extended families, from present-day to older friendship networks, and from child-hood classmates to parenting groups. It is worth noticing that this process of lodging in preexistent groups might be partly shaped by Argentina's strong associational culture. The *café* has long been both an emblem and a key locus of this process—which is why I chose it as a metaphor for WhatsApp, today's preeminent mediated space for the reconstitution of sociality in the country. As cultural historian Jorge Myers argues, already in the nineteenth century "the *porteño cafés* [coffee houses in the City of Buenos Aires] spon-sored a set of activities much more varied than the consumption of infusions and foodstuffs: books and newspapers were read and discussed, card games were played, public and private gossip circulated, and, according to some witnesses, there were activities less tolerated by contemporary morality."[27] Interviewees' experiences of WhatsApp—and other platforms—build upon yet also intensify and amplify Buenos Aires' *café* practices of the mid-1800s.

Thus, and contrary to Sherry Turkle's dystopic assessments stated ear-lier, the potential problems for interviewees were rooted not in a decrease of empathy, attention, and care but in the gap between the greater intention to empathize with, attend to, and care about many significant and not-so-significant others and what was experienced as limited time and energy. If anything, the heightened sense of attachment that was shown in this chapter and the previous one signals the contemporary difficulties that many individ-uals have in parting ways even transitorily with their social relationships—enabled by the screens and platforms that make such hyper-connectivity possible. The ever-growing reliance on media technologies in the ongoing re-constitution of sociality[28] has afforded the opportunity for people to be more, not less, social, and for solitude to become an increasingly rare source of per-sonal fulfillment.

Overall, the account in this chapter also underscores the heuristic power of the analytical approach adopted for this book in ways that complement prior work on information overload. First, issues of expression and relationality that are the very core of social media would have been lost with a focus on decision-making. Second, the centrality of leisure, news, entertainment, and everyday management in platform practices would have been missed by cen-tering on instrumental goals. Third, in light of the wide variety in the modal-ities and intensities of platform use that emerges from the interviews—and how much they are shaped by positional and contextual factors—attempting to figure out an optimal level of platform use might seem a noble goal but its practical realization would remain highly fraught. Fourth, as elaborated earlier, a default discourse of deficit would not do justice to the much more complex valuations that interviewees assign to roles of platforms in their lives.

As I have shown, the combination of screens and platforms is regularly used to access news and entertainment content. The volume of these types of content has also risen dramatically over the past few decades. It is to the everyday experience of consuming these two types of content that I turn to in chapters 4 and 5, respectively.

4

News

I get . . . news [stories], but have no time to read them.
I just see the links and get a sense of what the stories are
more or less about. But overall I feel that there is a
constant bombardment of information from the digital media.
                    Sandra, forty-eight years old, clerical employee.

The commercialization of the web a quarter century ago ushered in an era
of major growth in the volume of news outlets, the size of their audiences,
and the stories available to them. Long gone are the days in which people got
the news through a handful of broadcast channels, radio stations, and print
newspapers. People who access the internet can check the news on thousands
of sites, the vast majority with no cost other than their time. Gone are also
the days in which the largest news organizations assembled publics of a few
million people, each of them being able to consume only a handful of stories
at a time. Nowadays, the most powerful news companies have hundreds of
millions of users digitally. For instance, *Clarín*—which has been the highest
circulation daily in Argentina for several decades—had an average Sunday
circulation of 362,410 in July 2020.[1] By contrast, Clarin.com, the newspaper's
website, reached 71,500,000 visits that month.[2] Even if *Clarín* had different readers every Sunday of the month—a scenario that is exceedingly
unlikely—and most site visits were undertaken by a core group of visitors,
it is reasonable to assume that the digital public was several orders of magnitude larger than its print counterpart. Not only are digital publics much
larger than those of traditional media, the volume of news at their disposal
has also skyrocketed. For instance, a search with the keywords Lionel Messi
on Lanacion.com—the site of the main print rival of *Clarín*—performed
on October 17, 2020, yielded 16,685 stories published over the past quarter
century. Accessing this number of stories would have required dozens if not
hundreds of visits to a library before.

Abundance. Pablo J. Boczkowski, Oxford University Press. © Oxford University Press 2021.
DOI: 10.1093/oso/9780197565742.003.0004

The experience of this staggering growth in the volume of audiences and stories available is compounded by the speed at which information circulates in the contemporary world. The era of the daily news cycle seems long past in a context in which any major news development can spread online almost instantaneously. Although leading journalistic outfits continue publishing scoops, the period that such stories remain the exclusive property of a given organization has gone from a day or several hours to minutes or even seconds. The mundane experience of seeing news stories, true and false, go viral has led to a commodity expectation for most of the public: they are confident that most stories, in particular the high-profile ones, will probably be available in any and all of their outlets of choice. Moreover, these stories will almost certainly show up in their social media feeds even before they turn on the television set or visit their preferred news sites. This means that people are more exposed to news than ever before and can hardly escape the reach of news even when they would rather not be bothered—since most social media users do not visit platforms primarily to learn about current events, with the exception of Twitter, as was shown in chapter 3. It is no wonder that in light of this combination of volume, speed, commoditization, and ambiance, interviewees like Sandra feel bombarded by news stories but barely pay attention to them.

In this chapter I examine key structural and cultural factors that shape how people experience an information environment in which the news is plentiful. Regarding structural variables, I continue the exploration of the roles played by socioeconomic status, gender, and age regarding access and attitudes to news. Concerning cultural matters, I switch the analytical gaze to center on routines, which the existing scholarship shows is important in the reception of print and broadcast news. For present purposes, I draw upon three sets of findings from this scholarship to make more visible patterns of historical change in the contemporary scenario.

First, researchers have argued that most news consumption is highly routinized.[3] Thus, communication scholars David Gauntlett and Annette Hill have observed that "patterns of news consumption . . . were often based around scheduling and how this fitted into daily routine, rather than whether respondents found one channel more biased or intelligent than another."[4] Second, the high degree of routinization is organized alongside fairly predictable temporal and spatial coordinates: newspaper reading in the morning at home and also in public transit; similarly with radio listening, also present to a certain extent in the workplace; and television viewing at home in the early morning and, primarily, in the evening.[5] Media studies expert Roger Silverstone (1994) forcefully made this point for ordinary television viewing: "Television is a domestic medium. It is watched at home. Ignored at home. Discussed at home" (p. 24).[6] Third, the high degree of routinization and its organization alongside stable temporal and spatial parameters have been tied to a deep integration of news consumption into the fabric of social life.[7] Sociologist Leo Bogart (1989) noted that "perhaps the most important social function of newspapers is to be a catalyst for conversation and human contact. The news is an integral part of daily life" (p. 169).

Beneath these three patterns lie two under-examined common denominators that are essential for the analysis in this chapter: news was something that individuals had to obtain, and once they did that, the routines they enacted to consume it were primary. That is, they had to either buy a newspaper or turn on the television or radio set in order to get some news. Furthermore, once they acquired that information, its consumption was the primary focus of their attention: when someone sat down to read the news or watch a television newscast, that was often the main thing they did. These three patterns of findings and two common denominators form an initial background that will help bring into sharp relief patterns of continuity and discontinuity in contemporary dynamics of news reception.

The remainder of this chapter continues as follows. In the next section I will address the structural factors that shape access to, and attitudes toward, the news. I will spend the following two sections analyzing the reception routines of news in traditional and digital media, respectively. I will then address two issues that have become particularly salient regarding news reception in both kinds of media: the role of affect and the perception of bias. I will conclude by summarizing how the main findings help answer the questions stated in the preface, and reflecting on their implications for broader issues that motivate this book.

The Landscape of News Consumption

Access to news is almost universal among survey respondents: 97.43% percent of them said they look at news on a typical day. Unsurprisingly, with this level of access there is not much variance by age, socioeconomic status, or gender. However, there are major differences when it comes to the popularity of various news sources, with broadcast media clearly at the top of consumers' preferences, and the newer, digital alternatives surpassing their older, print counterparts (Figure 4.1). Television and radio were the two most popular choices, with 94.43% and 47.51% percent of the respondents saying that they get the news via these media, respectively. They were followed by social media at 38.71%, newspapers at 37.54%, websites at 25.95%, and magazines at 9.53%.

When asked to name their main source of news, 65.98% of respondents named television, reinforcing its dominance (Figure 4.2). Furthermore,

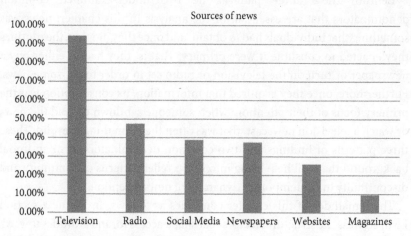

Figure 4.1. Sources of news.

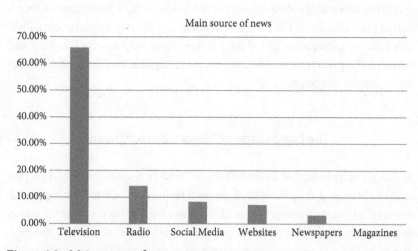

Figure 4.2. Main source of news.

there is a wide gap between television and the next most popular source. The main follower, radio, was 52 percentage points behind, at 14.22%. Thus, these two broadcast media combined are the key access point for news for four out of every five people in Argentina. Moreover, digital media have become the main alternatives to broadcast with a combined 15.54%, and with social media having a slight edge over websites. Finally, print media have almost entirely vanished as a principal entry door into the world of current events: a meager 3.23% named print newspapers as their top choice, and none of the 700 survey respondents named magazines. The contrast between the 37.54% who said they read newspapers and the 3.23% who choose them as their main source of news is a strong signal of the receding presence of print culture in the contemporary landscape of news consumption.

There are significant differences between those who identified broadcast media as their main sources of news, and those who named digital media.

Broadcast media is favored by people who are older and have lower socioeconomic status (Figures 4.3 and 4.4). But there are also major disparities between the survey respondents who listed television as their top choice versus those who expressed a similar preference for radio. First, there is a significant gender divide: women tend to favor television—73.45% versus 58.96%—and men radio—19.53% versus 8.85%. Although in absolute terms the gender spread between these two media is within a comparable range, in relative terms more than twice as many men as women named radio as

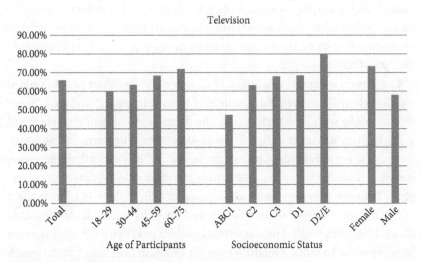

Figure 4.3. Television as the main source of news.
ABC1: High; C2: Middle; C3: Lower Middle; D1: Low; D2/E: Extreme Low

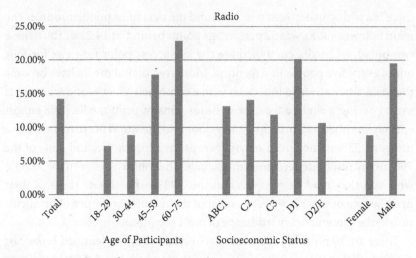

Figure 4.4. Radio as the main source of news.
ABC1: High; C2: Middle; C3: Lower Middle; D1: Low; D2/E: Extreme Low

their top choice. This is a very strong gender disparity. Second, a similar pattern applies to the age variable. While in absolute terms, the differences between the oldest and the youngest respondents who prefer television— 71.93% versus 59.88%—and radio—22.81% versus 7.19%—are some- what comparable, in relative terms this pattern is vastly more pronounced for radio: its prevalence is more than three times greater among older than younger people. Finally, on the one hand, there is a clear and linear socioec- onomic factor shaping who chooses television as their top access point for news. On the other hand, even though it appears that a more impoverished socioeconomic strata choose radio, the tendency is not nearly as strong as in the case of television.

Conversely, a higher proportion of younger and wealthier people singled out digital media as their main source of news (Figures 4.5 and 4.6). In ad- dition, unlike with broadcast media, the distribution of gender preferences is fairly even across the digital media spectrum. Furthermore, although there are some differences between those who privilege social media versus websites, these discrepancies are not nearly as stark as in the case of the diver- gence between television and radio consumers. First, there is a linear effect of age: the spread between the younger and the older respondents who iden- tified either of the digital media options as their top choice for news is much larger than for broadcast media—even for radio. In the case of social media the disparity is twenty-seven times—15.57% versus 0.58%—and for websites

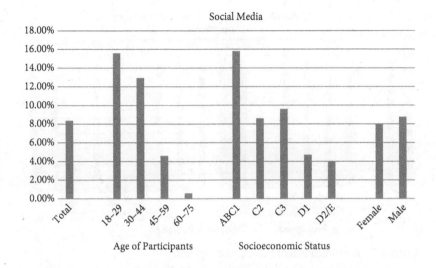

Figure 4.5. Social media as the main source of news.
ABC1: High; C2: Middle; C3: Lower Middle; D1: Low; D2/E: Extreme Low

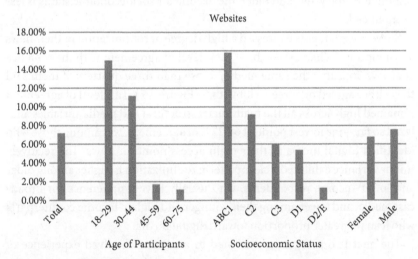

Figure 4.6. Websites as the main source of news.
ABC1: High; C2: Middle; C3: Lower Middle; D1: Low; D2/E: Extreme Low

it is thirteen times—14.97% versus 1.17%. A similar, albeit weaker, pattern can be seen in the case of socioeconomic status. The spread between those at the top and at the bottom of the income ladder is slightly less than four times for social media—15.79% versus 4.00%—and almost twelve times for websites—15.79% versus 1.33%. Finally, while the decrease is quite steep for

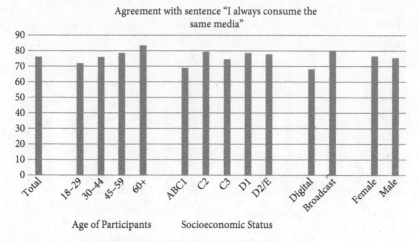

Figure 4.7. Routinization of news consumption.
ABC1: High; C2: Middle; C3: Lower Middle; D1: Low; D2/E: Extreme Low

respondents forty-five and older, the decline for socioeconomic status is less pronounced.

Survey respondents expressed a high degree of routinization in their news consumption. When asked about their level of agreement with the sentence "I always consume the same media," more than three quarters of them said they either agreed or agreed a lot with it (Figure 4.7). This level of agreement remained high across all the main social structural and media variables analyzed so far—the lowest point, at 68.27% of agreement, was among those who identified digital media as their main access point for news. The relatively minor variance exhibited a clear pattern: routinization is higher among older and lower-income respondents, who usually have a preference for broadcast media, and lower among their younger and higher-income counterparts who lean in greater proportion toward digital media.

The next two sections are devoted to analyzing the lived experience of these routines of news consumption by dividing the options into two major categories: traditional and digital media.

Traditional Media

The consumption of news in traditional media such as television, radio, and newspapers is highly routinized. However, while the habits of the first two are quite similar, those that pertain to print journalism differ in some notable ways and therefore provide an informative contrast. Thus, I will first address broadcast news consumption habits, then move on to reading newspapers, and finally briefly touch on mixed-media routines as a transition into the following section devoted to digital media.

The morning, between waking up and leaving for work, appears to be the main time for both television and radio news consumption among many interviewees. This pattern becomes stronger among interviewees starting in their mid-thirties, and further intensifies among those in their fifties and older. Mariana, a thirty-nine-year-old architect, illustrates the notion of television-as-company introduced in chapter 2 and adds a news dimension to it by saying, "I wake up and turn on television news to inform myself, [and] because it keeps me company; before leaving [for work] I like to have a sense of what's going on outside." Ezequiel, an attorney who is the same age as Mariana, has a similar routine and notes that for him "it's a habitual practice, especially because I have two little kids who go to kindergarten so I inform myself [about the weather] to see how I should dress them . . . and the same for me."

Getting the news is tightly integrated into the morning routines of many other interviewees, like Fabian, a forty-three-year-old doorman, who has "the alarm clock through the television; so, it turns on automatically and the *Crónica* [newscast] shows up on the screen. [I watch it] until I finish preparing coffee or *mate*, and then I go to work." Mara, who is forty-eight and works as an administrative assistant at an accounting firm, also weaves morning news consumption on television into her broader daily routines: "It's automatic; I have to take a medication before eating anything, so I turn on the television [as a prompt to do that]." Mabel, who is sixty-two and retired, does not need to leave her home rapidly for work. Yet, she enacts a similar pattern of behavior in a way that highlights its ambiance—a key feature of consuming news on broadcast media that I will address in greater depth later:

In general, [and] I do this routinely, I turn on the newscast every morning while I drink *mate* and have breakfast, [but] without volume. If there is something that interests me, then I put the volume higher and find out more.

Routinization is also high in the case of morning radio news consumption. Emanuel, a thirty-year-old employee at a store, comments that "the radio is always on when I'm having breakfast. I'm about to go to work and the radio is on, I inform myself [that way]. It's always on. It's a habit, like brushing my teeth." Alberto, who is sixty-two and works as a management consultant, echoes Emanuel's morning ritual by noting that in "[my] daily routine I listen to the radio early in the morning while I have breakfast." Some interviewees said that they do not even have to turn the radio on to listen to the news in the morning because they go to sleep while listening to the radio, and keep it on all night long—a practice that ties to the notion, first introduced in chapter 2, that some people use broadcast media to counter silence at home. Miriam, a sixty-nine-year-old housewife, sleeps with the radio on "because I don't like silence, it bothers me. . . . So there's always a news story [on air] when I wake up." Celia, a seventy-seven-year-old retiree, turns the radio on "at midnight, when I go to bed." She "sleep[s] with the radio [on]. I sleep well most of the night. I don't hear it, but I like to wake up and have the radio there [and turned on]."

Miriam's and Celia's practices point to the evening as an important, yet comparatively secondary, time of news consumption on the radio. This also applies to news on television. Mariano, who is thirty-five and works in the kitchen of an empanadas store, goes back home after work, and "always watch[es] television in the evening and [keeps it on] when it's time for the newscast [since] I like to be in the know." If Carolina, a twenty-four-year-old student, is at her home in the evening, she watches "the 8:00 pm newscast on Channel 13 and sometimes [also] the one at midnight, before going to bed, as a summary" of the day's current events.

When it comes to the radio, interviewees also consume news during their commute to and from work, and in the workplace itself. Alcira, who is fifty-four and works as an administrative aide at an elementary school, says that when she "goes in the bus [to and from school] she listens to radio news on the cell phone." Gabriel, a thirty-two-year-old insurance salesman, comments that "because of [my] job I spend a lot of time either in my car or in my office, and I always have the radio on." When asked about the most recent time she had consumed news, Marta, a fifty-two-year-old psycho-analyst who has her private practice in a separate room at her home, said it was on the radio while she was "doing household chores waiting for a client," adding that for her this is a "habitual" form of learning about current events.

Contrary to lofty ideals about civic duty, most people cite practical purposes such as the management of daily logistics and of social relationships as their main reasons for news consumption. Daniela, who is twenty-eight

and works in an ad agency, says that the "basic reason why I watch the newscast in the morning" is to "get a general overview and [to see] if there is a
major news story or a natural disaster or a subway strike or other things related to the transit in Buenos Aires. Just to start the day aware of how people's
emotional climate is going to be." Even when interviewees focus on public
affairs news content, they do it motivated more by a desire not to be left out
of social conversations than by a deep and self-sustaining interest in the content. Isabel, a twenty-four-year-old student, addresses this matter by making
a distinction between being updated and being informed. She talks about
watching television recently and learning "about the electronic dance party
[in which several young people lost their lives] and the [political corruption
case of] Lázaro Báez. I want to be more or less updated. . . . I wouldn't say
that I'm informed [about these topics], because if you ask me [about them],
the truth is that I have no idea." A key factor behind this desire to be updated
is being able to contribute to conversations about news stories with family,
friends, and co-workers. When Teofilo, a thirty-five-year-old construction
worker, was asked why it was important for him to know about what was
going on in the news, he answered: "Because, as I was saying, we get together
at work to have breakfast or lunch, and people comment 'hey, have you seen
this?' 'do you know about . . .?' And we start chatting. So, you can participate
in the conversation if you have some knowledge of what people are talking
about."

As it is evident from several of the quotes introduced in this section so
far, one of the attractions of getting the news on radio and television is its
ambient character: most interviewees do not watch and listen to the news as
their primary activity and main focus of attention. On the contrary, they inform themselves through these media in ways that enable them to do other
things that appear to be more important to them. Thus, broadcast news consumption habits become secondary to other daily routines, and therefore
are adapted to them. The ambient quality of broadcast news consumption
is easy to see when it is consumed at work—as the work itself should be the
center of the worker's attention. But this also applies, as we have seen from
the interviews, to the morning routine—when tasks such as preparing breakfast and getting dressed take precedence—and, needless to say, during sleep
time—unless someone has insomnia.

Sandra, the clerical employee, conveys the ambient character of news consumption succinctly and powerfully: "I have a habit. I almost don't watch television, but it is always on and tuned to a news channel." In a similar vein,

Lucas, who is thirty and works as an attorney, notes that "I have the newscast as background in the morning . . . but it's mostly a companion, something that is on, more a waste of energy which is a lifelong habit than something I pay attention to." Needless to say, not all television watching has an ambient character. Interviewees illustrate this by comparing the consumption of news with that of entertainment content—an issue that I will continue addressing later in this chapter, and also in chapter 5. Josefina, who is twenty-five and works in a public-sector agency, says that "at night I eat while watching [popular newscast] *Telenoche*. That is, I watch it, but it's not that I'm sitting on the couch as I do with the soap opera." She adds that she "concentrates more on the latter. Yes, yes, I sit down. I try to eat before it starts so that I can be fully focused on the soap opera [laughs]."

Ambiance is also a paramount feature of radio news consumption. Norberto, a fifty-three-year-old high school teacher, gets the news on the radio "while I'm doing something else, as company. [You know], while I'm cooking, mowing the lawn, other stuff. I consume the radio but in the background. I don't sit down to listen to the radio." In a similar line of reasoning, Cristina, a fifty-nine-year-old housewife, notes the superior ambient quality of radio over television by saying that "radio is practical in the sense that you can move your hands and sometimes even your head [laughs]. So, you go back and forth. Whereas television is more static." Thus, as Carlos, who is fifty-eight and a certified public accountant, reflects, radio news requires the least amount of routine disruptions of all media options: "Radio gives me the possibility of entertaining myself all day long without major distractions from other activities." This is a key reason that some interviewees enjoy radio news, like Juliana, a forty-nine-year-old schoolteacher, who comments that if she "had to choose a form of consuming news . . . I prefer it to be audio . . . and not sitting down to read. If I sit down to read, I don't read news but other things."

Juliana is not the only interviewee who does not read the news. Print newspapers were a polarizing topic among those interviewed for this book. Young people, even among those who had daily access to print newspapers, strongly reject the medium. Sabrina, a twenty-one-year-old student, comments that her parents "buy the newspaper at home, but rarely ever use it." Romina, who is nineteen and also a student, espouses a similar notion and adds an environmental objection to the idea of newsprint that was shared by some other young interviewees: "[We get the newspaper] every day at home. . . . It's very bad ecologically, very wrong."

The leading Argentine dailies, like *Clarín* and *La Nación*, have so-called readers' club programs whereby the monthly subscription comes with a loyalty card that provides benefits such as discounts at movie theaters and restaurants. Several interviewees commented that this is the main reason their households receive a newspaper on a daily basis. One of them is Patricio, another college student, whose parents purchase a subscription "just for the benefit of *La Nación* [readers' club]." However, having daily contact with a newspaper does not necessarily mean that those interviewed read its content. "I almost never read [the news] on paper. That is, I have the print copy and I read it on the computer. . . . It's crazy. . . . But [the computer] seems more practical to me because I can choose which [stories] to read." Kevin, another student, used to get the newspaper daily because he had purchased a subscription to *Clarín*'s loyalty program, "even though I don't like print." Like Patricio, he also goes "on the internet and read all the headlines that are there. I look at the news story that I want to see and that's it. . . . And even if I read the print paper from start to finish, I don't know what to do with all that paper. . . . It's not like a book, which is an object I want to keep."

But rejecting the print newspaper is not something that only young interviewees say they do. Older ones do this too. Soledad, a fifty-four-year-old speech therapist, comments that "I believe *La Nación* is being delivered to my place, but just as it comes . . . it is used for the various things that newspapers are good for!" Esteban, who is forty-five and has a clerical job, reads the paper "very sporadically. Nowadays digital technology advanced so much that . . . I only maybe read a print magazine when I'm waiting in a medical office." Alberto, the management consultant, says that for him "the newspaper went out of fashion because I'm more comfortable with the internet or digital media. . . . I used to enjoy getting the newspaper to do the same thing that I do now on my cell phone: read the news and entertain myself when I'm on the train. . . . But it was really uncomfortable!"

However, print newspapers also have their regular readers among those interviewed for this study, and in the population at large—even though, as the survey data show, very few of them single it out as their main source of news. They include some young adults such as Pedro, a twenty-four-year-old public-sector employee, who regularly reads the newspaper at a McDonald's restaurant that he visits twice a week. "I always go there on Tuesday and Thursday so I read *La Nación* in the morning. . . . There's always a copy available by where they have the hand sanitizer and the napkins." Sergio, who is sixty and has a coffee cart at a major public park, shares a comparable ritual: "I like to go to a coffee shop, order a coffee, and ask for a copy of the newspaper." In a similar vein, Elena comments that she "always ask[s] for a newspaper at a bar. And I read whichever newspaper is available." When asked why she likes the print newspaper, Elena says that she is "fifty-seven and used to reading the news. It's comfortable for me to read on paper. . . . I'm not very technological, so it's hard for me to locate the news on my cell phone." Some interviewees espoused a certain nostalgia for the artifact that they cannot access through television and radio. "I'm telling you, the smell of ink [and] getting your hands dirty with ink elicits a very special emotion that perhaps . . . young kids don't feel because they're more used to digital [media]," says Hector, who is forty-seven years of age.

Several interviewees commented that another reason they enjoyed their papers is that reading the news in print is tied to a slower pace of information intake. Lucas, the attorney, puts it as follows: "I get the newspaper on Sunday and devote more time to it. . . . When I read digitally it's faster because I'm reading at work, while I get calls. It's not the same to read calmly the print paper for one hour and a half." Patricia, the high school teacher, thinks of reading the news on paper as a unique "ritual" centered on "generating a different context that for lots of people continues to be satisfactory and therefore it's going to last for a long time." Finally, Marcelo, who is sixty-one and works at a convenience store, contrasts the focus and calm associated with reading the print paper with the ambiance of television and radio news consumption: "I read the print paper when I have spare time, so I'm more at ease, more relaxed. Whereas with the television I'm maybe doing other things as well, and with the radio even more so."

Marcelo's comment points to an additional theme common across interviews: most people do not consume news exclusively via one medium but, on the contrary, get their news through multiple media. Horacio, who is fifty-one and is a pharmaceutical sales representative, says that he gets the news through "three basic media. Television in general in the evening or the morning after I wake up. . . . The radio during the day. . . and I have lunch on the go, in restaurants, so I read whichever newspaper is available where I eat." Carla, a forty-five-year-old attorney, also begins "the day with the television newscast . . . and then the computer when I get to the office. I make myself a cup of coffee and read the news [online]." The next section goes in depth into this experience.

Digital Media

The consumption of news in digital media is less routinized than in traditional media. Moreover, the degrees and kinds of routinization, and the overall practices, vary substantively between social media and websites for learning about current events. Thus, for analytical clarity in the remainder of this section I will examine each option separately—as well as briefly comment on the role of search engines as news sources. I will also point out situations in which it is common for interviewees to use one option in relation to one or both of the others. A second difference is that, consistent with the survey findings summarized earlier in this chapter, digital news consumption appears to be more intense and significant in the lived experience of young people than in that of their older counterparts. Accordingly, the paragraphs that follow will be filled mostly with illustrations from the experiences of interviewees who were thirty-five years of age or younger at the time of the interview.

Some people enact news consumption routines on social media that resemble those common for television and radio. They check the same platforms, and in habitualized ways at certain times every day. Lionel, a twenty-one-year-old professional sports player, says that he "gets the news in the morning, immediately after waking up; I generally read Twitter or watch the news [on television]." Ana, who is the same age and is also a student, comments: "I inform myself a lot via Twitter. The first thing I do in the morning is log in on Twitter and check the trending topics."

The importance of Twitter for news consumption is consistent with the evidence presented in the previous chapter about the extent to which interviewees viewed this platform primarily as an information source. But Facebook, as was also mentioned in that chapter, is a common access point for news, too. Julian, who is twenty-nine and works as a movie producer, comments that "there is a moment in the morning when I still haven't started my work day, so I check Facebook and Twitter to find out what's going on [in the news]." To some other interviewees, the routinization of news consumption on social media happens not before the work day but while they are at work—akin to listening to the radio in the workplace. Magnolia, who is twenty-two and works as a teacher assistant at an elementary school, "look[s] at Facebook, therefore the news, too, during recess, around ten in the morning. I get updated about whatever shows up first [on the Facebook news feed]."

For other interviewees, the consumption of news on social media is far from being routinized. While they have preferred platforms, they do not have fixed times or places when they access them for news. On the contrary, they check the platforms at random times and places, and encounter the news in a non-routinized fashion as a result. Asked about the last time she had accessed the news prior to the interview, Juana, a twenty-year-old student, says it was "this morning, before the start of class. I got to campus at eight in the morning approximately. I was reading the news on Twitter while entering the cafeteria. It was a tweet by *Infobae* about a news story." Patricio, also a student, says that he normally gets the news at his home, and at any and all times "since I'm constantly with my cell phone and my computer, so I go on social media and see the [stories], and I also get videos on WhatsApp and check them out." Teofilo, the construction worker, learns about current events from several news organizations he follows on Facebook. But, unlike Magnolia, the teacher assistant, he does not have a pre-established time when he does this. On the contrary, "it's whenever I have some free time." Ludmila, a thirty-six-year-old employee at a clothing store, has a similar practice:

> I open Facebook whenever I can. Maybe a little bit during my nap time. Or, if I go to the store in the morning and perhaps my boss comes later and I'm there waiting, so, well, I open it a little bit and look at the news. News [stories] always show up [on my Facebook wall]. Always. So, I look a little bit.

Ludmila's comments point to the incidental nature of news consumption on social media, which is prevalent among many of the interviews. As noted in chapter 3, people say that it is more common for them to encounter news stories on social media, as a by-product of being there, than to seek them out on the various platforms they use. In the words of Sofia, a twenty-nine-year-old student and administrative assistant, "I have to see a story [on my feed] to read it; I don't go there to look for it." Luciana, a thirty-year-old accountant, adds that if "I see [on Facebook] a headline that grabs my attention, I click and read it. Otherwise, I don't. . . . . It's not that I go on Facebook to learn about current events. But, if I see something, I read it." Sara, a twenty-one-year-old student, recalls a recent situation in which "I was in a social gathering with friends and went on Facebook. Stories from my hometown showed up [on my feed] and since one of them interested me, I checked it

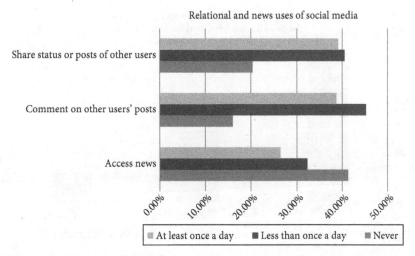

Figure 4.8. Frequency in which users undertake relational and news activities on social media.

out." Javier, the store employee, relays a similar situation: "I was on Facebook and it happened that somebody shared that story [about payments on national foreign debt by the Argentine government]. I checked it out because it interested me who were [the representatives] who made up a quorum in Congress to approve the payment."

Most people do not go on social media primarily for news—with the exception of heavy Twitter users—but for other purposes. Thus, news consumption becomes derivative from these other purposes which mostly have to do with self-expression, relational management, leisure, or simply killing time, as was described in chapter 3. Survey findings show that more than four out of ten respondents never get the news on the platforms they use (Figure 4.8); 56.32% of them disagree with the sentence "The information I access on social media about the news is more important than the information about family and friends"—and only 11.86% agree with it (Figure 4.9).

Julián, who is twenty-nine years of age and works as a film producer, is on social media constantly, and learns about current events this way. He notes:

With Facebook and Twitter there is like a spillover theory of the news . . . [in which] you eventually find out about what's going on in the world. Since everybody began sharing memes and news, and especially during electoral years, it's become like impossible not to find out about current events.

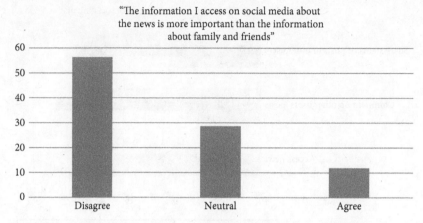

Figure 4.9. Interest in news versus social information on social media.

Julian's comments point to another salient aspect of the experience of consuming news on social media: the platforms often function as an alert system for important breaking news. Marisol, a thirty-one-year-old cook, says the most recent news story she had seen prior to the interview was through Facebook: "I consume Facebook a lot, saw the story, and got interested in knowing what had happened . . . because it was posted on the wall of not one, but of many people. So, that caught my eye." Lucila, who is twenty-seven and works in media, gives a powerful example related to the murder of district attorney Alberto Nisman in Buenos Aires:

> In January 2015 I was on Facebook [one day] and saw that everybody was saying something about Nisman. I asked myself "What happened with Nisman?" So, I went to *La Nacion*'s website and it was a huge story. . . . Like many times I tell myself, "Wow, something major has happened," and it's because I saw that lots of people are talking about it on Facebook.

The statements from Julian, Marisol, and Lucila are also evidence of the ambient character of news in people's everyday digital media experience. Many other interviewees also feel surrounded by information about current events, especially as a by-product of being on social media. Clara, a thirty-year-old psychotherapist, talks about her experience of "bombardment of information":

What happens a lot with Reddit or with Facebook is that it's like a bombardment of information. So, I know that I already saw several news stories
today, but there are things I don't remember directly because it was just
reading a headline and then seeing something else immediately afterward.

Estefania, a twenty-six-year-old employee at a non-profit, sees social
media as an alert system through which breaking news is always available:

Everything is so immediate today that, for instance, many news stories
I don't even have to go to *Lanacion.com*, because on Twitter . . . when something happens on the other side of the world . . . you do a refresh on your
Twitter [page] and you find out immediately because somebody retweeted
from someone else who was on the scene. . . . On Facebook too: you're there
and find out about everything in an instant.

As several quotes introduced so far in the chapter show, social media are
a major source of traffic toward news websites. But other interviewees say
they go to these sites directly. Those who do this tend to enact more routinized patterns of news consumption than those who resort primarily to either
social media or search engines. To some, visiting a news site is part of the
morning routine. Mora, a thirty-year-old industrial designer, says that "every
day I wake up and more or less . . . enter a news portal." Carla, the attorney,
comments that in her case "it's generally either during breakfast [in the computer at home] or on the phone if I have breakfast outside of the home. Or, on
the computer when I get to the office and [immediately] after I make myself
a cup of coffee. Those are the moments in which I see [online] newspapers."
She adds that "almost always I visit the same newspaper pages." Joaquin, who
is twenty-eight and works in the information technology unit of a large organization, gets the print newspaper daily, but "I consume the newspaper
every day on the Internet; it's one of the first things I do after I wake up." He
does this

on my cell phone during breakfast. I visit Todo Noticias, *Clarín*, *Perfil*, and
I have it a little bit as a habit. I check the pages from beginning to end. I see
if there is anything that has happened during the last few hours which grabs
my attention. That's [the news] I usually consume during breakfast. I'm a bit
like the updated version of the old man with the newspaper!

Not all interviewees visit news sites in the morning primarily. As with traditional media options, some enact their routines later in the day. Luciano, who is a thirty-six-year-old businessman, visits online news sites "religously every day in the afternoon." He reads the financial daily "*Ambito Financiero* every day on the internet. I don't buy the newspaper [in the morning]. But download it on the internet in the afternoon since at that time practically all the news stories are [well] developed. . . . I'm interested in economic and political matters, and there I have a perfect summary [of what's going on]." Patricia, the high school teacher, visits news sites starting "in general in the late afternoon. On my cell phone in the evening and on the computer in the afternoon. . . . I spend approximately 10 or 15 minutes [on news sites daily]."

Active search is the third main way in which people consume news in a digital form. While certainly prominent in terms of access to news sites, it was much less common in the responses of interviewees than the two previous alternatives. This might be an artifact of the rather unproblematic nature of this practice. When it did come out in conversation, or after it was probed, people most commonly mentioned search as a follow-up step from either encountering the news on social media or seeing an intriguing story on a website. In that case, the use of search engines was highly unroutinized in its timing. However, most people tended to use the same search engine, Google, to the point of turning this noun into the verb 'googling.' Camilo, a nineteen-year-old student, says he read an article after "googling it." In a few other cases, interviewees resorted to Google News as a way of organizing their news menu. Martin, who is twenty years of age and also a student, comments that he "has the Google News app that sends you all kinds of news, but divided by topic instead of by publication." In this case, search becomes a highly routinized source. Martin reads a selection of stories from this digest "every day in the bus, during the hour-and-a-half journey I have" to campus.

Cutting across all three main options of digital news consumption are reading practices that could be broadly characterized as brief and fragmentary. Josefina, the public-sector employee, says, alluding to Twitter, that the most recent story she read prior to the interview "had 150 characters, so it was very fast!" [laughs]. But a quick glance through the news is not the exclusive province of social media. German, a forty-one-year-old attorney, spends "minutes [on the news] . . . headlines." He adds that "once in a while I go deep into a given story that has a particular interest to me, but it's mainly headlines." Thus, regardless of which of the three digital options people use to get to a news story, it seems quite common for interviewees to focus primarily on the headline, secondarily on the opening paragraphs, and only very occasionally read the remaining text. Maria, a twenty-two-year-old student, normally "reads the headline, the lead, and the rest of the content diagonally. If there is a paragraph that catches my attention I re-read it, but, yes, in general [I read] diagonally." For instance, when talking about an important story on the Panama Papers involving President Mauricio Macri and allied legislator Elisa Carrió, Maria comments that she does not "really know what Macri said about this. I know, for instance, what Elisa Carrió said because somebody shared the story [on social media]. But I read the headline, I didn't click [on the link]." Similarly, Clara, the clinical psychologist, notes that she "look[s] at a lot of headlines, but doesn't open many stories." Marina, a twenty-two-year-old financial analyst, concurs: "I very rarely read a whole story, unless it interests me a lot." As Patricio, a nineteen-year-old student, puts it: "It's not that I read the whole article, but in general I take a look [just] to be somewhat informed."

The limited time and sparse attention devoted to the stories appears to be tied to the dominance of certain affective states related to the practices of news consumption.

Affect

Interviewees shared a wide range of emotions when talking about their experiences of reading, listening to, and/or watching the news. However, negative emotions tended to dominate their discourse. The adjectives that most commonly conveyed interviewees' emotional states give a glimpse into their dominant moods: anger, angst, fear, impotence, hatred, concern, horror, sadness, shock, poisoned, panic, and outrage, to name but a few. Most of these adjectives were often associated with the consumption of hard news, which people noted were overwhelmingly bad news. As the famous saying goes, "If it bleeds, it leads."

Sofia, the student and administrative assistant at a doctor's office, says that "today, I read on Facebook [a] Todo Noticias [story] that someone had found a newborn within a [garbage] bag. Why? What's the need [to publish that story]? They are all bad news, there isn't a single good one . . . it's pure angst." Agustina, a twenty-year-old student, concurs by confessing, "I get very sad when I watch the news. I feel like you can't do anything about it and that it's all bad." Martina, the law firm clerk, has "a five-year-old daughter, and since I had her, every time I see a news story of a kid kidnapped, stabbed, killed, raped, whatever, I get a lot of anxiety." Elsa, a sixty-six-year-old retired teacher and psychotherapist, says she experiences "fear" when watching the news: "I'm afraid for my kids, my grandkids, too. . . . My daughter works as a vet in the lower San Isidro (a neighborhood in the outskirts of Buenos Aires) and I ask myself: what if [thieves] rob there, what might happen to her?" Fabián, the doorman, switches the register to anger: "I can't tolerate [the news]. Nothing has changed for the past twenty years. . . . I've been working nonstop for the past twenty-four years, and whenever I stop I know I'll retire with the minimum pension." José, a forty-five-year-old clerical employee, is also angry and adds a dimension of impotence present in many interviews, too:

> The topic of insecurity makes me feel very angry. For example, the topic of when they kill people, like the father who was with his three-year-old son and they killed him. . . . Things like this give me a lot of angst. Do you want to know why it gives me angst? Because the worst part of this is that there're no prospects that they'll do something, that's the saddest thing.

Not all news consumption is linked to negative emotional states. Some people express fairly neutral feelings, like Martín, the student, who does not "give so much importance to the news for it to occupy an important space in my life. It's more like there is a gap, and I fill it with that (referring to news stories)." Others connect news stories to markedly positive affect. In most cases when this happens, the kinds of content people talk about are either soft news or commentary. Maribel, another student, asks the interviewer, "Did you see the story of the kid who used crutches to watch the [soccer] game? Well, that story really got to me. . . . They went to search for the kid, interviewed him, and he talked about his daily life. I don't know, it's like it moved me." Martín, who is also in college, noted that he recently watched an interview with soccer superstar Lionel Messi and "smiled when I saw Messi happy and talking. I hope he's in good shape and we win the America's Cup." Finally, Carla, the attorney, has a passion for the American magazine *The New Yorker*: "I love *The New Yorker*. I'm subscribed to it, so I read it when it arrives. I like the typography, that's really pure pleasure."

The dominance of negative affect tied to the news is in stark contrast to the consumption of entertainment content—a topic that will also be addressed in chapter 5. To some, this is because they see getting the news as something they have to do instead of something they want to do. Isabel, the student, watches televised entertainment in the evening and "alternate two soap operas, one in Telefé and the other in Channel 13. . . . It's like I sit down to watch it because it's fun . . . and I already fulfilled my duties: I got the news, I went to school [laughs]!" Sometimes people want to avoid the news to get away from an overwhelming reality, as is the case with Sara, another college student: "When you watch soap operas and things like that you unplug a bit from reality, from the things that happen, and you entertain or amuse yourself. Whereas, watching crime news or whatever, you get paranoid or fearful." These divergent emotional states tied to the consumption of news and entertainment are also related to different levels of attention paid to both types of content. Paola, a twenty-two-year-old professional model, compares watching news and series on television as follows:

> Even though I pay attention to the newscast, I don't pay as much attention to it as I do to the television series. I let [the newscast] go by a bit. . . . Whereas I pay a lot of attention to the series, I like it, I get into it. . . . I feel whatever is going on with the character, an adrenaline rush, and things like that.

Paola's comment points to the consequences of the dominance of negative affect for the consumption of news, which range from self-limitation to full withdrawal. Following up on the topic of entertainment, Lola, a seventy-seven-year-old retiree, likes *Animales Sueltos*, a popular political evening news program on television. However, she has recently limited her time watching it and filled that time slot with serialized fiction. She says that after watching *Animales Sueltos*, "I go to bed all wired up. . . . Everything is so ugly with the division [among political sides] and they go at each other time and again, that even though what they say is interesting, they overwhelm me a lot, so I go to sleep somewhat electrified. So, I haven't watched that program for a while." German, the attorney, has also limited his news intake, in this case by only glancing at the key stories: "I inform myself about the [main] topics or headlines, but since there are stories that are stressful I don't even know how they're framed . . . or the strategy behind the [media] discourses. No, I don't consume [much news]."

Other interviewees resort to almost complete withdrawal instead. That is the case of Ester, a sixty-one-year-old maid, who notes that "there is much news that makes you feel badly, you see? So, I prefer not to see them." Verónica, a forty-six-year-old school principal, shares a similar sentiment: "What happens to me many times is that I listen to so many things that make me feel sad that I prefer to take another path." Carmela, who is thirty years of age and lives in a small town near the city of Rosario, visits that city often so she prefers to avoid the stories about it altogether. "You generally look at the news and it's all robberies, car crashes, deaths. I don't look at those stories.... Because they terrify me. Perhaps I feel like there are so many [bad] things happening in Rosario, that it's best not to know what's going on."

Bias

Many interviewees take the existence of bias in the news as a given. Furthermore, to them, bias in news coverage is the norm and not an exception. Not only are statements about bias in the news common, but the opposite is virtually absent from the data set: none of the interviewees said that there was no bias in the news. This does not mean that all of those who were silent about this issue did not believe in the existence of objective, bias-free news reporting. However, it is telling that if they believed that, they chose not to say anything about it.

This trend across the interviews is bolstered by the survey data. Forty-one percent of respondents disagreed with the statement, "The news media of my country report the news independently of political powers" (Figure 4.10). This was the most popular option, followed by 30.98% having a neutral

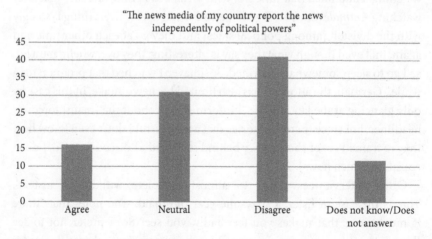

Figure 4.10. Perceived bias in the news I.

position and only 16.08% agreeing with it—the remaining 11.76% either did not know or did not answer. This means that there are one-and-a-half times more respondents who think the media are not independent of politics than those who think they are. Furthermore, perception of bias is highest among oldest and lowest among the youngest, thus suggesting that as time goes by and people have more contact with the news, their opinion of its possible independence from politics deteriorates (Figure 4.11).

Claudia, a forty-one-year-old clinical psychologist, addresses the existence of bias by noting that "one cannot forget the idea that news has an intention, a connotation of either political, partisanship, or business [reasons]." Casimiro, a thirty-one-year-old computer programmer, concurs by stating that "none of the Argentine newspapers seem to me objective enough to trust in the news. They mix news and opinion, [and] don't own [up to] the fact that they're biased." The existence of bias applies to both individual journalists and the news organizations they work for. Lucas, the attorney, thinks that "nowadays it's very difficult to believe in somebody [referring to both journalists and the media]. All of them speak from a particular point of view, with [a particular] interest, so it's impossible that someone is 100 percent objective." Martin, the student, argues that "it's clearly noticeable the point of view of each television channel. Sometimes even within the same channel there is a journalist who has a different idea from the main one." To Marta, the psychoanalyst, since "journalists present [news stories], they are never objective."

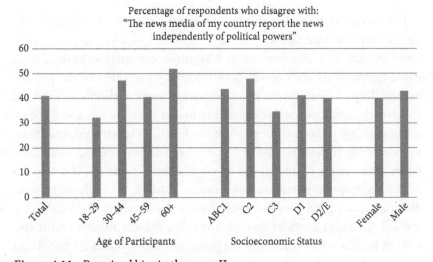

Figure 4.11. Perceived bias in the news II.

ABC1: High; C2: Middle; C3: Lower Middle; D1: Low; D2/E: Extreme Low

She continues by addressing this matter in the context of the public television news she occasionally watches: "Official channels are all the time entertaining and disorienting you, that's what I think. Then, you sort of end up a bit stupid from [watching] all of that."

Several interviewees refer to a recent deepening of both the existence of media bias and their awareness of it. They relate this trend to a long and bitter confrontation between the Néstor Kirchner (2003–2007) and Cristina Fernández (2007–2015) presidencies and media organizations perceived to be opposed to their policies, in particular, those tied to media conglomerate Grupo Clarín and the broadsheet La Nación. Humberto, a forty-nine-year-old businessman and attorney, puts it as follows:

HUMBERTO: During the past five years, as a result of the war they had with the "Kirchneristas" (the supporters of both presidents, Kircher and Fernández), Channel 13 (owned by Grupo Clarín) turned its newscast into a silly thing, no? Then, it is like a disinformation [newscast]. It was the only news show that provided you with information before. Nowadays you get more information from the news talk shows than from the newscasts.

INTERVIEWER: Do you trust the media in Argentina?

HUMBERTO: No, no. We have a lot of contact with everyday reality at work, and a lot of the news that you see on television has nothing to do with reality, nothing to do.

Humberto's statements point to two important issues that came up repeatedly in the interviews. First, a somewhat low level of trust in the news—which was also present in Casimiro's comments above. This is consistent with the data about news credibility presented in the preface. Second, Jorge-Luis raises the issue of whether when someone has personal experience with a particular event that makes it to the news, the subsequent coverage is seen as doing justice to what they experienced, and therefore decreases the assumption of bias, or the other way around. In all cases when interviewees shared stories about this issue, it was to the detriment of their perception about the news media. Carlota, a twenty-eight-year-old graphic designer, lives in a small town in the outskirts of Córdoba city, around 500 miles north of Buenos Aires. She reflects about a recent episode in her town that made it to the press, and about which she had direct knowledge:

It makes you think to say "What bastards!" Because they were saying a bunch of wrong things. And it makes you feel really badly; you know it's not [what they say], you have the true information, and I swear to you that I read a bunch of web pages of radio stations and it's all different, all wrong. So, if these things happen in [small town's name], I imagine that at a greater scale it's all super manipulated.

Sofia, a twenty-year-old student who lives in Buenos Aires, uses a similar line of reasoning when she talks about a high-profile event, the story of an electronic music party in which five people died and five others ended up in an intensive care unit in April 2016—a story also mentioned in a previous quote by Isabel.

I'm listening to the news less [these days]. . . . It all began with that tragedy. Because I frequent those social circles. . . . I began watching on television and reading in newspapers a lot of things that were half true and half a lie. Then, I began questioning other topics that I knew nothing about, and I learned [about them] from television and the media: would it be true or false what they say?

The widespread perception of bias reaches both the news and social media. Marisol, the cook, reflects that "in general, lots of things viralize [on social media] and they are not true or have something of an exaggeration in what they say. Then I prefer to double-check [that story] on news media since they're more trustworthy to me." However, resorting to the same trope of disinformation that Jorge-Luis used, she adds that "the news media also, rather than inform, they dis-inform you, or there are lots of things [published] that aren't real. Mmmm, so then I listen to the media between inverted commas." Rodrigo, a twenty-nine-year-old store employee, also utilizes the same trope. To him, Facebook is a "mass of . . . dis-information" because "there is a lot of information that people upload whatever they want, and 'what is the source?' I don't know."

To some of the interviewees, the stories that they encounter in the news media appear to be less biased than those on social media. Mariano, who is thirty-five years of age and works as a cook at an empanadas store, comments that "I've always trusted TV more because on social media there are . . . many false news stories." Ezequiel, a thirty-nine-year-old attorney, keeps "resorting to the news media and not to social media. Maybe afterwards I check the repercussion of the news story on social media. But the first option is to visit a news portal." However, other interviewees tend to trust more the stories on social media than on the news media. This usually is tied to the idea that the process whereby their social media contacts recommend and annotate stories is perceived as less biased than editorial selections, an idea that was first introduced in chapter 3. Miguel, who is sixty-five and works at a hardware store, trusts the news on Facebook "because I know what the origin is," by which he means the contact posting that story.

While interviewees enact an array of strategies to deal with the perception of systemic bias in the news, two of them appear as particularly prevalent: listening to multiple sides, and focusing on the known other. The first strategy centers on self-exposure to divergent viewpoints, frequently on the opposite ends of the ideological spectrum. Gustavo, a thirty-four-year-old consultant, explains the rationale behind this mechanism as follows: "Since all journalism consists of the construction of a narrative, [it's useful] to have both narratives to see how people are biased [by the news media]." Sebastian, who is also twenty-four and works in marketing, "tries not to listen to, as the saying goes, only one bell. . . . I read (left-leaning) *Página/12*, (conservative) *La Nación*, and (centrist) *Clarín*. I search for different viewpoints." Daniela, a twenty-eight-year-old publicist, applies a similar logic to television watching: "Todo Noticias . . . and then C5N, very much opposed, like the yin and the yang. . . . I feel it's necessary to play devil's advocate and always listen to the two sides." Rather than doing point-counterpoint, interviewees who pursue the second strategy concentrate on a news organization they disagree with ideologically but whose biases they feel able to identify beforehand. Lucas, the attorney, illustrates this strategy noting that "my default newspaper is *La Nación* and it opines totally different from what I think, but . . . I know from which stance it writes. And I know where to position myself to be able to analyze a news story." Clara, the psychologist, describes a similar practice and adds the complementary role played by her social media feeds:

> The only newscast I see regularly is that of Todo Noticias. Because what happens to me with Todo Noticias is that I'm not in agreement with lots of things they say, but at least I know where they're coming from and I have the [interpretive] filter prepared [beforehand]. . . . On top of that, my social circle is . . . center-left, or left, or progressive, so many times what I see on social media balances out a bit what I see or not see on Todo Noticias. Therefore, that works for me.

As with the dominance of negative affect toward the news, in particular hard news, interviewees say that the perception of systemic bias in news coverage diminishes their interests in that coverage. Luis, a twenty-seven-year-old race car driver, comments that "for many years the news media in Argentina haven't been neutral. . . . You don't have a neutral perspective and information comes distorted. This generates less interest, at least for me." Soledad, who is fifty-four and works as a speech therapist, shares a similar sentiment: "What happens to me on Facebook is that I see a news story, read the first three sentences, and whenever I notice that I'm being led [somewhere I don't want to go] or is tendentious, I say 'bye' and leave. . . . So, I know only half of all the stories!"

Concluding Remarks

What is the experience of getting the news when the information is plentiful and highly commoditized, circulates at furious speed, and can hardly be avoided?

The analysis of structural factors sheds light on access conditions and prevailing attitudes that envelop the everyday routines of news reception. To begin, broadcast media are the most popular options as top news sources, especially television. Furthermore, socioeconomic status is the strongest predictor of someone choosing these media as their main source of information about current events. But this association does not apply to people who select digital news as their top choice—either on platforms or sites—for which there is a relative parity between socioeconomic status and age. These findings are consistent with prior research on the reception of news. For example, in his studies of newspaper consumption with evidence up to the 1980s in America, sociologist Leo Bogart found that the influence of income was greater than that of age.[8] However, analyzing data from seven European countries collected up until the end of the 1990s, mass communication specialist Edmund Lauf concluded that "in all countries studied here, age has become the most powerful discriminating variable between daily and non-daily reading."[9] Although to the best of my knowledge there is no comprehensive account comparing the role of various structural factors in news consumption, it is reasonable from the existent scholarship to posit that while there is no clear dominance of one factor over the other, the role of age might have increased in recent years in relation to the rise of digital news.[10]

The survey findings also showed the persistence of high levels of routinization in news consumption. However, the interview data revealed significant differences with the ideal-typical rendition of news consumption during the second half of the twentieth century summarized in the introduction to this chapter. In particular, the analysis illuminated the existence of four mechanisms that mediate between an environment with abundant information and how individuals experience its reception.

First, contrary to the notion that information has to be obtained, most interviewees perceived that news is ambient in the sense that it is so readily available in their daily lives—especially via social media—that whenever there is a relevant story they will rapidly learn about it.[11] Thus, paraphrasing the notion put forward by political communication scholar Homero Gil de Zúñiga and his colleagues, the news "will find them" instead of them having to obtain it.[12] Second, this is coupled with the presence of largely derivative routines in which individuals get access to news content as part of another activity that is the main focus of their attention—being on social media, cooking, doing household chores, and so on.[13] The salience of derivative news consumption routines constitutes a historical break from the scholarship about print and broadcast media summarized above, and even more recently. When I conducted fieldwork for *News at Work: Imitation in an Age of Information Abundance*[14] in Buenos Aires and its suburbs roughly a decade prior to the empirical research for this book, I uncovered the existence of a series of primary digital news consumption routines. Third, there was a shared acknowledgment that bias in the news is both widespread and systemic.[15] Therefore, interviewees devised and implemented strategies designed to counter it—such as triangulating across multiple sources and focusing on the known other and discounting its ideological position. These strategies highlight the role of critical reception practices in Argentina discussed in the preface and which are consistent with preexistent low levels of trust in the news. Regardless of the strategy pursued and its apparent effectiveness, the notion that bias is widespread and systemic contributes to further erode the overall trust in journalism as a social institution. Fourth, the news not only appeared to be heavily biased, but its consumption was also deeply connected to feeling overwhelmingly negative affect.[16] This was often tied to news avoidance issues.[17]

The compounding effect of the perception and practice of ambiance, the enactment of derivative routines, the acknowledgment and management of widespread bias, and the processing of predominantly negative affect is the

experiential devaluation of news in everyday life. It is not that people explicitly say that they do not appreciate the news, but that the way they treat it
within their daily routines espouses a low level of valuation. This is bolstered
by the fact that while, as I showed in chapters 2 and 3, many people experienced relatively high levels of attachment to screens and platforms, and some
also to serialized fiction in case of binge watching, there was very little of this
connection regarding the news.[18] The main exception to this trend appears
to be among newspaper readers, some of whom expressed a deep, and tell-
ingly nostalgic, affective tie to the materiality of newsprint and the forms of
slow reading associated with its content.[19] In a sense, the presence of this
rather exceptional connection magnifies the absence of a comparable one for
the more dominant gateways to the news.

These mechanisms bring into sharp relief the role of agency: the growing
centrality of derivative routines, the development of creative strategies
to counter the perceived bias, and the presence of deliberate avoidance
connected to negative affect are different ways in which interviewees show
that they are far from the passive, mindless individuals implicit in the accounts of propaganda and manipulation that have gained remarkable
traction in the past decade—a resurgence that I will address in chapter 6.
Furthermore, an examination of the modes whereby interviewees enact this
agency questions the tenets of the transmission view of communication
applied to information overload in the news, including a focus on instrumental decision-making. This is because most interviewees prioritized expressive and relational information practices over learning about current
events. With this in mind, the notion of an optimum of information intake
loses its purchase. Since the majority of interviewees get the news to have
something to talk about with those in their social networks, the quantity and
content of that information depends on a host of positional and contextual
circumstances that make the idea of optimality an analytical goal that might
be desirable in the abstract to some, but highly problematic to realize concretely. Thus, despite the noble ambitions of certain normative perspectives
about the role of news in liberal democracy, a discourse of deficit that faults
either the information ecosystem for its abundance or the news consumers
for their oversight would miss the reality of both the routines of news reception and their imbrication into broader patterns of everyday life.

The perception and practice of ambiance, the enactment of derivative
routines, the acknowledgment and management of widespread bias, and the
processing of dominant negative affect shape the news reception routines

that mediate between the abundance of information about current affairs and their everyday experience. Thus, the experiential devaluation does not result exclusively from the existence of abundant information, but also from the presence of these distinct mechanisms and associated routines. The next chapter, focused on the correspondingly abundant entertainment content, shows how alternative mechanisms and routines can generate quite different experiential valuations.

5

Entertainment

On television I don't know the programming schedule of the
things I want to watch so it's hard for me to find something....
[And] I'm a slave because I don't like to miss the ending,
so whatever it's happening I have to watch it until the end....
With Netflix I can leave it hanging, suspended until I get back [to it].
Eugenia, forty-seven years old, college instructor

"Watching TV is America's favorite pastime." That sentence could have been a headline from the 1960s. However, it is part of a report published by the US Bureau of Labor Statistics in 2018, with data from the American Time Use Survey. "With nearly 80% of the population watching TV on any given day," the report continues, "one result has been clear since the survey began back in 2003: television dominates the time Americans spend in leisure and sports."[1] The resilience of television watching as a defining cultural practice is remarkable, not just in the United States but also in many other countries, including Argentina. Consistent with the data presented in chapter 2, the 2017 national survey of the Sistema de Información Cultural de Argentina (System of Cultural Information of Argentina, SINCA) shows that 96% of the population watches television, devoting an average of 3 hours and 10 minutes daily to this practice[2]—close to the 2 hours and 46 minutes of daily television watching in the United States.[3] Furthermore, the prevalence of this activity has been quite stable between the 2013 and 2017 surveys conducted by SINCA.[4]

The resilience of television watching is all the more striking in light of the technological, infrastructural, and regulatory transformations that have taken place over the past four decades. Key to these transformations has been a dramatic rise in the volume of content available. From a few national television networks with a handful of channels offering only live programming, the options have expanded to cable services with hundreds of channels as

Abundance. Pablo J. Boczkowski, Oxford University Press. © Oxford University Press 2021.
DOI: 10.1093/oso/9780197565742.003.0005

well as on-demand options and to streaming platforms featuring thousands of movies and tens of thousands of episodes of serialized fiction available for a monthly flat fee roughly equivalent to the price of a movie theater ticket.

The case of Netflix, the world's most popular streaming platform, is paradigmatic of this trajectory. Founded in 1997, for the first ten years of existence the company focused on DVD rentals. In 2007, Netflix expanded its services by offering content via streaming, first within the United States and later overseas. This line of business grew exponentially, and by the spring of 2020 it had subscribers in almost all countries with a wide array of titles available, as was noted in chapter 1. For instance, as of fall 2019, subscribers in Argentina had access to 640 shows and 2,394 movies.[5] In addition, a growing portion of Netflix's library is composed of original content. *Quartz* calculated that the company released around 1,500 hours of original programming just in 2018: "That's nearly nine consecutive weeks of binge-watching. It would have taken more than four hours of streaming per day, every day of 2018, to watch all of it."[6] Hulu, Amazon Prime Video, and Apple TV are other key players in the booming streaming sector. According to the online database JustWatch, as of October 2020 the content of all the providers in the United States combined amounted to more than 138,000 titles—many of them series with dozens of episodes each.[7]

How do people experience the abundance of audiovisual content?[8] To answer this question I continue looking at the roles played by structural and cultural variables. Concerning structural matters, I address how socioeconomic status, gender, and age influence access to mediated entertainment options. Regarding cultural factors, I build on the path started in chapter 4 and foreground various configurations of reception routines. I pay special attention to the intersections between these routines and dynamics of programming flow since, according to cultural analyst Raymond Williams, it was "the central television experience."[9] As he explained in *Television: Technology and Cultural Form*,

> In all developed broadcasting systems the characteristic organization, and therefore the characteristic experience, is one of sequence or flow. This phenomenon, of planned flow, is then perhaps the defining characteristic of broadcasting, simultaneously as a technology and a cultural form. In all communications systems before broadcasting the essential items were discrete. A book or a pamphlet was taken and read as a specific item. A meeting occurred at a particular date and place. A play was performed in

a particular theatre at a set hour. The difference in broadcasting is not only that these events, or events resembling them, are available inside the home, by the operation of a switch. It is that the real programme that is offered is a *sequence* or set of alternative sequences of these and other similar events, which are then available in a single dimension and in a single operation.[10]

Yet, for all the centrality of the notion of flow in research about television for almost half a century, there has been a dearth of studies about how viewers experience this characteristic of the medium.[11] According to social psychologist Sonia Livingstone, this is part of a larger scholarly trend: "In accounts of the mediatization of societal domains or fields . . . the lived experience of audiences is largely invisible."[12] Media studies scholar Jonathan Gray argues that this is particularly problematic in the contemporary context:

> The relative quieting of the qualitative audience in critical cultural scholarship, leave us knowing embarrassingly little about contemporary audiences. As much as we might all suspect that digitization, globalization, neoliberalization, and personalization have played roles in shifting the ground underneath the audience's feet in the last two decades, the field of media and cultural studies has too little documentation of these processes, and hence too much speculation.[13]

Eugenia's statement at the beginning of this chapter provides a glimpse about how the routines enacted to consume abundant entertainment information might challenge ideas about programming flow that were born out of a media environment marked by comparatively greater content scarcity. In addition, notions of convenience and choice, paramount to both the neoliberal and the personalization rhetoric of technological change by entertainment companies—and critiques about them prevalent in academic discourse—are central to the experience of Eugenia and other interviewees. Thus, the analysis I will present in this chapter contributes not only to the account of information abundance that is the focus of this book but also to filling some voids in studies of contemporary entertainment reception.

The remainder of this chapter is organized as follows. In the next section I will focus on the role of structural determinants of entertainment consumption. The analysis will reveal one key difference between the most and least chosen forms of main entertainment activities. On the one hand, the former, in particular watching television, takes place mostly within the household environment. On the other hand, the latter, such as going to the movies, to see plays, and to the museum, happen outside the home. Thus, in the following two sections I will draw on the interview material to analyze the experiences associated with key forms of entertainment within and outside the household. I will first focus on audiovisual entertainment on the small screens due to its popularity, then contrast it with going to the movies, a direct counterpart due to comparability in the content. Finally I address the theater and museum experiences to highlight similarities with moviegoing. Then, I will return to two issues addressed in previous chapters—affect and attachment—and devote one section to each. I will wrap up the chapter by elaborating on how the main findings contribute to answering the questions posed in the preface and reflecting on some of their larger implications.

The Landscape of Entertainment Consumption

Survey respondents were given a set of twenty activities and asked to indicate which one they spent most of their free time on. These activities ranged from watching television to going to the theater, and from getting together with people to taking a walk. Some of them can be classified as forms of entertainment, like the first two. Others are better categorized as types of non-entertainment leisure activities, such as the second two. Understanding the consumption of entertainment as one kind of activity in which people spend their free time helps to put these activities into the larger framework of everyday life. The analysis shows that 59.85% of respondents chose a form of entertainment as their main activity, while 32.85% of them selected a type of non-entertainment option—and 7.3% marked the option "other" (Figure 5.1). The entertainment options include watching television and videos online, listening to music and to the radio, being on social media, and reading books, among others. The non-entertainment choices include walking, running and playing sports, getting together, sleeping, playing soccer, and doing yoga and other fitness activities, among others. The remainder of this section looks at consumption of entertainment.

Watching television was by far the main way respondents liked to spend their free time—25.43% of the total sample—and therefore it also dominated their entertainment diet: more than four out of ten people named it their top choice within the entertainment options. Trailing behind watching television—and the only other option in double digits—was listening to

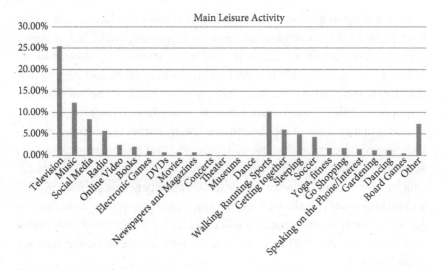

Figure 5.1. Main leisure activity.

music, at 12.29%. These two choices constitute a top tier of entertainment consumption that is followed by a second one composed of being on social media and listening to the radio, with 8.43% and 5.71% of the preferences, respectively. The remaining eleven alternatives were chosen by fewer than 5% of the respondents. Watching videos online, reading books, and playing electronic games were selected by at least 1% of the respondents, and could be clustered into a third tier. None of the other options were even in the single digits, including some of the most common forms of high-brow cultural practices—going to see a play, attending a dance performance, and visiting a museum—which were at the very bottom of respondents' preferences.

At least two common traits mark the activities in the top two tiers: ambiance and abundance. First, the activities have a potentially highly ambient character since they can be undertaken while doing something else. As I showed in chapter 2, it is not uncommon for people to have the television set turned on as either background noise or a second screen while they are on their phones. It is also typical for respondents to listen to either music or the radio while cooking, mowing the lawn, and even working. A similar pattern applies to the uses of social media platforms, as I argued in chapter 3. By contrast, it is more difficult to read a book and play a video-game in an ambient fashion, let alone go to the theater or the museum. Second, while in the twentieth century people had access to a handful of television channels and radio stations and limited collections of vinyl and CD records at home, people now have replaced these things, as the volume of content available has grown exponentially. From the thousands of series on streaming platforms to the millions of songs on Spotify to the billions of posts, pictures, and videos available across social media platforms, the top entertainment choices of survey respondents reflect the abundance of material available at their fingertips.

Additional analyses of top tier options reveal another important common trait across these entertainment activities, one that also marked the use of screens and platforms and the consumption of news: when it comes to accounting for variance in what type of leisure activity people prefer, age plays a more important role than socioeconomic status and gender. The effects of age are not only stronger but also more regular—since they tend to increase or decrease linearly—while those of socioeconomic status are comparatively more irregular.

The influence of age is remarkable in the case of television, the most popular entertainment choice. Whereas the difference in the likelihood of choosing this option varies by 23 percentage points between the youngest and oldest respondents, the gap between the richest and poorest is only 9 percentage points (Figure 5.2). Moreover, in terms of age, the sample is polarized into two camps: 44 years of age and younger, and 45 and older. By contrast,

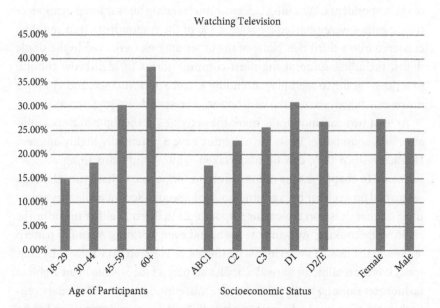

Figure 5.2. Watching television as main leisure activity.
ABC1: High; C2: Middle; C3: Lower Middle; D1: Low; D2/E: Extreme Low

there is no such stark polarization for socioeconomic status. Finally, the difference by gender is comparatively much smaller, with female respondents being more likely to choose television by 4 percentage points.

If watching television is more prevalent among older than younger people, having music as the top choice reverses this trend. The probability more than triples from oldest to youngest: it goes from 6.86% among the older to 21.14% among the younger (Figure 5.3). Furthermore, although the effect of age decreases linearly as people get older, there is a cleavage that separates the very youngest segment from the rest. By contrast, there is no clear effect in terms of socioeconomic status since the highest frequencies are registered at both ends of the pyramid, with 16.46% among the wealthiest respondents and 19.23% among their poorest counterparts. Moreover, there is no effect in terms of gender, with both female and male respondents signaling that listening to music was their top choice in 12.29% of the cases.

Consistent with the analysis presented in chapter 3, social media as a form of entertainment is also an affair of the young and the wealthy. The youngest respondents chose this option twelve times more than their oldest counterparts—13.14% versus 1.14%—whereas the wealthiest did so three times more than the poorest—15.19% versus 5.13% (Figure 5.4). Once again, the pattern is predictably linear in the case of age and less linear when it

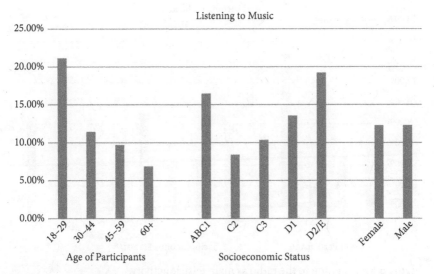

Figure 5.3. Listening to music as main leisure activity.
ABC1: High; C2: Middle; C3: Lower Middle; D1: Low; D2/E: Extreme Low

comes to socioeconomic status. Finally, there is a difference of 2 percentage points between female and male respondents—9.43% versus 7.43%.

In terms of age, listening to radio as a form of entertainment is the opposite of being on social media: it was the top choice of the oldest respondents

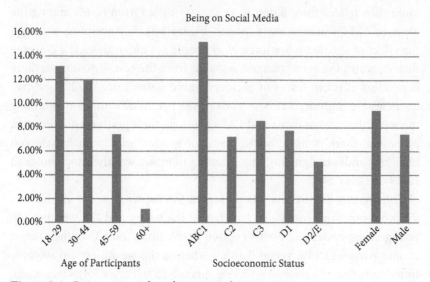

Figure 5.4. Being on social media as main leisure activity.
ABC1: High; C2: Middle; C3: Lower Middle; D1: Low; D2/E: Extreme Low

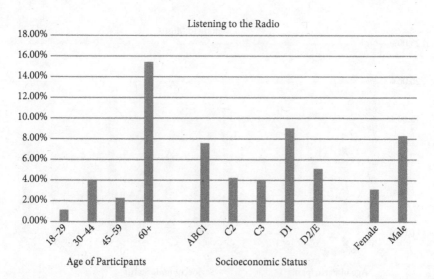

Figure 5.5. Listening to the radio as main leisure activity.
ABC1: High; C2: Middle; C3: Lower Middle; D1: Low; D2/E: Extreme Low

and fourteen times more than of the youngest counterparts, 15.43% versus
1.14% (Figure 5.5). By contrast, the differences across socioeconomic strata
are comparatively much smaller, and there is no major contrast between the
top and bottom of the income earning pyramid. Finally, listening to the radio
is where gender matters the most among the top four entertainment consumption activities. Male respondents were more than twice as likely as their
female counterparts to prefer this medium, 8.29% against 3.14%

This analysis of the survey results provides the macro-level structural
contours that shape access to entertainment and helps frame the meso-to-
micro-level patterns of the reception of various modes of entertainment that
come to life in the interview data—to which I turn in the next four sections.

Watching Audiovisual Content within the Household

Watching audiovisual content in the household has become a highly multifaceted experience. Contrary to the unidimensional image of the couch potato, what emerges from the analysis is the remarkable level of versatility of
this experience. This versatility applies to how people access the content; the
devices through which they watch it; with whom they do this; and the rituals
associated with this experience. Beneath this versatility lie patterns of entertainment consumption in an age of information abundance that shape not
only practices within the household, but also outside it.

Access

The responses of the interviewees show a proliferation of options to access
audiovisual content at home: network television, cable television, streaming
services such as Netflix, satellite television such as DirectTV, internet sites
like Cuevana, video repositories like YouTube, and DVD players, among
others. Furthermore, interviewees appear to have developed a series of routinized patterns to deal with this plethora of options.

Watching network and cable television is highly tied to the practice of
channel surfing and to an experience of a relatively unfocused and diffused
mode of consuming content. Julian, a twenty-nine-year-old film producer,
comments that "what I like about television is doing channel surfing. . . . I like
that television gives you that. . . . On the computer you navigate. On Netflix

you navigate the on-demand [services]." To which he adds, "On the television I like the act of being in front of the screen and flipping channels." Not all interviewees share this positive experience of channel surfing. Marta, a fifty-two-year-old psychotherapist says that she watches "very little [television]. It bores me. I do channel surfing, don't find anything, [and] turn it off (laughs)." Soledad, a fifty-four-year-old speech therapist, concurs: "Television tires me, doing channel surfing and that's it. It lasts two minutes."

Some interviewees have back-up alternatives to deal with the perceived scarcity of appealing content. Jorge, a nineteen-year-old student, comments that he does "channel surfing rapidly, and if there's nothing [interesting], I put *The Simpsons* [on]. . . . Or I start with the phone while I leave the most tolerable content [on the television screen]. . . . And then I do channel surfing again to see what's there." By contrast, others either continue doing channel surfing for longer periods or settle on content not particularly exciting. Ricardo, another nineteen-year-old in college, says that he persists doing channel surfing "because maybe I skipped something during commercials . . . and when I get back there is something interesting. Otherwise I stop [channel surfing] on something (referring to a program) that interests me more within the little all the rest interests me." Flavia, a forty-eight-year-old interior designer, comments that the evening before the interview took place she "started doing channel surfing . . . until I found a picture I don't remember the name. It was very old, very bad, but it was a comedy and I got hooked on it and watched it."

Regardless of whether it is experienced as something positive or negative, most interviewees agree that channel surfing—and therefore watching network and cable television—is connected to an unfocused and diffused uptake of audiovisual content. Mariano, a thirty-five-year-old cook, says that he watches "whatever I find at the time I turn the [television] on." When Dora, fifty-five-year-old clerical employee, is asked what she had watched on television most recently, she answers by saying, "Whatever was there." Marcelo, a sixty-one-year-old who works at a convenience store, says that for him, watching cable television means doing "channel surfing, and whatever I like, I stay [in that channel]."

This experience stands in stark contrast with watching satellite and streaming services, of which Netflix was a popular choice among interviewees. This option of accessing audiovisual content at home was connected to a focused and tailored experience marked by its convenience, adaptability, and flexibility, as anticipated by Eugenia's quote at the beginning of the chapter. Patricia, a fifty-one-year-old high school teacher, comments that "lately I use Netflix more than doing channel surfing on cable." This is because of "the freedom that Netflix gives you to choose the title, stop it, and continue watching it another day if I couldn't finish it. Yes, freedom." Victor, a twenty-three-year-old student, concurs: "I think that Netflix is so easy that I end up searching a movie there before anything else." Clara, a thirty-year-old psychotherapist, emphasizes the importance of the convenience factor by noting that "it's always more convenient to have things [available] and sit down to watch them whenever you want or can." Cecilia, a forty-nine-year-old housewife, says that she watches "very little network television ... because it's boring, always the same!" She adds that "because of family [activities] I can't maintain the time of a television show. On the contrary, you can stop the series [on Netflix]; it's superior. .... You can use [the service] during the time of the day when you're free, and if you want to stop it, either you do it or you go on."

Additional types of access to audiovisual entertainment content at home include satellite services, the internet, and DVDs. Lola, a seventy-seven-year-old retiree, comments that she has been following a Spanish soap opera "for seven years. . . . Every year! And when I'm not available [to watch it], I record it . . . on DirecTV." Lola's practice shows that the different modes of access sometimes are not mutually exclusive but complementary. That is, some interviewees take advantage of multiple modes of access, albeit not with the same frequency. Juliana, a forty-nine-year-old teacher, combines internet and streaming services to access films: "I use Netflix a lot, But . . . the movies that interest me aren't always there. In that case . . . I look them up on an internet site." For others, newer alternatives seem to have displaced their older counterparts. Marisol, a thirty-one-year-old cook, notes that "nowadays there isn't anything that grabs my attention to watch or entertain myself. Maybe a series, but I watch it on the internet, not on television." Leila, a nineteen-year-old student concurs: "I don't watch television anymore as a showcase of entertainment content because the internet surpassed it." However, on occasion, older options seem to overshadow newer ones, as is the case for Claudia, a forty-one-year-old psychotherapist:

I have everything to have Netflix, but I prefer to purchase movies [on DVD]. I don't know, the truth is that I'm a bit independent. I like to say "I stop by [a place selling DVDs], I see the movie that I like, I purchase it. Also, they're usually movies with a high quality of content so I keep them.

I consider them equivalent to books [in that sense]. I like to save everything that is film.

Devices

Patricia's practice ties together issues of access to content with the materiality in which it is embedded. For her, the quality of the content deserves to be stored, thus DVDs become the preferred option. But there is also a plethora of device options to consume content, including television sets—smart and not smart—desktop and laptop computers, tablets, e-readers, smartphones, and game consoles, among others. As is the case with access options, there are some distinct patterns in terms of how people use the different devices to consume audiovisual entertainment in the household, most notably around issues of convenience, mobility, and sociality.

David, a twenty-four-year-old employee at a paint shop, states that for him it's "more comfortable to watch [audiovisual content] on the cellphone, because I [can] have it in bed. The computer is a desktop and I have to be standing [to use it]. Maybe it's more relaxed to watch in bed." In addition to the convenience factor, David's comment brings up the issue that there is mobility not only outside the home environment but also inside it. Whereas the cellphone and the laptop computer are easily movable from one room to the next, the television set and the desktop computer are not. But for others the division is between inside and outside, as is the case of Sebastian, a thirty-two-year-old insurance salesman, who watches Netflix "on the television and also on the cellphone. If I'm at home it is the television, and if I'm with free time in any other place I use the cellphone." Mauricio, a fifty-one-year-old security guard, watches series "on the television, the computer, and the cellphone." He pauses and shows the interviewer the smartphone screen with the app open, and then adds that he watches "everywhere. I have Netflix. Look!"

Sociality also intersects with mobility in the choice of device. Martina, a thirty-seven-year-old clerical employee at a legal firm, says that she watches series "in the television set because of my daughter. But, in general, I take the computer to bed when I lie down. I don't have a television set in my bedroom, so I take the computer with me." Martina's statement also points to the perception that the television set is more conducive to collective viewing, whereas the computer, tablet, and smartphone are tied to individual viewing.

When asked if she watches a particular series on either the television set or the computer, Lucila, a twenty-seven-year-old administrative employee in a media company, answers that it is "on the computer. It's a more solitary consumption." Estela, who is twenty-six years of age and works at a non-profit, says that when she watches *House of Cards* with her girlfriends, she does it "on the computer, but connected to the television set." However, if she is by herself "everything I watch . . . I do it lying down on my bed [and] I don't have a television set in the bedroom . . . so it's on the computer because of . . . convenience." Juanita, a fifty-six-year-old teacher, sums up the perceived role of devices in matters of sociality as follows:

> The television set gives you this possibility of sharing, of enjoying a soccer game, a sports event. . . . Something that you want to share with somebody is on the television, not the tablet or the cellphone. The tablet and the cellphone are individual personal media, no? The television set continues being what gathers people around; if there is a World [Soccer] Cup everybody gathers around the television set.

The statements by Martina, Lucila, Estela, and Juanita not only shed light on the connection between devices and sociality but also point to the versatility of the latter tied to the consumption of audiovisual entertainment within the household.

Sociality

Interviewees watch audiovisual entertainment both by themselves and with others, including partners, family members, friends, and co-workers. These options are not mutually exclusive. On the contrary, most interviewees enact a range of sociality practices. In some cases, collective viewing is planned while on other occasions it is improvised. Watching television in the company of others sometimes leads to negotiations over content; this is especially prevalent in the context of romantic relationships. Regardless of the choice of company, sociality often contributes to shape issues of selection, time, and place of audiovisual entertainment consumption in the household.

Victor, a twenty-three-year-old student, prefers to consume television alone. "In general, I've always watched series and movies and all of that by myself. . . . Maybe if I'm with other people I prefer to do other things than watching a screen." Sabrina, who is twenty-one years of age and also in college, concurs: "I watch almost all [series] by myself." But she adds that "we watched *Lost* with my boyfriend, and now we're watching *Orange Is the New Black*. . . . And on Saturdays, especially in the evening, when we don't go out, we stay [home] watching a series." The coexistence of multiple sociality options that is apparent in Sabrina's case is also prevalent among many other interviewees. Carlota, a twenty-eight-year-old graphic designer, comments that she watches some shows "in the workplace at lunchtime, with my partners. . . . Others with my boyfriend. And by myself, too. I see what comes up." Claudia, a forty-one-year-old psychotherapist, notes that "the kids' program is on as background many times during dinner, which means we all share it. But then each one can have a little bit of time . . . to relax, and we all use this time differently."

Claudia's comments point to the issue of family life, once the iconic locus of co-viewing and still deeply intertwined with watching audiovisual content at home. This form of sociality is particularly hailed by middle-age interviewees. Barbara, a forty-nine-year-old information technology specialist, comments that she has "a plan with my daughter: we eat and watch [soap opera] *Las Estrellas* (laughs)." Horacio, a fifty-one-year-old pharmaceutical sales representative, ties family co-viewing and eating, too, by noting that "it's part of a combo of various things. . . . The three of us [referring to his wife and child] are at home, so we say 'Well, what do you think if we order something that we like, such as sushi . . . and watch a series?'" Manuela, a fifty-five-year-old housewife, emphasizes the enjoyment of family co-viewing: "We like the [moment] of 'let's sit down, let's watch,' of maybe doing something with part of the family."

Younger interviewees emphasize the pleasure of collective viewing with their friends rather than their families. Emanuel, a thirty-year-old employee at a retail store, comments that "we always watch movies with [my] friends. More in winter than in summer, [which] is more for going out." Francisca, a twenty-two-year-old student, says that with her friends "we all watch the same [series] and then we gossip about them." She adds:

> I got really obsessed with *Narcos*, for example. I talked to them all the time [about it] and they did that too. What we see in programs like [the gossip television show of Jorge] Rial is also a topic of conversation. . . . We chat a lot about that in the WhatsApp group. That is, the most stupid thing, but well . . . the life of [local model] Pampita. So, you can imagine!

Perhaps in no other kind of social tie is audiovisual entertainment content at home more central than in the case of romantic relationships. It helps organize time together and shape content choice. Lorena, a forty-one-year-old teacher assistant, notes that she and her partner routinely watch television together because "we like it. . . . We almost don't share anything during the work week, [so] this is something we share during the weekend." Cecilia, a forty-nine-year-old housewife, confesses that "when I watch something by myself it's different topics, more female topics" than when she watches with her husband. In a related vein, Julian, a twenty-nine-year-old film producer, states: "My girlfriend doesn't like thrillers, dramas, horror movies. . . . [T]hen, when we watch together we watch comedies or romantic films or *Master of None*, series like that we watch together." Carlota, the graphic designer, tells that "the other day my boyfriend was criticizing me because I went ahead in one of the series [we watch together] since he went on a business trip for a couple of days." She adds that "we watch an episode per day . . . well, sometimes I go ahead because I'm kind of addicted [and want to watch more]."

Beneath the different types of social ties lies the pattern that sociality dynamics shape the experience of consuming entertainment at home. Luciano, a thirty-six-year-old businessman, says that "I watch animated films with my daughter all the time and . . . the movie ends and I don't even remember if I watched it or not (laughs)!" Bruno, an eighteen-year-old student, comments that "when I get together a lot with somebody, for instance, we run out of things to talk about and we start watching Netflix. We begin a series and there's an implicit pact that you can't watch it without the other person." More generally, as Manuela, the housewife, puts it,

> With one of my daughters we watch *Desperate Housewives* [and] with another of my daughters and my husband *Designated Survivor*. . . . When I'm by myself I used to watch another one that I already finished. Then, depending on whom I'm with, I watch different series.

Rituals

The versatility in access modes, device constellations, and sociality configurations coexist with rituals enacted to structure the plethora of audiovisual entertainment options available in the household. Going back to the issue introduced in the previous section, while some of these rituals are individual, others are collective. Furthermore, several interviewees appear to turn highly popular shows into media events, and structure co-viewing and second-screen activities accordingly. Finally, some people organize their consumption during the afternoon and others in the evening, with a third temporal frame taking place immediately before going to sleep.

Ramiro, a twenty-one-year-old architecture major, is a "fan of *Friends*. I've seen the whole series, I know the dialogues, but [watching it] is helpful to me . . . to decompress." Because of this he has developed

A routine. . . . Since I came [to the City of Buenos Aires] for college, I began working this year, so the three previous years . . . I'd get back home from classes at noon, and from 12:00 to 1:00 they show [*Friends*] on TV, so I watch it there. . . . Nowadays I'm getting home around 6:30 pm, and I believe that at 6:40 *Friends* is being aired. . . . So, I watch it for a while.

While Ramiro's ritual is individual, for others it is collective. Consistent with the importance of family co-viewing among many interviewees introduced in the previous section, some rituals bind various family members together. Roman, who is fifty-three years of age, recalls that in his household they used to watch the miniseries *Moses*, "religiously . . . at the time when it aired [on television]." Ludmila, a thirty-six-year-old employee at a clothing store, states that "I'm very constant if I like a program. I try to be back home on time and have everything organized to be able to watch it when it is shown." When asked if this is by herself or others, she answers that it is

With my son, haha. Not with my daughter, the oldest one, because she does not like soap operas. But my son does. My son and my husband. He also got hooked. The three of us are there, glued to the television.

The popularity of some programs is such that they can turn into media events, which are then tied to collective rituals. The most popular among the interviewees was *Game of Thrones*. Manuela, the housewife, says that in her household, "the only routine that we have is on Sunday at 10:00 pm . . . when it's *Game of Thrones*. . . . The world stops and the four of us sit down [to watch it] . . . From April to June, at 10:00 pm . . . We watch it live." Similarly, Maribel, a twenty-one-year-old student, watches the show every Sunday by "getting together with a friend who subscribes to HBO. . . . It's one hour, so I go [to his place] since he lives close by and I don't lose any time. I go, we eat during the show, and then I get back." She adds that the conversation continues with other friends over WhatsApp:

Three other friends who also watch it included me in a group [about the show] (laughs)! Not while the show is being aired, but afterwards we always comment something . . . and if there is a piece of news or a preview that is released during the week, we also talk about it in the group.

As Ramiro's story illustrates, sometimes media rituals take place during the daytime. This is more commonly the case for students, people who work at home, and retirees. Sara, a twenty-one-year-old student, states that "I used to watch the same [television] shows. In the afternoon, for instance, I have [the television set] on and [watch] gossip shows and things like that. However, it's not that I'm paying that much attention. But in the evening, yes, it's the weekly soap opera." Thus, for Sara, the transition from daytime to evening watching is marked by a shift in patterns of attention. This shift, which is also prevalent among other interviewees, is in part a result of the notion that evening viewing is an activity to close the day, and that there is a desire to devote the last bits of energy to a relaxing activity. Marina, a twenty-two-year-old financial analyst, says,

The moment that I have for watching television is mostly the evening and it is to relax from [what happened earlier] in the day. And I don't want to watch the news. I watch [Argentine soap opera] *Los Ricos No Piden Permiso*, haha. And, on Netflix I follow *Gossip Girl*.

Mabel, a sixty-two-year-old retiree, also experiences a shift in attention as the day unfolds, but in her case it is marked by the passage from the evening to bedtime. "I tell you," she starts, "the computer is over in the evening and the television set shows up again. . . . I have a routine so that I'm eating [dinner] during primetime. . . . and I watch a network television channel, whatever there is, a soap opera, an entertainment show . . . but I don't give much importance [to the content]." Then she adds

But, when I go to bed, I search for a documentary, or a movie, or [something on the] Discovery [network]. Something that grabs my attention a bit more. I don't watch network television because I don't find anything that interests me. . . . I watch until I fall asleep. . . . If I'm not tired and find something interesting, I can stay up until, say, 2:00 am. Easily.

The ritual of watching audiovisual entertainment on the screen while in bed and right before going to sleep is so prevalent among many interviewees that it serves as a mediatized sleeping aid. To Patricio, a nineteen-year-old student, bedtime is marked by a transition from playing games on the computer to watching entertainment in bed. "It's the moment in which I get tired of playing games and want to be in bed. I don't want to be sitting in front of a screen, so I play a video [on the television set] and fall asleep while watching it." As television is a companion and guardian of the night time—an idea first introduced in chapter 2—Agustin, a nineteen-year-old factory worker, confesses that "I can't fall asleep without the television turned on. I fall asleep with that on, otherwise I can't sleep." Teofilo, a thirty-five-year-old construction worker, watches "a movie from 10:00, 11:00 pm onwards . . . to go to sleep at 1:00 am. It's almost like not feeling sleepy before that." As, Carlos, a fifty-eight-year-old accountant, puts it in a quasi-meditation frame of reference:

> The moment of watching television during the work week . . . is almost an indispensable step before going to sleep. It's not about watching something in particular, but about doing something [like] turning your mind blank, distracting yourself a little bit, before saying "I'm going to sleep."

Entertainment Outside of the Household

In this section I examine three well-known kinds of cultural activities undertaken outside the household: going to the movies, to see a play, and to the museum. The first kind has been most directly affected by the abundance of audiovisual content within the household. The second and third options have been only somewhat indirectly affected by the trends shaping content availability at home; thus they serve as a useful contrast to the moviegoing experience.

Going to the Movies

The analysis of the interviews shows that as the volume and range of shows, series, and movies available at home has risen, the practice of going to the movies has become more complicated and less desirable to undertake. Interviewees commonly state that their interest in watching a movie in the theater is much higher than the frequency with which they do this—which pales in comparison to the frequency of at-home viewing. Some of the typical complicating factors include the trouble of getting to the theater; the cost not only of the ticket but also of the larger experience of which watching a movie is usually considered to be part; and the need to find companions who agree not only on the movie but also on the complementary plans before and/or afterward, since going to the movies is normally considered to be a collective activity. Because of the combination of these complicating factors, many interviewees regularly substitute the movie outing with at-home audiovisual entertainment, and articulate a discourse of convenience regarding the latter.

It was common to hear interviewees say that they like going to the movie theater but do not get to do it as often as they would want to. Ana, a twenty-one-year-old student says, "I love to go, but do so approximately once every other month." In a related vein, Estefania, a twenty-six-year-old employee at a non-profit, states, "I like the movies, but in truth I don't go a lot. It's been a while. . . . Recently we had winter break and you weren't going to see me stepping into a movie theater . . . not even drugged [laughs]!" When asked if he goes to the movie theater, Mariano, a thirty-five-year-old cook, answers:

MARIANO: Sometimes I go, but it's been a while since I've gone . . .
INTERVIEWER: So, do you like going?
MARIANO: Yes, I like it, I like it. The only movie I've seen was Titanic. . . .
    I think in the theater.
INTERVIEWER: Oh, it was a long time ago!
MARIANO: No, just kidding [laughs]!

Mariano's joke illustrates not only the mix of high interest with low frequency, but also serves as a window into what these frequencies mean in the context of going to the movies and how they compare with watching audiovisual content in the household. Even among those who say they go to the movie theater a lot, the frequency with which they say they do this is much lower than the amount of time even an average person devotes to entertainment consumption on their personal screens. Adriana, a twenty-two-year-old student "goes a lot, I'd say maybe twice a month." Likewise, Juana, who is two years younger and also in college, says she goes to the movie theater "a lot." And adds that this means every "two, three weeks."

One reason interviewees give for their not-so-frequent visits to the movie theater is distance to the venue. This factor is most prevalent in small towns in the provinces that have the fewest theaters, while people in the suburbs of Buenos Aires and other large metropolises fall in the middle between the small towns and the City of Buenos Aires, which has the most theaters and most frequent attendance. Lucila, a twenty-seven-year-old clerical employee in a media company, comments that "there was a moment in which I used to go a lot because I lived in [the Buenos Aires neighborhoods of] Caballito, Boedo. . . . I'd go twice a month to the Gaumont [movie theater]. . . . I really liked the Gaumont. . . . It has a great neighborhood vibe." At the other end of the spectrum is Luciano, a thirty-six-year-old businessman in a small town in the province of Santa Fe. "We go very little . . . because we don't have [a movie theater] in town. . . . We've gone a few times to the movies in [the town of] Casilda, and in [the city of] Rosario two or three times, not more." Somewhat in the middle between these two ends of the geographic spectrum lies the significant portion of the interviewees who live in the suburbs—mirroring what happens with the population-at-large. Furthermore, those who are in the suburbs complain that most theaters are concentrated in a few geographic centers—usually in large malls—and screen mostly blockbuster films. Elsa, a sixty-six-year-old retired teacher and psychotherapist, says,

> Nowadays to go to the movie theater you have to go to [shopping malls] Unicenter or Showcenter, and that's far away. . . . Otherwise, you have to go to [the gated neighborhood] Nordelta, which is far. . . . It's not like before that you could go to [the densely populated suburb of] San Isidro, watch a movie, and come back. We have a car, but it takes time [now].

Silvina, another sixty-six-year-old who is a retiree, is frustrated about the selection of films in addition to issues of distance:

> I would like to go to the movie theater because I like movies a lot . . . but you have to go to the city. . . . Or around here in [the shopping mall] Las Toscas [in the municipality of Canning, in the province of Buenos Aires]

you also have [a movie theater]. But I don't know, they don't always show good movies.... They show only the most popular ones.

A second reason people do not go to the movies often—or at all—revolves around economic matters. Carolina, a twenty-four-year-old student, states, "I seldom go, though I love it. But I don't go a lot . . . mostly for economic matters." Leila, who is nineteen years of age and also a student, says that "my boyfriend and I were going to go yesterday, but we decided to eat out [instead]. Between the fact that movie tickets are expensive . . . and that sometimes you aren't satisfied with the movie, then you have to have a really good review for me to go to the theater." Sebastian, a twenty-four-year-old marketing employee, further elaborates on the price-quality relationship:

It's been a while since the movie [industry] got into a complicated crisis because a lot of the great creative minds migrated to the universe of the series. . . . Then, this means that you go to the movie theater to see a film with a lot of special effects. . . . So, I go to see special things in the theater, not as often as I used to go because it's an expensive outing.

A third factor keeping people from movie theaters is sociality. Contrary to the social versatility of watching a movie at home, going to the movies is almost always seen as a collective activity. "I'd say that the last time I went to the movie theater by myself was in 2008," states Julian, the film producer. In a similar vein, Maria, a twenty-two-year-old student, comments that "I've never gone by myself.... There have been times I wanted to go by myself, but I didn't have the courage [to do it]." Flavia, the interior designer, says that "I've gone by myself but . . . when I was with my dad and he had to run an errand, I was by myself in the theater." And then she adds, "But it's not that I go by myself if [a movie] interests me and nobody comes with me. In those cases, I don't go." Estanislao, a twenty-seven-year-old clerical employee, shares a similar stance: "I choose to go to the movie theater with company. . . Either with a partner or with my little brothers. . . I don't go to the movies by myself." Thus, to most interviewees, not finding company equals not going to the movie theater. As Manuela, the housewife, puts it: "I like going to the movie theater a lot, but it's been a while . . . because I don't have anybody to go with."

There is a strong taken-for-granted association between going to the movies and doing it with others. "I don't think it's an activity to do by yourself," states Rosario, the Pilates instructor. Pedro, a twenty-four-year-old public-sector employee, agrees: "I think it's a group outing ... or at least with someone else. Not by yourself." Because this convention is so strong, the majority of the handful of interviewees who have broken it felt somewhat uneasy. Juana, a twenty-year-old-student, confesses to have gone "two or three times by myself, but it's kind of sad." "It's somewhat strange when you show up by yourself at the movie theater; people look at you," adds Victor, the college student. Luciana, who is thirty years of age and works as an accountant, comments that the first time she went to the movies by herself "it was strange. To begin with, it was a comedy and I felt that I was laughing alone. . . . So, at the beginning you're too self-aware, but then [you realize] that nobody cares." Marcela, a seventy-two-year-old widow, notes that

> I have discovered that I like [going to the movies] by myself. . . . I used to go with my late husband. We liked to go together. And then it was hard to do things by myself. Some more than others. And recently I discovered that I like going to the movies by myself. . . . I enjoy that nobody talks to me during the movie, for instance. I go to the theater, buy my ticket, sit down, leave the theater, and I go back [home]. I'm not wondering around ... [because] I don't like to get a drink alone. That's something that I still don't like. Still, and probably never. Get a coffee by myself? No, I'd rather be at home.

Marcela's reflections about her experience are important not only because they challenge the idea that going to the movies is a collective activity, but also because they make visible the fact that going to the movies is often part of a larger social outing that involves grabbing a bite or a drink either before or after the film. Estela, a twenty-six-year-old employee at a non-profit, reflects that "you don't talk during those two hours [of the movie], but I don't know, I take advantage of going to the movies to get together with somebody and maybe we have dinner." David, a twenty-four-year-old who works at a paint shop, says that "it's an outing. First you grab a bite, then you stroll around, get into the movie theater. . . . It's more to go out and about, than to go to the movies per se." Fabian, a forty-three-year-old doorman, goes to the movies quite often. When he is asked what is it that he likes about it, he says it is "the whole combo: go to the theater, buy popcorn, watch the movie. The whole outing. Then, you go out to dinner, get back [home] full, tired, and fall asleep." He adds that this is "totally different" from watching a movie at home.

But the majority of the interviewees do not share Fabian's preference for going to the movie theater over watching audiovisual entertainment within the household. "It seems to me that since I have Netflix I haven't gone to the movies as often," reflects Eugenia, a forty-seven-year-old college instructor. Then, she adds "I'm thinking that the latest movies I've watched, I did so at home either on Netflix or another one in particular we went to buy [the copy on DVD]." Similar to Eugenia's experience, fifty-three-year-old Roman also notes that "now that we have Netflix and stuff like that, I consume more movies that way." When asked to choose between going to the movie theater and watching Netflix, Matias, a thirty-two-year-old community manager, replies with a strong "No! I stick to Netflix. As a matter of fact, we were about to go to the movies yesterday, and decided to watch a movie at home and then go out to dinner. The movie theater is done." In a similar vein, Claudia, a forty-one-year-old psychotherapist, says that she "doesn't believe" she would go to a movie theater because "the television gives you a lot! And if you want, well, you can search on the internet! Nowadays you have a lot to wonder around, search, look. The internet opens up a world." Marisa, a fifty-nine-year-old housewife, tells the story that when she was dating the person who later would become her husband,

> we used to go to the movie theater every Sunday. And even during the work week. Because we like films a lot. . . . We still do it, but less than before. That's why we subscribed to Netflix, because in a sense it's not the same but it's similar. . . . [And] we can watch [movies] every night.

"Convenience" and "comfort" are the keywords that interviewees most commonly mention when they explain why the abundance of audiovisual entertainment within the household has led them to decrease the frequency with which they go to the movies. "It's a matter of convenience," says Cristina, a fifty-nine-year-old housewife, to watch "Netflix or . . . purchase a movie [on DVD]. . . . Habits change, you see?" Mauricio, the security guard, "likes to go to the movie theater," but getting there is cumbersome. Thus, "instead of going and coming back, I better stay at home watching Netflix. I have my own couch, forget about it. I stay there comfortably, sipping some *mates*, eating something. There is nothing like being comfortable." Similarly, Cecilia, a forty-nine-year-old housewife, says she and her husband go to the movie theater "little-to-nothing. I'm more comfortable watching [a film] at home." She adds that "it's too much movement. . . . I prefer other kinds of outings . . . such as eating out or getting together with friends, instead of locking myself inside a movie theater, which is something I can do at home and more comfortably." Miguel, who is sixty-five years of age and works in a hardware store, goes to the movie theater

> Once in a while, little, little . . . because of convenience, of being tired after the work week. So, you say "How nice the movie theater, the ambiance there," but sometimes the will [to go] doesn't coincide with how tired you are, and you keep postponing. Then, they show the movie on television, on Netflix . . . and then you don't go to the movie theater anymore.

Money and time are two additional factors that interviewees mention when they talk about how their movie-viewing habits have changed. Laura, a twenty-year-old-student, says that she "used to go [to the theater] a lot, all the time." However, "Nowadays, I watch a lot of new releases on Apple TV. I don't have it, but when I go to my boyfriend's they always watch it. And that way I save [the money] for the theater." Clotilde, a twenty-nine-year-old maid, confesses that "if it was for me, I'd go to the movie theater. But because it's so expensive, we watch at home. That's the truth." Sara, the college student, says she "downloads movies from the internet. Otherwise, I go to the movie theater, but very little. Because it's hard to find the time." Marcelo, a sixty-one-year-old who runs a convenience store, says that "it's been a long time," since he has gone to the movie theater. "Maybe I don't have time. It surely is easier to watch a movie at home," he adds.

Going to See a Play

Most of the patterns that characterize the moviegoing experience also mark how frequently people visit the theater to see a play. But this happens in a more intense fashion: the frequency of the activity is lower—even if the interest is high; the cost of the ticket matters more; the issue of distance becomes even more important as theaters are more geographically concentrated in location than are cinemas; and the collective character of the outing remains, but when combined with the higher economic costs and transportation hassles, it becomes even more challenging to find company to see a play. Although the abundance of available audiovisual content does not have a direct impact on theater activity—the products are not comparable—it does offer a powerful alternative; and the various complications associated with going to see a play, coupled with the wealth of other options available to the household, indirectly contribute to making theatergoing less appealing.

"I like theater a lot. . . . But normally I don't go. The last play I've seen was . . . I don't know, a year ago," confesses Horacio, the pharmaceutical sales representative. Carlos, a fifty-eight-year-old accountant, shares a similar sentiment: "Theater? Not little, very little. Very little given that I like it. I don't recall exactly, but it must be a year or more than a year since we've gone to see a play." Zoraida, a twenty-two-year old student, also shares a high level of interest but sees plays infrequently: "I like it, but it's been a long time since I've gone. . . . A month ago, I was going to go and . . . I was like 'No, I have to study,' so nothing." Paola, a twenty-two-year old model, says practically the same: "I don't go to see plays a lot. I like them, but I don't go often." Estela, the employee at a non-profit, echoes her words by noting that "it's not that I don't like it, but I don't do it."

Other interviewees not only do not go to plays, but they are not even interested in them. "I would like to say that I go to the theater often, but the truth is that I don't," says Lucas, a thirty-year-old attorney. Asked why he would say that, Lucas answers, "Because it's politically correct to say 'I consume theater.' . . . But the truth is that it's been a long time since I've gone." Marisa, who lives in the small town of Arequito, in the Santa Fe province, comments that "there are plays here in town, and I've heard they're good. . . . But I don't go." Mateo, a twenty-two-year-old student, similarly states, "I don't go to the theater, never. It's not that I don't value it, I think it's a nice genre. But I don't know, I don't have the habit or anybody who encourages me to go." Ezequiel, a thirty-nine-year-old attorney, reflects that in his case, "the outings to the theater that we had in the past, have practically disappeared nowadays."

But even among those who are interested in seeing a play, and do it sometimes, the frequency is lower than going to the movies. "I don't go as often as I go to the movies, but much more than the average," says Santiago, a thirty-year-old businessman. Ana, the college student, is "more distrustful of the theater than of the movies. The ticket is much more expensive, so I do some research before going. It's not like in the movies where I say, 'Well, I see whatever and if I don't like it, it's no big deal.'" Ana's remarks point to the importance of cost in understanding the theater experience. While ticket price is also important for movies—as was shown in the previous subsection—it is even more pronounced for plays. Manuela, the housewife, says that the theater "interests me, but I don't go . . . because the cost is high." Florencia, a nineteen-year-old student, comments that she has "gone to Teatro San

Martin to see a play with my mom. The truth is that I was left with a lot of interest to go back." This is a municipal theater which offers more reasonably priced options than those of for-profit competitors. However, to Lola "the thing is mostly the price of the ticket. . . . It's expensive, even more so these days." Josefina, the public-sector employee, also likes going "to the theater, but the tickets are expensive." Jorge, a nineteen-year-old college student concurs: "It's more expensive [than the movies and] you have to travel farther."

Jorge's statement ties together money and distance, another factor that was also salient in the moviegoing experience. This is because theaters are so much more geographically concentrated than theaters, thus increasing the associated transportation challenges. Kevin, a twenty-three-year-old student, says that going to the theater "is something I enjoy a lot but simply don't do it. Maybe it's because it's too far from where I live. . . . What I consume a lot is movies, [because movie theaters are] much closer comparatively. . . . I go around twice a month." Eleonor, a fifty-year-old receptionist, lives in a northern suburb of the City of Buenos Aires and "would like to go more, but there are no [theaters] in the area." She adds that "there was one [nearby] Tren de la Costa [station], but they closed it. And others farther away, like the Astro, where I used to go, and the Bristol, which burned down, were never reopened." Laura, a twenty-year-old student, lives in another northern suburb and says that because "it's super expensive and it means going downtown," she does not see plays nearly as often as she would like to. In addition, "you have to find someone to go with, which is a whole issue. It's more difficult that someone joins you [than in the case of going to the movies]."

Laura's remarks point to the social dimension. Seeing a play is considered a collective activity by the vast majority of interviewees. Thus, Celia, a seventy-seven-year-old retiree, and Juanita, the teacher, go to the theater "always with company." Similarly, Esteban, a forty-five-year-old administrative employee, does it "always with my family." Andrea, a thirty-one-year-old photographer, goes "with friends, maybe with my mom." Tatiana, the librarian, also "likes that somebody comes with me." The collective mandate, coupled with the deterrence of economic and geographic issues, decrease either the likelihood or the frequency, or both, of respondents' going to the theater. Gerardo, a fifty-two-year-old astronomer, "likes the theater. . . . But my wife doesn't like it . . . so, we don't go." As Romina, a nineteen-year-old student, puts it, "It's tough to find someone to go with."

Going to the Museum

The practice of going to museums shares some of the patterns that characterize going to the movies and to see plays, such as a higher level of espoused interest than frequency of attendance, and the pervasive notion that museumgoing is a collective activity. But there is also a significant difference with these other two forms of entertainment consumption: going to the museum is almost always seen as something to do not only outside of the household but also out of town. There is a sense that museums are a unique window into the other— city, country, culture—rather than an expression of a person's own experience; thus museum visits are associated with travel. Although there is no direct or indirect impact of the abundance of audiovisual entertainment content in museum activity—other than the availability of online access to collections, which was not mentioned by a single interviewee—a brief examination of the routines enacted in relation to this form of high-brow activity helps to both underscore the role of routines shaping cultural practices and also to denaturalize the conventions associated with going to movies and to plays.

"I'd like to have the visit to museums more incorporated [into my routine], but something always comes up that seems better than going to a museum," says Carolina, a twenty-four-year-old student. She reflects the dominant tendency among interviewees: a stated yet unrealized interest. Sebastian, the marketing employee, comments that "I don't go very often. I would like to go a bit more frequently . . . but the truth is that it's not one of my most frequent outings." Similarly, Barbara, the systems analyst, also says that she "likes it, but doesn't go very often."

However, a minority of interviewees say that they visit museums quite frequently. "I go to museums a lot!" exclaims Laura, a twenty-year-old student. Adding, "Even more so with my Humanities major we're always trying to see the exhibits that are available." Casimiro, a thirty-one-year-old programmer, says that he goes "quite a bit, every other month or two I visit [a museum]." On the other end of the spectrum are the interviewees who have no interest in this cultural practice. "I haven't gone to museums for a long time, since elementary school I haven't done it," confesses David, the employee at a paint shop. Estanislao, the clerical employee, has "zero interest in going; if it happens it is merely by chance." Fidel, a fifty-eight-year-old attorney, bluntly says: "Museums? No. I think the last time I went to a museum was abroad because I was part of group of forty people. It wasn't my choice. . . . I leave it very low in my preferences [of cultural activities]."

The collective aspect of the museum experience is quite pervasive among interviewees. Marisa says that she goes to museums "with my husband because he likes it better than me, so he takes me. Because if it was up to me maybe I wouldn't go." In a related vein, Mariana, a thirty-nine-year-old architect, comments that "I like to go with company, so when I don't find anybody that can come with me maybe I don't go." Similarly, Mateo, the student, does not go "because I don't have anybody to go with." For some interviewees, the collective aspect of visiting museums is associated with parenting and grandparenting, as a form of educational experience. Fabian, the doorman, "went to the Museum of National Sciences . . . because my daughter wanted to see [the dinosaurs] and now I have to take her to the Fine Arts one. She goes out of curiosity, and I do it to keep her company." Lola, the retiree, and her husband recently visited a rural museum in the municipality of Luján, some forty miles away from the City of Buenos Aires, "to take our grandkids, because we wanted them to see it."

Although it is something he does not like to do, Fidel went to the museum as part of a trip. This association between museums and traveling is key to understanding not only when people go to museums, but, more important, why they do it. Bruno, the student, says: "When I travel, I go often to museums because it is a way of appreciating the culture of a place." Museums, in other words, are constructed as windows into the other. "If I go on vacation or to a place I don't know, it's a mandatory visit," laughingly comments Sara, the student. Similarly, fifty-eight-year-old Matilde says she does not go to museums in her own town, but "if I have to travel, then yes. I visit all possible museums—that I do." According to Cecilia, the housewife:

> You take more advantage when it's overseas, and not so much here, at home. . . . Because here you have your daily routine and it doesn't include museumgoing a lot. By contrast, during a trip you incorporate it more because you have to take advantage that you're abroad.

The tie that binds museums and traveling applies to both domestic and overseas trips. Mateo, the student, says that he does not go to the museums that exist in the city of Córdoba, the second most populous of Argentina, "but I've gone when I've been to other cities [in the country]. . . . You're more like a tourist." Norberto, the high school teacher, comments that he goes to museums only when I come to Buenos Aires. . . . Because maybe you live in Buenos Aires, and walk by the entrance of Teatro Colón and see it as another part of the city. But when you come from somewhere else you become much more interested [in museums].

Angeles, the retiree, who lives in the City of Buenos Aires, echoes Norberto's sentiment though in her case talking about foreign travel. And she illustrates her thoughts also making reference to Teatro Colón, the famed opera house and museum:

If I'm visiting another country, yes. But in my own country, no. The other day I was asking myself why I've never been to the Colón. . . . That is, if I go to another country . . . the first thing I do is to visit [the equivalent of] that country's Colón, but not here.

Although present in domestic tourism, the link between museums and traveling is particularly strong in foreign trips, as illustrated by Maribel—who lives in a city with plenty of museums to choose from. Sandra, a forty-eight-year-old clerical employee, comments that she recently went to a lot of museums "because I went to Italy. . . . If I go places where there are museums I [visit them]. But here in Buenos Aires I don't remember when the last time was I went." When Carolina, the student, is asked whether she goes to museums, she says:

CAROLINA: Here, unfortunately not.
INTERVIEWER: Why do you say "here"?
CAROLINA: In Buenos Aires.
INTERVIEWER: And where do you go?
CAROLINA: When I travel overseas. I don't know if it's because of the fact of traveling.

Even though a large portion of the museums in Argentina do not charge an admission fee, this tie to tourism imbues museumgoing with a significant social class component—particularly in a country where almost a third of the population lives below the level of poverty. The interviews reveal that visiting museums is further connected to possessing certain levels of cultural capital, an issue that is less prevalent when people consider going to see plays and, especially, going to the movies. "I never went to museums as a kid; I thought it was very boring," confesses Adriana, a twenty-two-year-old student. "But after taking an arts class [in college], we went to the museum all together and it was interesting. Maybe it didn't interest me before because I didn't know much about art." Soledad, a forty-four-year-old speech therapist, thinks that because she does not have that knowledge it is difficult for her to enjoy the museum experience, which she labels a "pending assignment." She asked a friend who is well versed in art history "to teach me, but like a kid . . . one little step at a time. Because I didn't grow up in a household with that cultural level, it's hard to for me to incorporate it." Roman concurs, also referring to his "pending assignment," and adds that "in reality I'd like to go to museums . . . but I don't know anything about painting." Thus, the notion that enjoying museums requires a certain level of cultural capital, which in most cases is seen as difficult to acquire, ends up further deterring people from taking part in this experience.

Affect

The emotional states that interviewees express when talking about their entertainment activities are overwhelmingly positive. This is a stark contrast to the emotions that are tied to news consumption, as I showed in chapter 4. Furthermore, in a continuum of emotional expression, the consumption of audiovisual content at home is at the higher end and going to the museum at the lower end, with movies and plays in the middle. This manifests in both the number of times interviewees mention emotional issues tied to entertainment activities and the intensity of the positive states they experience. Although the spectrum of emotions mentioned was quite wide, there was a handful of highly prevalent ones: relaxation, disconnection, enjoyment, and wonder.

The association between relaxation and consuming audiovisual content within the household is quite common. Pedro, a twenty-four-year-old public-sector employee, says that watching Netflix "is the part of the day that relaxes you a little." Barbara, the system analyst, concurs by noting that watching television allows her "to relax . . . distend myself." When asked what the moment of watching television means to her, Patricia, the high school teacher, answers: "It's the moment I have for myself, to relax, to enjoy. . . . I like it because I have freedom to choose, to enjoy, I love it." Patricia, the high school teacher, replies to a similar question by stating that, "Well, it's like being peaceful at home, calm, like the day is over and I sit down to watch television."

This feeling of relaxation is often linked to an experience of disconnection, once again quite prevalent in the case of at-home entertainment. Hector, a forty-seven-year-old, watches television "to put my mind in blank, [and] sometimes to see things that make me laugh." Sara, the student, contrasts this feeling of disconnection with her experience of watching news content: "When you watch a soap opera and things like that, well, you disconnect a bit from reality, from things that happen. . . . Whereas, when you watch crime news or whatever, it's like you become more paranoid or afraid." She adds that this difference in emotions leads her to want entertainment content instead of news stories. Similarly, Veronica, a forty-six-year-old school principal, says that entertainment shows are "a way of exiting from reality." When asked to compare how she feels watching political programs and entertainment shows, she answers: "It's like entering and exiting reality." Regarding entertainment shows, she particularly enjoys celebrity and gossip programs, because "I laugh! I laugh! And, well, I see that the same things happen to all of us, that in the end we're all human." Mariano, the cook, comments that he really likes the show How I Met your Mother because "it makes me laugh a lot."

Veronica's and Mariano's comments point to the importance of enjoyment, which is another common emotional state mentioned by the interviewees. "I enjoy it, I enjoy the guy, [Marcelo] Tinelli. . . . I laugh, because I know it's all a show," comments Emanuel, the store employee, about the highly popular network television program Showmatch, hosted by Marcelo Tinelli. Juanita also talks about enjoyment, in her case in relation to the comparison between entertainment and news consumption. She says that she "enjoys" entertainment since "it makes me see different realities, I laugh for a while. . . . [T]he newscast [has] things you have to know [and] I like to know, but you watch so many things that you are not interested in, or that it's always the same . . . that I prefer not to watch [the news]." When asked what she likes about going to the movies, Mora, the industrial designer, says that "the whole program seems really enjoyable to me. . . . I like the whole experience: I go and buy popcorn, it's like the whole thing seems really good to me."

Other interviewees also comment how much they enjoy the experience of going to the movies, in some cases linking it to a sense of wonder. German, the attorney, says that the movie theater "is fascinating to me." He adds that he likes going to the movies "because I feel really comfortable; I like the climate it generates, the darkness, the good sound. I enjoy going to the movie theater a lot. It's like ecstasy when I really score with the movie." Similarly, to Matilde going to the movies "can't be compared to anything you watch at home.... The screen, darkness, silence, the atmosphere of the theater.... There are movies that lose their magic if you watch them in any other place that isn't the large screen." Mara, the administrative employee, relays a similar sentiment, with a nostalgic touch: "I've always liked going to the movies. . . . I remember that there was an outdoor movie theater and we used to go (laughs). An antique [experience]. . . . I'm very passionate about the moment of being in the movie theater." On occasion, interviewees link that sense of wonder and intense connection to going to see a play or an exhibit. The latter was the case for Santiago, the teacher: "I was in Russia. I went to Moscow and Saint Petersburg, and I spent three full days at the Hermitage. . . . I got crazy about it." This feeling also surfaces in conversations about programming for the small screen, as when Agustín, the factory worker, comments that he's watching "*Breaking Bad*, I'm in love," and Lucila, the clerical employee at a media company, says that the release of the new season of *Game of Thrones* made her feel "so emotional . . . [even though] the first episode terribly disappointed me."

Attachment

Many interviewees made comments about their practices that evinced a significant level of attachment to the audiovisual content they watched at home. There was not a comparable pattern that applied to going to the movies, to see a play, or to a museum. This, in turn, marks another significant difference between entertainment consumption within and outside the household. Furthermore, the analysis reveals a strong connection between this level of attachment, on the one hand, and the abundance and constant availability of content perceived as appealing, on the other hand. This is particularly prevalent in the case of serialized fiction on streaming platforms; it is mildly present for soap operas, and does not apply at all to watching movies at home. Attachment shapes not only the content people watch but also indirectly the programming they choose not to consume. Finally, even though it tends to be tied to a perception of low levels of self-efficacy, some interviewees comment about limiting their viewing practices to counter what they consider to be the negative effects of being attached to audiovisual entertainment content at home.

The following dialogue took place during the interview with Marcelino, a forty-one-year-old teacher:

INTERVIEWER: When was the last time you watched television, but not for news?

MARCELINO: A couple of hours ago.

INTERVIEWER: How was it, on the computer or on the television set?

MARCELINO: No, on the television. I watched eight episodes in a row of a series that is driving me crazy.

INTERVIEWER: Which one, can you tell?

MARCELINO: *Limitless.*

INTERVIEWER: Is it new?

MARCELINO: Yes, yes, it's amazing.

INTERVIEWER: Well, I'm going to . . .

MARCELINO (INTERRUPTING): No, no, I recommend it to you. You don't know what it is!

INTERVIEWER (LAUGHING): Do you like series a lot?

MARCELINO: I'm a fan of series, but in addition to that Netflix allows you to watch an entire season at once.

. . .

INTERVIEWER: And, how much time do you devote to [watching] television?

MARCELINO: Huh (thinking) . . . Well, in general I get home between 9:00 and 10:00 pm. I live by myself. I cook, I finish dinner or sometimes make myself a little sandwich, I go to bed, turn on the television, and until 2:00, 3:00 in the morning . . . [I watch] episodes!

Besides the irony of being attached to a series called *Limitless*, this dialogue illustrates the existence of an intense bond between people and content—both in terms of time spent and also emotional connection—and the association of this experience with the abundance of available programming. Joaquin, a twenty-eight-year-old systems analyst, "consumes Netflix until dying ('hasta morir') and it can be several hours. On weekends that I don't want to do anything, I consume Netflix from the time I get up until the evening." When Ramiro, the student, discovered *Game of Thrones*, "it blew my mind. I began late . . . and I watched two seasons during one week on vacation." Laura, the student, comments that the day before her interview she watched a series on Netflix "all day. What a disaster! I'm very addicted if I get hooked on a series." Tatiana, the librarian, confesses: "I'm not one of those people who can watch a little episode per day. That is, if I watch something, I have to finish it." She considers that discovering a series that she likes is "an obstacle in my life. . . . Because all of a sudden, I have to finish it. That is, you have the complete series on Netflix." Lucila, the clerical employee, shares Tatiana's sense of ambivalence, even though this does not make her stop: "Last Saturday evening I watched six episodes of *Girls*. . . . But it stops being a source of enjoyment to becoming a commitment."

As the statements of Joaquin, Ramiro, Laura, Tatiana, and Lucila show, the attachment to audiovisual content is particularly strong in the case of serialized fiction. Interviewees say that this is because of the confluence between two factors. On the one hand, there is a lack of closure at the end of any given episode and a continuity across episodes—which also applies to other television genres such as soap operas. On the other hand, the availability of entire seasons on streaming services, satellite television, and online sites marks a difference with watching series and soap operas on network and cable television. As a result, attachment shapes not only which content people watch, but also what they choose not to watch—series versus soap operas and movies. Furthermore, it is tied to the perception of relatively low levels of self-efficacy. Mariana, a thirty-nine-year-old architect, says that she prefers series more than movies on television because

a movie takes longer [to watch] than a series, an episode of a series. And it's like there is something pending in the series, always. So, I want to know what happens, how it continues. . . . It's like with series, until I don't finish them. . . . There is a thread [across episodes], I want to keep watching it, until the end.

By contrast, Estanislao, the clerical employee, prefers to watch soap operas on network television over series on streaming because "the soap opera finishes, whereas the series doesn't. . . . You have the possibility to keep watching. . . . With the soap opera you're forced to wait until the next time to watch it [again]." He adds that with the series on streaming, "Maybe it's difficult to stop and say [to yourself], 'No, I stop here and watch a single episode.' . . . It's tough to have self-control." Humberto, a forty-nine-year-old businessman and attorney, prefers movies over series not because he likes the former more than the latter but "because series hook me up a lot, and they force me to want to see all episodes at once. And I don't have the patience or the time available to do it." Similarly, Carla, a forty-five-year-old attorney, states:

I don't watch series, because [they] absorb me a lot and generate avidity. And since I have to work the next day and I need to sleep, I try not to watch series. Unless we set aside a whole weekend devoted to watching a series, I prefer to watch a movie that begins and ends.

The comments by Estanislao, Humberto, and Carla illustrate not only the perception of low levels of self-efficacy but also that people devise measures to limit their exposure to content they feel they might get attached to. Some of these measures are seasonal, limiting exposure to times of the year with fewer obligations, such as holidays. Juana, the student, says that "the only period in which I consume [Netflix] is over the summer, when I don't have any classes to take and things like that." She adds that during that time, "I watch one series after the other, spend the entire day hooked on Netflix.... Pum, pum, pum, you finish a series in less than a week, three days." Other measures are temporally based. Marina, the financial analyst, comments that when she wrote her undergraduate thesis, she had the rule of "four hours on the thesis every day [and] forty minutes of Netflix." But others are more extreme and withdraw from watching serialized fiction on streaming altogether, as was the case for Isabel, the student described in the preface.

Concluding Remarks

In this chapter I examined key structural and cultural factors that shape how members of the audience experience a world of abundant entertainment information.

The analysis shows the dominance of watching television, followed by listening to music, being on social media, and listening to the radio. Furthermore, as has been the case with screens and platforms, and contrary to that of news—examined in chapters 2, 3, and 4, respectively—age plays a more important role than socioeconomic status and gender in shaping entertainment choice. Television and radio are more strongly preferred among older segments of the population, with comparatively weaker effects of social class, and lower disparities in terms of gender—women side with television, and men with radio. By contrast, listening to music and being on social media are more common top choices among younger respondents—with no effect of either class or gender on listening to music, and comparatively milder effects of both on social media use.

These findings resonate with current work on cultural consumption. After many decades in which accounts of the reception of cultural goods and services primarily revolved around issues of class and their relationships to education and income, more recent research has emphasized the rise in the structuring role of age.[14] Cultural sociologists Omar Lizardo and Sara Skiles examined the evolution of musical taste in the United States from 1993 to 2012, and concluded that "newcomers into high-status classes are finding ways to extend their esthetic gaze towards cultural forms that older generations may have considered out of bounds."[15] Thus, assessing the findings from this and other related studies, stratification expert Sam Friedman and his colleagues underscore "the centrality of age and generational divisions in structuring cultural tastes and participation."[16]

Within these broad structural patterns, the account presented in this chapter highlights the versatility in the routines of watching audiovisual entertainment within the household. This affects modes of access, types of devices, sociality configurations, and consumption rituals. It is also intertwined with the ability to watch televised fiction in an ambient fashion at times—and to fold this practice into broader routines within the home environment—and making it the primary focus of action on other occasions. In part, versatility is somewhat independent of any individual, such as the varieties in access and devices available. Multiple options exist beyond the control of interviewees, who then choose to realize one or more of them, shaped by their means, knowledge, skills, and preferences. Yet, versatility is also partly an expression of the agency of interviewees, especially in the cases of sociality and rituals. There is nothing in the nature of the technology and/ or the content that dictates individual versus collective viewing or the prevalence of using televised fiction as an integral part of the going-to-sleep routine. Finally, ambiance and versatility are tied to a common ideology among the interviewees that places a premium on convenience and choice, which is also in part a manifestation of agency of interviewees.

By contrast, the consumption of entertainment outside the household is experienced as having a greater sense of rigidity regarding issues of distance, cost, and sociality—it is also more difficult to undertake these activities in ambient fashion since they require a dedicated level of attention. All of this is particularly prevalent in the cases of going to the movies and to see plays. When it comes to visiting a museum, the rigidity in relational manners is also coupled with an almost taken-for-granted association with traveling. While it is objective that in the majority of cases going to the movies requires overcoming distance barriers and entails a financial expense, the convention that turns moviegoing into a collective endeavor is another manifestation of agency tied to prevailing notions of sociality. The rigidity in the social dimension adds a layer of complication to this activity—from choosing suitable partners to agreeing on film, time, and place options—that goes against the frequency with which it is undertaken. A similar logic applies to going to the theater and visiting a museum. Furthermore, in light of the prevailing prioritization of choice and convenience, the comparably lower level of versatility of entertainment outside the household makes it a less appealing alternative to its counterpart within the home. This is consistent with data from Argentina's SINCA, which reports a 12.5% decline in the proportion of the population who watches movies in the theater, from 40% in 2013 to 35% in 2017.[17] Despite the differences in the economic means of people in the Global South and Global North, the trend in Argentina resonates with data from North America. That is, there were over 1.576 billion movie tickets sold in the United States and Canada in 2008, but that figure dropped to 1.300 billion in 2018.[18] Meanwhile, the combined population of both countries rose from 337 million to 364 million in this period. Thus, the per-person annual movie tickets sales went from 4.67 in 2008 to 3.57 in 2018, which represented a 24% drop.

The differences in the routines associated with inside- and outside-the-household practices are tied to variation in issues of affect and attachment. Concerning affect, while entertainment consumption is usually linked to positive emotional states, the frequency with which this association appears and the intensity with which it is expressed is much greater for watching audiovisual content within the household than for the other forms of cultural consumption examined in this chapter. Regarding attachment, it is solely noticeable for television, and mostly in the case of binge-watching serialized fiction. This level of attachment is lower than that regarding smartphones and platforms. The differences in affect and attachment contribute to further account for the divergence in the experience of consuming audiovisual entertainment content on the small and big screens, inside and outside the household. In addition, they also help shed light on the divergent paths of abundance of information between news and entertainment. If, as it was argued in chapter 4, people have enacted routines that depreciate the news within their everyday lives, it could be said that the routines undertaken in the case of entertainment reveal the experiential appreciation of watching televised fiction. Interviewees enact this appreciation in manifold ways through the perceived versatility of this practice, in connection to positive emotional states, with sometimes significant levels of attachment, and in consonance with an ideology of convenience and choice.

The attachment to serialized fiction on streaming platforms also provides a suitable window to revisit the notion of programming flow, especially its contemporary experience from the standpoint of the audience. The analysis of the interviews shows both a decomposition and an acceleration of flow dynamics: watching one episode of a favorite show on a streaming platform skips the quintessential multi-program sequence of linear broadcast television, and going over a season in less than a week—sometimes even less than a day—eviscerates prior temporal parameters. This amounts to a shift in a logic of programming structured around the dynamics of media organizations to another one increasingly structured around the interplay between audiences interests and the broader conditions of their everyday lives. This analysis also contributes to filling the more general void about scholarship on contemporary audience entertainment practices alluded to above by Sonia Livingstone and Jonathan Gray in at least two ways.

First, it shows the importance of contextualizing the attachment to serialized fiction by connecting it to comparable phenomena regarding mobile phones and social media platforms—and the absence for news content. The level of attachment to the serialized appears to be lower than in the cases of mobile phones and social media platforms. The object of attachment is also different: mass-produced entertainment versus relational and expressive content. The greater pull of relational/expressive content tied to the reconstitution of sociality examined in chapters 2 and 3 might account—at least in part—for the lower level of attachment to mass-produced entertainment. However, there is a common root of experiencing a certain lack of control with respect to the abundance of information available and the associated attempts to regain control by establishing a series of routines free from screens, platforms, and entertainment. In addition, there are compounding effects that occur when mobile and platform communication are linked to either incentivizing additional viewing or engaging in co-viewing and/or second screening at a distance. Thus, to make sense of audience practices it is useful to put them in the context of relevant non-entertainment ones. This relates to the value of integrating objects and domains of inquiry that have been traditionally kept apart—an issue I introduced in the preface and to which I will return in chapter 6.

Second, the analysis highlights the key role played by the versatility of watching television—in its many forms—within the broader ecology of entertainment practices. Despite the often critical perspective of most television audience scholarship, and consistent with the stance of emergent valuation espoused in chapter 1, the account presented in this chapter highlights the worth that interviewees usually attribute to matters of convenience and choice, two values often associated with personalization and neoliberalism in everyday life. From the vantage point of the interviewees, watching television is taking advantage of this versatility by mixing modes of access, types of devices, sociality options, and watching rituals. This contributes to a significant re-appreciation of the worth of watching television. As with news, this experiential revaluation is not something interviewees often explicitly articulate; it emerges from an analysis of the centrality and worth it has acquired within the context of their everyday practices. Adopting a discourse of deficit tied to both the prevailing research on information overload and the critical perspective common in cultural studies of audiences would miss how the interviewees agentically appropriate these issues of convenience and choice and the extent to which that informs their reception routines. Going back to the opening quotation of this chapter, whereas the scarcity of the pre-neoliberal, mass ethos of linear television "enslaved" Eugenia— a sentiment echoed by other interviewees—the abundance represented by streaming platforms like Netflix was experienced as an emancipation from the tyranny of programming flow. While this experience is not immune to broader marketing and ideological discourses, discounting it as a mere by-product of them would ignore the power of individuals' agency—something which, as I have demonstrated repeatedly in the course of this and the previous chapters, amounts to nothing short of analytical blindness.

6

Scarcity

The number of pages in this book is no more or less
than infinite. None is the first page, none the last.

Jorge Luis Borges[1]

The written journey that started with the description of two people living in
the streets of Buenos Aires is coming to an end. In this final chapter I will take
stock of the main lessons learned and reflect on their key implications for
media, culture, and society.

I will elaborate on how adopting a ritual view of communication sheds
light on facets of the experience of information abundance that previous
work in this area left unexamined; how challenging some prevailing intellectual divisions of labor in the study of media and communication
generates knowledge gains; how embedding culture within structure, and
the present within the past helps put micro- and meso-level contemporary
patterns in broader macro-level and historical perspective; and how being
self-reflexive about the location of the inquiry helps avoid the blind spots
of studies undertaken with a view from nowhere. In the final section of this
chapter I will switch the frame and foreground critical dimensions of scarcity in both theory and practice. To this end, I will highlight the need for
rebalancing the dynamics of institutional power and individual agency in
accounts of the social consequences of digital technologies, and for dealing
with the lack of certainty about the structural and cultural basis of contemporary society.

To bring the account full circle, I will close the text with a serendip-
itous encounter that marks the final destination of this journey, in an
Argentine landmark located some twenty blocks away from where the book
began.

Abundance. Pablo J. Boczkowski, Oxford University Press. © Oxford University Press 2021.
DOI: 10.1093/oso/9780197565742.003.0006

Findings and Implications

In this section I summarize the main findings about the questions posed in the preface and elaborate on their implications by dividing them into three parts: the structuring power of age, sociality-in-the-making, and the poverty of facts and the wealth of fictions.

The Structuring Power of Age

The analysis presented in chapters 2 through 5 reveals that age is the main structural determinant of access and use of personal screens, social media platforms, and mediated entertainment whereas socioeconomic status plays that role in the case of news. Broadcast, rather than digital, media represent the top news source for most people, a result that is largely shaped by age as a variable. There are two broader considerations that contextualize these patterns. First, most people devote much more time to platforms—mostly via their smartphones—and entertainment than to news. But it is not only about time spent. The high level of attachment to smartphones, platforms, and—to a lesser extent—serialized fiction, and the positive affect often tied to their consumption, stands in contrast with the absence of attachment to news and the negative affect that usually accompanies its reception. In other words, for most people the worth of information for sociality and entertainment purposes far exceeds that of news. Second, the growing role of technology in the consumption of news makes it reasonable to predict that age increasingly will shape access to and attitudes about current affairs reporting in the foreseeable future. Therefore, even while taking into account the exceptions, age is the most important structural factor in determining how we navigate abundant information in daily life. At the time of this study, a third of Argentina's population lived below the poverty line, and one in sixteen households was in a situation of indigence—a figure that had risen to over 40% and one in nine, respectively, by fall 2020. That the aforementioned patterns of access prevail there makes the greater structuring power of age over socioeconomic status all the more remarkable as a sociological fact, and the current situation all the more pressing and concerning as a humanitarian crisis.

Age has a unique quality relative to other key social structural factors such as socioeconomic status and gender. Whereas most people so far experience little class mobility and do not alter their gender identities repeatedly during their lifetimes—if at all—they feel the impact of age every day of their lives. The passing of time is unstoppable and shared by all members of society. With aging come both life stages and generational shifts that position how individuals navigate their social worlds variously as time goes by. Thus, when age is a defining structural organizer of media access, change becomes en-. demic and unsettles previously more stable social formations. This, in turn, is tied to an increase in the overall sense of uncertainty in mediated experience that I will address later in this chapter.

Almost a century ago, classical sociologist Karl Mannheim wrote the foundational text about the role of generations in structuring social life. To him, "its practical importance becomes clear as soon as one tries to obtain a more exact understanding of the accelerated pace of social change characteristic of our time."[2] The current centrality of age is tied to Mannheim's intuition about a society undergoing a period marked by rapid transformations. At the time he wrote, the existence of shared defining experiences organized cohorts for a twenty-to-thirty-year period. In the contemporary situation, it seems that a generation' duration is in the single digits of years. This phenomenal acceleration in the pace of change triggers unsettling social experiences. Perhaps nowhere is this more evident within the findings presented in the previous chapters than in the issue of the reconstitution of sociality, to which I turn next.

Sociality-in-the-Making

The account in chapters 2 and 3 highlights the role of attributions of meaning in the appropriation of personal screens and social media platforms. Specific meanings emerged around particular screens and platforms, and these meanings contributed to how interviewees use and do not use the screens and platforms alone and with other people. These meanings also had implications for how interviewees understood and practiced their sociality.

The smartphone became akin to a prosthetic device, indispensable and difficult to part with; the computer is a tool, helpful but cold and easier to dispense with; and the television set is a companion, somewhat dated yet warm and dependable. Relatedly, WhatsApp embodies the cherished coffee place, with its atmosphere of public intimacy; Facebook is the all-purpose shopping center, convenient and multifaceted yet impersonal and somewhat uncool; Instagram is the promenade where one goes to see and be seen, with all the aesthetic pressures that come with that; Twitter is the newsstand where information-hungry individuals converge and relate to each other around news topics; and Snapchat represents the carnival where informal interactions take place, usually in relation to playful and mundane imagery.

This account also reveals the centrality of agency and attachment in shaping the contemporary experience of information abundance. The role of agency becomes evident in a broad range of practices and interpretations: from conscious decisions to post certain messages on one platform but not on others and undertake certain tasks on the smartphone but not on the computer, to concerns about spending too much time with these screens and platforms, thus devising strategies to self-limit exposure and use. The latter set of issues points to the significant level of attachment that many interviewees felt to their smartphones and the social media they accessed—and also, though to a lesser extent, serialized fiction on streaming services. This attachment was salient not only in the time devoted to screens and platforms, and the emotional intensity of the connections, but also in how difficult the absence of such connection was to many.

The combination of agency and attachment that ties screens and platforms in everyday life leads to the emergence of a society of screens and platforms.[3] This trend manifests in three interlocking connotations of this turn of phrase: the ubiquity and centrality of these technologies in everyday life; the dense and multifaceted ecosystem that weaves the various screens and platforms into a whole much greater than the sum of the parts; and the way this ecosystem affords social connections that then socialize the ecosystem's materiality by folding it into the lives of the users. As media theorist José van Dijck puts it, "The construction of platforms and social practices is mutually constitutive. Sociality and creativity happen while people are busy living their lives."[4] All in all, this amounts to a reconstitution of the understandings, practices, and norms whereby individuals enact their sociality.

This process of reconstitution is evident in the existence of both rising interest and perceived pressures to engage in additional interaction, in particular with groups of people anchored in meaningful institutions of daily life. The focus of this interest and pressure represents a significant historical break with the experience of other periods marked by information abundance: in the pre-modern period, the attention was directed to the wonders of the natural world, and in the modern era to elite information centers such as publishing and mass media; in the contemporary world, it is mostly centered on the lives of ordinary others. I will address the sociopolitical consequences of this historical discontinuity in a subsequent section, but for present purposes a key implication of this shift in the locus of attention is the multiplication in the potential sources of attention.

These quantitative pressures often trigger qualitative challenges to the individual's self-perceived ability to control the flow of communication. There is the sense among many interviewees that there are simply not enough waking minutes in the day to keep up with what others are doing and sharing one's life with them. Furthermore, the combination of more communication and the demands they make on our time gives us a heightened reflexivity about our interaction patterns, something that used to be more taken-for-granted. This reflexivity, in turn, feeds back into both the management of the volume of interactions and our strategies and perceptions of control. Contrary to common dystopic tropes about how the combination of smartphones and platforms has contributed to a decrease in sociability, the typical content of the reflections shared by the interviewees suggests the opposite: we have become more, not less, social. Moreover, this is a major source of concern for many—as can be seen partly in the challenges of solitude and also in the recurrent use of mediated information to quell the angst triggered by moments of extended silence. It is likely that the strong associational culture that has characterized everyday sociality in Argentina has partly shaped these findings and made them more visible than in locations marked by more individualistic and instrumental ways of life. Further research should delve into the role that different associational cultures might have in shaping the consequences of smartphone and platform use for sociality, rather than unreflexively assuming that what happens in countries of the Global North is the norm everywhere—an issue I will address more extensively later.

Issues of solitude and silence tie to the role of ambiance in the contemporary experience of information abundance. We increasingly seem to perform our sociality within a digital environment rather than merely use the discrete artifacts that constitute it.[5] Thus, the experience emerging from screens and platforms is more like being immersed within an environment than using artifacts in a stand-alone fashion, such as reading a newspaper or watching a movie. Borrowing from media theorist Mark Deuze, "Media are to us like water is to fish."[6] This ambiance of media is particularly meaningful to understanding patterns in the reception of news and entertainment content.

The Poverty of Facts and the Wealth of Fictions

The analysis presented in chapters 4 and 5 reveals a spectrum of routines and divergent experiential valuations tied to reception of abundant news and entertainment content.

Regarding this spectrum, most interviewees appear to have treated the surge in the volume and availability of information about current affairs by folding them into preexisting news consumption routines and emerging digital media use routines. Furthermore, the novel news consumption routines tend to be secondary to other personal and work habits, and social media routines, too. This is in part because most people seem to consume news for fairly practical purposes rather than for lofty ideals of civic duty, and they quickly accomplish these goals while undertaking routines that are more important and central to their daily lives. In addition to the relevance of practical goals, contemporary news consumption in Argentina is also shaped by the widespread perception of systemic bias in news coverage and the dominance of negative affect tied to the encounter of journalistic content. As the news has become part of the symbolic ambience of contemporary society, its relevance has largely deteriorated within the experience of everyday life.

Concerning the reception of entertainment, the majority of the interviewees favored audiovisual entertainment consumed in the home in no small part due to the versatility of the routines that organize this activity. This versatility manifested itself in four dimensions. First, individuals took advantage of a number of modes of accessing televisual content, including linear broadcasting, on-demand cable programming, DVDs, internet distribution, and streaming services. Second, they watched this content using multiple devices, such as televisions sets, computers, tablets, and mobile phones. Third, sometimes they engaged in this activity by themselves, while on other occasions they did it in the company of others—partners, family members, friends, and so on. Fourth, they enacted a variety of rituals, from taking advantage of popular shows as opportunities for co-viewing media events to turning end-of-the-day programming into a non-medicinal sleeping aid. This versatility contrasts with the perceived rigidity of the most typical entertainment options outside the household, such as going to the movies, seeing a play, and visiting a museum. These activities are different among themselves but additionally they all occur outside the household, in the physical company of others, and as part of more complex outings. In contrast, the versatility of audiovisual entertainment experienced in the home is tied to the dominance of positive affect and the presence of attachment, in particular to serialized fiction. All of this amounts to a state of experiential appreciation related to the reception of mediated entertainment in the home.

Thus, the account in chapters 4 and 5 suggests the coexistence of the poverty of facts and the wealth of fictions in the contemporary experience of information abundance. The evidence presented to make this assertion comes from a peripheral Global South country with a complicated political and economic history, and with levels of distrust in the news media that are higher than in the majority of the countries where this trust has been measured in a comparative fashion—as noted in the preface. However, since those measurements also indicate a trend toward rising levels of distrust globally, it is possible that the above mentioned evidence is a more extreme manifestation of a trend nonetheless widely shared across many nations, including some of the Global North. In this sense, perhaps there is no more apt metaphor for the divergence in experiential valuation between fact and fiction than the election of Donald Trump as president of the longest-standing democracy and the largest economy in the world: a leader who became a household name through a reality television show and whose penchant for twisting facts amounted to 22,247 "false or misleading claims" during his first 1,316 days in office—according to one fact-checking organization.[7] What is even more remarkable from a sociological standpoint is that given this volume of mis- and dis-information, it is difficult to imagine a scenario in which his supporters might not have encountered at least several dozens of examples. However, facts appear to be devalued so that this level of fact-twisting did not seem to have alienated the electoral support of a sizable portion of the voting population of the United States during the 2020 electoral contest.

The analysis of the interviews also suggests that the experiential wealth of serialized fiction has been partly realized at the expense of related activities of cultural consumption. Perhaps what might be lost in this rebalancing between within- and outside-of-the-household entertainment activities is not only, and not even primarily, the actual content of these experiences but a particular form of urban social life in mediated and unmediated settings. Thus, the wealth of fictions might ultimately entail the impoverishment of the cultural practices that marked the social and symbolic texture of the twentieth century.

More generally, both sets of differences in the reception experience of technologically mediated content—between news and entertainment, and between content consumed within or outside of the household—do not appear to be shaped decisively by either technology or content factors. On the contrary, the analysis presented in chapters 4 and 5 underscores repeatedly the key role played by non-media factors in shaping media practices.[8] First, while there is more news content available than ever, the access to it has in most cases greatly improved, and the combination of multimedia and database applications has yielded coverage of major stories with unparalleled breadth and depth, the interviews showed that the routines enacted to consume the news are largely derivative and premised on folding information acquisition into primarily non-media practices—from mowing the lawn to cleaning the house, and from cooking to filling time, for even just a few seconds of idleness. Second, even though technological innovations have greatly enhanced the quality of watching films in the movie theater, the interviews revealed that people often do not take advantage of this for reasons apart from the films themselves: the widespread belief that going to the movies requires company and should be part of a larger outing, plus the rising admission fees and the trend toward geographic concentration of theaters in a few urban areas—which further complicates transportation and other logistical issues. Thus, highlighting these non-media factors reinforces the heuristic power of the invitation made by cultural studies scholar David Morley "to 'decentre' the media, in our analytical framework, so as to better understand the ways in which media processes and everyday life are interwoven with each other."[9]

Revisiting the Four Distinct Features of This Book

Having taken stock of the main findings and key implications, I now assess the extent to which the four features discussed in the preface affected the experience of information abundance in particular, and larger issues related to the uptake of digital media in society more generally.

Enacting a Ritual View of Information Abundance

At the outset of this book I argued that the ritual view of communication's joint meaning-making provided a much needed counterbalance to existent research on information overload, which has usually espoused epistemic tenets consistent with the transmission view of communication. In chapter 1, I further elaborated on six specific limitations of the relevant prior scholarship that the approach adopted in this book aimed to overcome. Two of them center on matters of analytical focus, another two on interpretation of findings, and a third pair on methodological concerns. In the reminder of this subsection I will address each of these pairs in turn.

First, against the backdrop of the scholarly focus on the use of information for decision-making, in particular with instrumental goals, I have shown that other uses and purposes are more central in the contemporary experience of information abundance. Interviewees sometimes use content to make decisions and for either work or study reasons. However, more often they appropriate smartphones for managing everyday life, platforms to express and socialize, news to have something to talk about, and entertainment for leisure. There is also an interconnection in modalities of reception as in, for instance, when a Facebook group is established for students taking a particular class in college but a subset of them who develop a friendship switch to their own WhatsApp group—one in which patterns of communication are more intense and central to them. Understanding these various reception modalities and their different meanings in people's lives would have been hindered by an approach that privileged one type of use and purpose over the others.

Second, contrary to the notion of an optimum of information intake beyond which negative effects ensue, the evidence presented in the preceding chapters shows that the wide spectrum of positional and situational circumstances among interviewees makes it very difficult to establish parameters of optimality that would do justice to the diversity of lived experience. Because of this, the normative underpinnings that lead to the prevailing discourse of deficit do not often adequately capture the realities of the subjects that it is supposed to understand. As I demonstrated in the interpretation of the findings from chapters 2 to 5, a more mixed valuation emerges from listening to the stories of the interviewees. This emergent valuation replaces the black-or-white connotations of the dominant discourse of deficit with the gray tonalities that are more typical of everyday life. This does not mean that there are no black and white extremes, but that the great gray middle would have been missed—or at least mis-interpreted—with the predominant notions of optimality and deficit.

Third, this emergent valuation results from an emic perspective that centers on the stories of the subjects and is self-reflexive about the contextual characteristics of the location of the research. This methodological stance contrasts with the dominant use of survey and experimental designs formulated from an etic perspective and its usual tie to a view from nowhere. Had I adopted this latter perspective I would have likely overlooked the role of meanings and routines in shaping the research subjects' experience of information abundance in their situated contexts—I will further elaborate later in the chapter on the knowledge gains that result from remaining mindful about key features of the research location. One of the salient findings from this attention to meanings and routines, and the variability of the contexts in which they exist, has been the extent to which the subjects interweave objects of inquiry that are often studied separately by different scholarly communities. It is to this matter that I turn to next.

Challenging Intellectual Divisions of Labor

The second distinct feature has been to examine within a single project objects of inquiry—technologies such as screens and platforms, and types of content such as news and entertainment—that are normally studied separately. To this end I integrated insights from scholarly communities that are also not usually in conversation with each other about their respective objects of inquiry.

Analyses of the structural determinants of information access, use, and reception have usually focused on either personal screens, social media platforms, news, or entertainment, and often delved into a single key set of variables—such as age, educational attainment, gender, and race and ethnicity. However, inquiring into these matters across old and new technologies, and news and entertainment content, and contrasting the roles played by different sets of variables, showed the overall dominance of age over socioeconomic status and gender for determining technology use and entertainment habits, but not for news consumption. The very fact that news consumption on television is largely driven by socioeconomic status, but entertainment consumption on this medium is decisively shaped by age, points to the value of examining different types of content in relation to the other, thus challenging the rationale for maintaining intellectual distance between accounts of journalism and of popular culture. Furthermore, the interviews underscored the relative centrality of relational, expressive, and leisure communication, and the parallel peripheral nature of news in people's lives. This enabled the analysis to better assess what this discrepancy means for a broad spectrum of mediated experience.

This is also critical to understanding the divergent experiential valuations assigned to the consumption of news and entertainment. The mere availability of abundant content does not have uniform effects in people's lives, because consumers often enact different routines with respect to different types of content. Furthermore, the analysis also revealed significant differences even within the same type of entertainment content depending on whether it was consumed on television or in the theater. Thus, the multiplication of options for watching a given movie at home has been integrated positively into broader everyday routines, but it has also been negatively associated with watching that movie in the theater. This has little to do with content per se, and more with non-content factors that diverge according to where a person is watching the movie. Whereas the relational and temporal versatility of at-home options increases the positive valuation of its experience, the belief that outside-the-household entertainment has to be enjoyed in the company of others and as part of a larger social outing presents all kinds of logistical complications that decrease its occurrence. This, in turn, shows the limits of the long-standing division between media studies research on television and sociological scholarship on cultural consumption. Had the account only examined either watching television or going to the movies, the analysis could not have identified the interpenetration of the routines for consuming different kinds of entertainment, the role of non-content factors organizing these routines, and the broader implications of these dynamics for the urban and symbolic fabric of daily life.

In sum, the decision not to take for granted the separation between objects of inquiry has yielded accounts with better descriptive fit and stronger explanatory power. Thus, bringing experience back into the study of digital media can help shed new light on objects of inquiry that used to be more easily separated in terms of both technological and social constructions. If in the past there were clearer divisions between interpersonal communication on the phone and mass communication via print and broadcast media, social media platforms have all but obliterated the neatness of this division. If the lines that divided news and entertainment—even in the same medium, either newspaper or television—were more easily identifiable in the past, the last twenty years have seen a relentless experimentation with genres variously crossing these lines. Thus, the intellectual divisions of labor that might have worked better then seem quite dated now. Therefore, understanding information abundance, and the reception of digital media more generally, is in dire need of data collection efforts that start with the practices of the subjects—instead of assuming them beforehand—and interpret the findings through analytical lenses that creatively integrate what used to be quite separate intellectual communities.

Integrating Culture and Structure, and Present and Past

The third distinct feature has to do with embedding the cultural focus typical of the ritual view within a structural sensibility, and foregrounding the contemporary moment in relation to a rich background of historical trends.

The scholarship adopting a ritual view of communication has often resorted to a cultural lens to examine micro- and meso-level matters of practice, interpretation, and affect. However, this focus does not exist in a social vacuum. On the contrary, this weaving takes place within macro-level patterns of access to, and attitudes about, various technological and content alternatives. To examine these patterns I complemented the ethnographic interviews with the survey. Without this complementarity the account would not have uncovered how age structures access to screens, platforms, and entertainment—and to a much lesser extent, news—as well as attitudes regarding the indispensability of platforms for subjects, the low degree of credibility assigned to journalistic coverage, and the prevalence of television over other mediated forms of entertainment. Furthermore, within these broad parameters, the interviews show both how these structural variables are enacted in everyday life, and how these attitudes are tied to specific practice, interpretation, and affect configurations—from the different perspectives of grandparents and grandchildren about the uses of mobile phones at the dinner table to the strategies enacted to counter the perception of systemic bias in mainstream news. Thus, had the book focused only on micro- and meso-level data gathered from the interviews, the analysis would not have been able to shed light on how they are partly shaped by macro-level formations that they variously reproduce and alter in relation to larger dynamics of everyday life.

The vast majority of the studies on information overload have concentrated on present times and paid limited attention—if at all—to how the phenomena under examination might relate to comparable phenomena in past times. The main problem with this approach is that it opens the possibility of a contemporary bias that takes for granted a sense of novelty about the current moment. It ignores historical patterns that might show both continuity and discontinuity. To help prevent this bias, I have resorted to historical scholarship providing a background against which to evaluate the contemporary moment. This has enabled the analysis to show that there has been a shift in the locus of the gaze from the natural world and elite knowledge to information about ordinary people gathered primarily through personal screens and social media platforms. This is in part made possible by a many-to-many communication infrastructure whereby the ordinary person can produce information accessed by micro-publics made up of a combination of family, friends, co-workers, and strangers. While these micro-publics are rarely the size of those that consume mass media content, their aggregation and interconnection results in a significant displacement in how attention is organized, from around a small number of elite players to around a much larger number of peer communicators. As I will elaborate in greater detail below, a cumulative effect of this historical discontinuity seems to be a turn away from elites and toward the ordinary other, and a concomitant shift in appreciation of content from the former to the latter. Had the analysis not put current matters into historical perspective it would have missed the finding that one of the defining aspects of the contemporary experience of information abundance is about the focus and content of our info-lust, to return to Ann Blair's evocative concept, and not solely about matters of quantity.

Locating the Inquiry in the Global South and Being Reflexive about This

The fourth distinct feature of this book is that contrary to the tendency of previous studies on information overload to draw on data from countries in the Global North and to interpret the findings with a view from nowhere, I conducted the research on Argentina and remained attentive to the location of the inquiry in making sense of what I found.

In the preface I highlighted three attributes of the Argentine context that made it especially suitable for the questions asked in this book. First, the greater material scarcity—relative to countries in the Global North—underscored how important connectivity appears to be for people who go to great pains to secure it. It is worth noticing that this is the norm rather than the exception since the standards of living in the handful of nations that constitute the Global North are not widely shared around the world. Furthermore, the presence of high levels of material scarcity makes even more meaningful the finding that age prevails over socioeconomic status as the main structural factor shaping access to screens, platforms, and entertainment. Second, the presence of a strong associational culture provided fertile ground to look into the contemporary reconstitution of sociality. It also called into question the broad applicability of the theorizing drawing on more individualist and instrumentalist national contexts exemplified by the work of social scientists such as Barry Wellman and Sherry Turkle discussed in chapter 3. It also delineates possible scope conditions of the findings presented here, since the situation in Argentina might not be applicable everywhere, thus serving as a general cautionary note about the limits that a view from nowhere presents to theorizing. Third, the high level of distrust in the news and the concomitant presence of highly critical consumption habits constituted a suitable terrain to probe the role of agency in media reception. Because, as noted above, levels of trust in the news have declined in many countries around the world recently, Argentina might be an avant-garde in comparative terms, and preview what might happen in other locations as consumers refine their critical skills to counter perceived systemic bias in ways that resonate with what many interviewees for this study did.

Beyond the specifics of the case at hand, shifting the location of the inquiry from the center to the periphery, and being reflexive about this, helps to produce knowledge that is politically empowering. To begin, it showcases the voices to subjects who have been largely absent in studies of digital culture, often authored by scholars located in institutions of the Global North and fascinated with what happens in their respective countries but often silent about comparable phenomena in the rest of the world. Because the results of these studies are often taught and discussed in the Global South as if they were universal, this pattern of silence reproduces long-standing dynamics of inequality in the production and circulation of knowledge. In this sense, showcasing the voices of subjects who have been largely silent can be emancipatory. By implication, making sense of alternative realities, and doing so while being reflexive about the location of the inquiry, also suggests that the dominant scholarship is location-specific. Therefore, the broader applicability of its findings has to be demonstrated rather than assumed.

This leads to another politically empowering effect: challenging the exoticization of the experiences prevalent in the Global South as of "the other." As noted above, the common—and often implicit—stance is that scholarship about countries in the Global North is universal, and therefore no reflexivity about the location of the inquiry is needed. This is usually matched by a belief that the function of studies on nations in the Global South is to shed light on the particular, and therefore reflexivity about locational matters is expected and demanded in the peer-review process—typically leading to a so-called double standard that further widens inequality between Global North and South publication patterns. I argue that if not all dynamics emerging from studies on the Global North are universal by default, then not all patterns of practice revealed by accounts about the Global South are unique to those particular settings. On the contrary, there was a common reaction of surprise about many of the findings that I encountered when giving talks about this book and sharing earlier versions of its chapters: "They were about Argentina, but they could have easily been about here"—"here" meaning the location of the interlocutor. Thus, this book challenges the twin assumptions that knowledge about the Global North is universal by default and that complementary studies about the Global South shed light on the exotic; this amounts to decentering scholarship on digital culture. It invites the analyst to demonstrate rather than to assume both what might be shared and what might be unique in the findings—neither universals at home nor exotics abroad. As my colleague Eugenia Mitchelstein and I have argued, when research "has been decentered, fully contextualizing our scholarship . . . is not only methodologically sound, heuristically imperative, and normatively balanced, but also becomes politically empowering."[10]

From Abundance to Scarcity

The previous discussion points to the more general issue of how this analysis of information abundance in the contemporary media environment sheds light on the scarcity of cosmopolitanism in much of the existent relevant scholarship. It also indicates that matters of scarcity are critical to making sense of the broader theoretical and societal import of the account presented in this book. This does not mean, as sociologist Andy Abbott puts it, "that excess of one thing is simply scarcity of another,"[11] but that a focus on the former can also help to bring the latter into sharp relief. I will conclude this book by reflecting on two kinds of scarcity that appear to be particularly relevant, one theoretical and the other societal: the lack of balance between institutional power and individual agency in analyses of digital media's societal implications, and the lack of certainty in the experience of information abundance.

Rebalancing Media Power and User Agency

Going back to the value of interpreting findings about the contemporary moment through a historical sensibility, prior periods marked by a significant increase in the availability of information were often accompanied by widespread concerns about the potentially deleterious social consequences of this trend. However, research has shown, time and again, that these concerns were unwarranted. On the contrary, accounts such as those by Ann Blair[12] and Chad Wellmon[13] have shed light on the positive benefits that sometimes accrue from a society struggling to adjust to a new information environment, including an array of information management techniques that are still in use today, and the institutionalization of disciplines in the modern university. However, the existence of this historical record has not prevented contemporary commentators from expressing concerns with the current surge of information availability, as I also illustrated in chapter 1.

This is part of a more general pattern: periods of major technological developments have often been marked by moral media panic. This panic subsequently triggers scholarly assertions about the deleterious effects of these technological developments in part because the concerns are consistent with the expectations of politicians, funding agencies, journalists, and the public.[14] In the preface I illustrated this general pattern with a concrete and high-profile example regarding current debates about the role of social media in democratic life. In it I included a quote by Siva Vaidhyanathan, media scholar and regular contributor to *The Guardian*, in which he asserted that Facebook users have become "cows": "data-producing farm animals, domesticated and dependent. We are the cows. Facebook clicks on us."[15] What is striking about this statement and its underlying metaphor is not the deterministic and unidirectional causal chain, but the utter de-humanization of the users: they are deprived not only of agency but also of language, the single most important condition that distinguishes humans from other species. If, paraphrasing the pathbreaking book by George Lakoff and Mark Johnson,[16] we live by metaphors, the one chosen by Vaidhyanathan expresses a worldview that populates the worst nightmares of horror films—as well as the fantasies of autocratic thinking on the left- and right-side of the ideological spectrum.

Vaidhyanathan is far from being alone in de-humanizing the experience of information abundance. As noted above, this way of addressing the issue has gained currency in part because it is consistent with the expectation of vast sectors of society, including the media which in recent years have repeatedly framed their coverage in deterministic and dystopic ways. One example of this kind is an article published in Spain's *El Mundo* in early 2019, entitled "From Bolsonaro to Vox: How WhatsApp Has Become the Most Effective Weapon of Political Propaganda."[17] Of particular relevance, given the location of the research presented in this book, this article includes an illustration showing the late Eva Perón speaking to a large audience. This illustration is based on a photo of Eva Perón in 1951, addressing a crowd of women—although the article makes no mention of the source and situation, thus conveniently de-historicizing the event. The illustration superimposes a WhatsApp icon over the microphone and the "read-receipt" feature of this platform over the heads of the women in the crowd. This reinterpretation of the event in light of current media artifacts and discursive sensibilities denotes a direct connection between the app under the control of the sender and the minds of the receivers—with no other signaling of their interpretive capacities. Like Vaidhyanathan's users-as-cows trope, the people in the crowd are de-humanized, their brains substituted by a technological artifice in ways that resonate with related discourses that have described Eva Perón's supporters as ignorant and easily manipulated.

Yet nothing could be further from the truth. As the historical record shows, the people who attended rallies such as the one depicted in that image did so because they felt interpellated by a leader who spoke of their concerns like no one else before in the history of the country, and who ushered in a series of policies to improve their standard of living. Among other historical achievements, and of particular relevance with regard to this picture and the subsequent illustration, Eva Perón played a key role in women's getting the right to vote and she led the creation of the Women's Peronist Party, which had over half a million members around the time the picture was taken. Regardless of one's ideological preferences, overlooking the agency of the supporters—and the consequences of the enactment of their agency—would be a gross underestimation of their role as political actors. To put it bluntly, the poor and the marginalized had agency in the era of the mass media as much as they do in the era of social media.

Something similar could be said about the billions of users currently on social media, including three quarters of the population of Argentina at the time of this study. To think that they spend one of every five minutes of their awake time on platforms in the same way that cows graze the pastures before being milked and/or slaughtered would be to tragically misunderstand their existence as social beings, something that is anchored in their use of language—which the users-as-cows analogy denies and which this book puts front and center with its focus on meaning-making. The myriad of creative practices and interpretations of the interviewees, and even their mindfulness about the struggles with unsatisfactory situations, illustrate the manifold expressions of agency in dealing not just with platforms but also with screens, news, and entertainment. This does not mean that this user agency exists within a vacuum of media power but that an examination of the former helps put the latter in perspective. As Sonia Livingstone suggests:

> Inquiring systematically into the experience of audiences (people) will not always produce happy answers. But it will help us check and qualify grand claims, and it will remind us of the many potential levers for change, including but also going beyond the technological.[18]

From a historical standpoint this rebalancing of the media power and user agency equation is particularly relevant since a key distinct characteristic of the contemporary wave of information abundance is the ability of users to be sources and distributors of communication and not mere recipients of it. This contributes to the overall increase in volume and in diversity of content creators, which is a bedrock of user agency that marks the contemporary media landscape. This does not mean that some of the organizations providing the infrastructure of information abundance do not have unparalleled reach—and the very deep pockets that come with it—and that some of the news and entertainment companies that generate the mass-mediated content that circulates through it do not have some of the largest audiences in history. What it means is that the ultimate social consequences of media power are filtered through structural and cultural dynamics such as the ones examined in the book, and that this filtering is key to, as Sonia Livingstone notes, being able to qualify grand claims of deterministic and dystopic nature.

Contending with Uncertainty

A close attention to these dynamics of media power and user agency leads to the other kind of scarcity foregrounded by this analysis: the lack of stability and, therefore, certainty in the experience of the interviewees. This lack of stability is tied to the three main patterns of findings unearthed by this inquiry.

First, the strong structural role of age, as I noted above, is an unsettling force. In contrast to comparatively less mutable factors such as socioeconomic status and gender, age is a variable in motion: we all age every day, and cohort effects keep happening. Furthermore, the acceleration in the pace of technological change has contributed to the shaping of media generations that last for a shorter time than previously. Thus, a society in which media access and use are marked by age is unsettled at its core, and unsettling to its members. In addition, given the rising ambiance of media and the increase in the number of hours of awake time connected to them, these unsettling dynamics are not marginal but central to people's lives.

Second, the reconstitution of sociality that is tied to the uptake of screens and platforms adds to this sense of instability and, ultimately, uncertainty about how to relate to significant and not-so-significant others. In the face of this uncertainty, individuals resort to meanings and routines that are anchored in preexisting markers of social life. These orient their appropriation of novel communication opportunities made possible by technological innovations in screens and platforms. These meanings and routines do not eliminate uncertainty but make it more manageable by combining the new with the old. But because of the unsettling character of present times, where old conventions remain but lack automatic applicability, and new conventions are only partly shared and are therefore provisional, there is a sense that we are living during a moment of transition where the past is behind and the future is not yet in the horizon. Thus, individuals carry on with their lives but not without a baseline of unease about how to practice and understand their sociality and that of their significant others—an unease that was not nearly as vivid just a couple of decades ago.

Third, the devaluation of news further contributes to issues of instability and uncertainty. The information lust about the lives of others is tied to a shift in attention from institutionalized news media to the trials and tribulations of the common person. This has an antecedent in the rise of reality television but undoubtedly has exploded on social media. Furthermore, this has been coupled with a second displacement, in this case from the ability of a handful of elite players to organize the attention of large publics to the emergence of a myriad of non-elite players that gather the interest of many micropublics.

In relation to these two historical trends, public discourse has become increasingly discordant and fragmented, and the knowledge institutions of modernity that were in charge of producing it—including journalism, but also medicine, science, and the law—have suffered a significant erosion in their cultural authority. This erosion, as I showed in chapter 1, was characteristic of prior periods of information abundance but has intensified in current times. We see evidence of this trend in the recent rise of concerns about mis- and dis-information not only regarding political news but also health and science news—from vaccinations to climate change. Perhaps the most striking recent example of this erosion took place in Washington, DC, on April 23, 2020. During a press conference related to the evolution of the COVID-19 pandemic, the sitting United States president Donald Trump made the following remarks after a presentation by William Bryan, acting head of the United States Department of Homeland Security's Science and Technology Directorate:

THE PRESIDENT: Thank you very much. So I asked Bill a question that probably some of you are thinking of, if you're totally into that world, which I find to be very interesting. So, supposing we hit the body with a tremendous—whether it's ultraviolet or just very powerful light—and I think you said that that hasn't been checked, but you're going to test it. And then I said, supposing you brought the light inside the body, which you can do either through the skin or in some other way, and I think you said you're going to test that too. It sounds interesting.

ACTING UNDER SECRETARY BRYAN: We'll get to the right folks who could.

THE PRESIDENT: Right. And then I see the disinfectant, where it knocks it out in a minute. One minute. And is there a way we can do something like that, by injection inside or almost a cleaning. Because you see it gets in the lungs and it does a tremendous number on the lungs. So it would be interesting to check that. So, that, you're going to have to use medical doctors with. But it sounds—it sounds interesting to me.

So we'll see. But the whole concept of the light, the way it kills it in one minute, that's—that's pretty powerful.[19]

Because of its twin implications for the health of the polity and the politics of public health in the middle of the worst pandemic in a century, what is particularly remarkable about this example is that the source of anti-scientific mis-information is not some obscure actor but the president of the country, and the occasion is not a private exchange but a press conference aired on national television. At a time in which the citizenry needed the certainty and stability that emanates from trusted facts and institutions with high levels of cultural authority, it is instead exposed to content that takes the idea of "alternative facts" from the fringe of the contemporary political vernacular into the mainstream of presidential messaging.[20] Although they were not a subject of inquiry for this book, developments of this kind have undoubtedly contributed to an overall experiential devaluation of the news—and facts and institutions more generally—in everyday life.

Because of its anchoring in major ongoing trends—the structuring power of age, the reconstitution of sociality, and the poverty of facts and the wealth of fictions—the uncertainty that marks the contemporary experience of information abundance will not go away rapidly and easily. Therefore, learning to live and cope with it has emerged as one of the defining challenges of our time, a challenge that will require resilience as well as creativity.

The Book of Sand, a collection of short stories by acclaimed writer Jorge Luis Borges, was published in 1975, two years after his retirement as director of the National Library of Argentina. Included in this collection is a story that shares the title with the book. It begins with a book seller visiting the apartment of the author, who had recently retired from his position at the National Library. The seller shows the author a peculiar manuscript with a seemingly infinite number of pages and an organization that follows no apparent logic—skipping numbers and making it virtually impossible to return to any one of them. The seller explains that it is "called the Book of Sand, because neither the book nor sand has any beginning or end."[21] The author acquires the manuscript and becomes obsessed with it. He spends his days and nights perusing it, does not leave his apartment, and becomes socially isolated. Aware of the dangers that this obsession might pose to him, he summons the willpower he has left and decides to get rid of it:

I recalled reading that the best place to hide a leaf is in a forest. Before retirement, I worked on Mexico Street, at the Argentine National Library, which contains nine hundred thousand volumes. I knew that to the right of the entrance a curved staircase leads down into the basement, where books and maps and periodicals are kept. One day I went there and, slipping past a member of the staff and trying not to notice at what height or distance from the door, I lost the Book of Sand on one of the basement's musty shelves.[22]

I had read this story for an assignment during high school. I encountered it again, somewhat serendipitously, a few months after the June 2018 visit to Buenos Aires when I realized that the main theme cutting across the interviews was the abundance of information in contemporary life. Borges's story immediately struck a chord in me. From the vantage point of the interviewees, the experience of information abundance seemed to be made of sand, not silicon: material but formless, malleable but difficult to grasp in its vastness, and structured but constantly changing. Trying to build a social world out of sand entails an enormous amount of individual and relational effort. This can be both exhilarating and frustrating, and contending with its instability and uncertainty is nothing short of a remarkable cultural accomplishment. What kind of future awaits? Borges's story concludes on a cautionary yet optimistic note. The mesmerizing quality of sand is powerful and its appeal takes a toll on the author's life. However, he is ultimately able to enact agency and limit his exposure.

The National Library of Argentina moved to a new location in Buenos Aires almost two decades after Borges retired from its directorship. The building on México 564, between Perú and Bolívar streets, now houses the National Center of Music and Dance. Its second floor, though, is home to the Center for Studies and Documentation on Jorge Luis Borges, which includes collections about his life and work. I wonder if the next time I am in Buenos Aires I should stop by. Perhaps *The Book of Sand* might be there. Or maybe it is still in the basement of the building, waiting to be rediscovered by readers for whom conventional texts might have become insufficient to render their lived experience of information abundance believable.

Notes

Preface

1. García Márquez, 1982, n.p.
2. Whenever an interviewee is quoted, the person's name has been changed for confidentiality purposes.
3. Carey, 1992 [1988].
4. Carey, 1992 [1988], p. 14.
5. Carey, 1992 [1988], p. 15.
6. Carey, 1992 [1988], p. 18.
7. Carey, 1992 [1988], p. 18.
8. Carey, 1992 [1988], p. 19.
9. Bruner, 1990, p. 13.
10. Boczkowski & Siles, 2014.
11. Waisbord, 2019, p. 124.
12. Latour, 1987.
13. Romero, 2002, p. ix.
14. World Bank, 2020a.
15. World Bank, 2020b.
16. Mesche, 2018.
17. OECD Economic Surveys, 2017, p. 10.
18. Consejo Nacional de Coordinación de Políticas Sociales, n.d.
19. Devoto & Madero, 1999, n.p.
20. See, for instance, Gayol, 1999, 2000; González Bernaldo, 1999; Míguez, 1999; and Myers, 1999.
21. See, for instance, Archetti, 1999; Beccaria et al., 2002; González-Bombal, 2002; and Gutierrez & Romero, 1995.
22. Winter, 2017.
23. Vaidhyanathan, 2018, p. 19.
24. Vaidhyanathan, 2018, p. 203.
25. Newman, Fletcher, Kalogeropoulos, Levy, & Nielen, 2017, p. 105.
26. Newman, Fletcher, Kalogeropoulos, Levy, & Nielen, 2017, p. 105.
27. Newman, Fletcher, Schulz, Andi, & Nielsen, 2020, p. 14.

Chapter 1

1. Boczkowski & Lievrouw, 2007, p. 955.
2. Wikipedia, 2020a.

3. Wikipedia, 2020b.

4. Statista, 2020.

5. We Are Social, 2020.

6. SimilarWeb, 2020a.

7. SimilarWeb, 2020b.

8. Wikipedia, 2020c.

9. Moody, 2020.

10. Cook, 2020.

11. Blair, 2010, p. 3.

12. Blair, 2010, p. 20.

13. Blair, 2010, pp. 45–46.

14. Blair, 2010, p. 11.

15. Bushnell, 1996, p. 118.

16. Levitin, 2014, p. 14.

17. Gleick, 2011, p. 402.

18. Wellmon, 2015, p. 112.

19. Ellison, 2006, pp. 12–13.

20. Gitlin, 2002, p. 17, emphasis in the original.

21. Andrejevic, 2013, p. 3.

22. See, for instance, Bawden & Robinson, 1982; Buckland, 2017; Hunt & Newman, 1997; Meier, 1963; Vollmann, 1991; Wurman, 2001.

23. Miller, 1956, p. 90, emphasis in the original.

24. Simon, 1971, pp. 40–41.

25. See, for instance, Hu & Lai, 2013; Klingberg, 2008; Levitin, 2014; Misra & Stokols, 2012; Pennington & Tuttle, 2007; and Swar, Hameed, & Reychav, 2017.

26. See, for instance, Chen, Shang, & Kao, 2009; Cheng, Sun, & Zeng, 2010; Herbig & Kramer, 1994; Jacoby, 1984; Jacoby, Speller, & Berning, 1974; Lee & Lee, 2004; Li, 2017; and van Zandt, 2004.

27. See, for instance, Bawden, Holtham, & Courtney, 1999; Hall & Walton, 2004; Olsen, Sochats, & Williams, 1998; Rudd & Rudd, 1986; and Savolainen, 2007.

28. See, for instance, Hiltz & Turoff, 1985; Jones, Ravid, & Rafaeli, 2004; Karr-Wisniewski et al., 2010; Lee, Son, & Kim, 2016; Maes, 1994; and Saunders, Wiener, Klett, & Sprenger, 2017.

29. Simmel, 1950 (1903).

30. Milgram, 1970, p. 1461.

31. Milgram, 1970, p. 1462.

32. See, for instance, Aldoory, & Van Dyke, 2006; Holton & Chyi, 2012; Ji et al., 2014; Lee, Lindsay, & Kim, 2017; Schmitt, Debbelt, & Schneider, 2018; York, 2013.

33. See, for instance, Chewning & Harrell, 1990; O'Reilly, 1980; Schick, Gordon, & Haka, 1990; Schultze & Vandenbosch, 1998.

34. See, for instance, Deutsch, 1961; Klapp, 1986; and Meier, 1962.

35. See, for instance, Keane, 2013.

36. Roetzel, 2018.

37. Hargittai, Neuman, & Curry, 2012, p. 162.

38. Eppler & Mengis, 2004, p. 326.
39. Shenk, 1997, p. 15.
40. Schwartz, 2004, p. 2.
41. Carr, 2011, p. 170.
42. Levitin, 2014, p. 15.
43. Gleick, 2011, p. 11.
44. Roetzel, 2018.
45. Eppler & Mengis, 2004, p. 330.
46. Dewey, 1916, p. 5.
47. Carey, 1992 (1988), pp. 18–19.
48. Hutchins, 1995.
49. Geographically, the majority of the interviews took place in the City of Buenos Aires and its suburbs, but a sizable minority was undertaken in the provinces of Córdoba, Salta, San Juan, and Santa Fe. Overall, I did not find geography to be an important factor shaping the experience of information abundance—and, whenever relevant for the analysis, I will address geographic issues in the respective chapters.
50. Trost, 1986.
51. Wellmon, 2015, p. 10.
52. Gitlin, 2002, p. 10.
53. See, for instance, Correa, 2014; Friemel, 2016; Lauf, 2001; Lizardo & Skiles, 2015; and Friedman et al., 2015.
54. See, for instance, Akrich, 1998; Douglas, 1987; Fischer, 1992; MacKay & Gillespie, 1992; Oudshoorn & Pinch, 2003; and Suchman, 1987.
55. See, for instance, Ang, 1985; Bird, 2003; Hall, 1980; Livingstone, 2008; Morley, 1980; and Radway, 1984.
56. See, for instance, Eglash, 2004; Jenkins, 1992; Kline, 2000; Kline & Pinch, 1996; Liebes & Katz, 1990; and Wyatt, 2003.
57. Emirbayer & Mische, 1998, p. 970. For additional scholarship on the notion of agency, see, for instance, Bourdieu, 1977; Bourdieu & Wacquant, 1992; Depelteau, 2008; Fuchs, 2001; Giddens, 1979, 1984; and Wang, 2008.
58. Webster, 1998.
59. Blair, 2010, p. 12.
60. Blair, 2010, p. 45.
61. Wellmon, 2015, p. 16.
62. Wellmon, 2015, p. 210.
63. Blair, 2010, p. 57.
64. Wellmon, 2015, pp. 40–41.
65. Andrejevic, 2013, p. 3.
66. Horrigan, 2016.
67. Simmel, 1950 (1903), p. 424.
68. García Marquez, 1982.
69. Thomas &Thomas, 1928, pp. 571–572.
70. Most people in Argentina consider WhatsApp a social media platform rather than a messaging app.

71. See, for instance, Bogart, 1989; Dayan & Katz, 1992; Gauntlett & Hill, 1999; Lull, 1982; and Silverstone, 1994.
72. Berger & Luckmann, 1967.
73. Couldry & Hepp, 2016, p. 4.

Chapter 2

1. Haraway, 1991 (1985).
2. Navarro, 2020b.
3. Wikipedia, 2020d.
4. Internet World Stats, 2018.
5. Sistema Nacional de Información Cultural de la Argentina, 2018.
6. Negroponte, 1996, p. 18.
7. Jenkins, 2006.
8. See, for instance, Baumsinger, 1984; Bogart, 1955; Chan & Goldthorpe, 2007; Graber, 1984; Jensen, 1990; Lull, 1982; and Robinson & Levy, 1986.
9. boyd, 2014, p. 8.
10. As are other social media platforms, which will be the subject of chapter 3.
11. See, for instance, Chan, 2018; David-Barrett et al., 2016; Feng et al., 2019; Fortunati et al., 2019; Olsson et al., 2019; and Quan-Haase et al., 2018.
12. Correa, 2014, p. 104.
13. Friemel, 2016, p. 328, emphasis in the original.
14. Licoppe, 2004, pp. 135–136.

Chapter 3

1. Navarro, 2020a.
2. Kemp, 2018.
3. Kemp, 2018.
4. Constine, 2016.
5. Carey-Simos, 2015.
6. Tung, 2017.
7. Internet Live Stats, 2020.
8. Kemp, 2018.
9. For studies about artifacts and infrastructures as varied as telephony, television, and computers see, for instance, Farman, 2018; Fischer, 1992; Gergen, 1992; Hampton, 2016; Hampton & Wellman, 2003; Kraut et al., 1998; McPherson et al., 2006; Meyrowitz, 1986.
10. For various treatments of this issue see, for instance, Burchell, 2015; Campbell. 2018; Fortunati, 2002; Humphreys, 2018; Katz & Aakhus, 2002; Kobayashi et al., 2015; and Ling, 2012.
11. For different perspectives on this topic, see, for instance, Baym, 2015; Duffy, 2017; French & Bazarova, 2017; Gillespie, 2018; and Turkle. 2015.

12. Ling, 2016, p. 9.
13. Rainie & Wellman, 2012, p. 12.
14. Turkle, 2017 (2012), p. xxi.
15. For research on the role of meaning in the use of social media see, for instance, Karapanos, Teixeira, & Gouveia, 2016; Papacharissi, 2009; Pittman & Reich, 2016; and Quan-Haase & Young, 2010.
16. This rate of penetration is slightly higher than the 65% revealed by the survey conducted throughout the country by the System of Cultural Information of Argentina—part of the country's Ministry of Culture—with 2,800 adults in 2017 (Sistema de Información Cultural de la Argentina, 2017). It is likely that the difference of 6 percentage points is due to the fact that overall access to digital goods and services is lower in rural than in urban areas.
17. Even though Google+ had a 45% rate of access in the survey, it was not mentioned a single time in the interviews. Thus, I conclude that this figure is a function of the name recognition of Google among survey respondents, not of the actual use of this platform.
18. Smith, 2019.
19. Milonga is a musical genre related to tango.
20. Neff &Stark, 2004.
21. See, for instance, Clark, 2011; Katz, 2010; Livingstone, 2009; Nelissen & van den Bulck, 2018; and Tripp & Herr-Stephenson, 2009.
22. Nelissen & van den Bulck, 2018, p. 383.
23. Correa, 2015, p. 1180.
24. Scholarship on the notions of repertoires (Kim, 2016; Livingstone, Van Couvering, & Thumim, 2005; Taneja, Webster, Malthouse, & Ksiazek, 2012; Webster, 2011; Wolf & Schnauber, 2015) and polymedia (de Bruin, 2017; Madianou, 2014; Madianou & Miller, 2013; Peng, 2016; Renninger, 2015) has highlighted the observation that people tend to use multiple media options in relation to each other rather than isolation.
25. For different treatments of this issue, see, for instance, Bayer et al., 2015; Blackwell et al., 2015; Hancock et al., 2009; Litt, 2012; Marwick & boyd, 2011; and Trieu et al., 2019.
26. For various perspectives on this matter, see, for instance, Duffy & Chan, 2019; Halfmann & Rieger, 2019; Hall, 2017; Litt et al., 2014; and Oeldorf-Hirsch et al., 2017.
27. Myers, 1999, p. 134.
28. See Couldry & Hepp, 2016, on the notion of "deep mediatization."

Chapter 4

1. Instituto Verificador de Circulaciones, 2020.
2. SimilarWeb, 2020.
3. See, for instance, Bogart, 1989; Gauntlett & Hill, 1999; Jensen, 1990; Lull, 1982; and Webster & Phalen, 1997.

4. Gauntlett & Hill, 1999, p. 77.

5. See, for instance, Bogart, 1955; Dayan & Katz, 1992; Silverstone, 1994; and Webster & Phalen, 1997.

6. Silverstone, 1994, p. 24.

7. See, for instance, Bausinger, 1984; Chan & Goldthorpe, 2007; Graber, 1984; Jensen, 1990; Martin, 2008; Palmgreen et al., 1980; and Robinson & Levy, 1986.

8. Bogart, 1989.

9. Lauf, 2001, p. 239.

10. See, for instance, Debrael et al., 2019; Elvestad & Blekasaune, 2008; Hmielowski et al., 2011; Malthause & Calder, 2006; Matsa, 2018; and Thurman & Fletcher, 2019.

11. On various perspectives about ambient journalism in relation to social media, see, for instance, Hermida, 2010, 2014; Papacharissi & de Fatima Oliveira, 2012; and Sheller, 2015.

12. Gil de Zúñiga et al., 2017.

13. The centrality of these derivative routines is perhaps nowhere more salient than in the rise of incidental news consumption on social media, as Feezell, 2018; Fletcher & Nielsen, 2018; Gil de Zúñiga et al., 2017; Mitchelstein et al., 2020; Valeriani & Vaccari, 2016; Weeks et al., 2017; and Yadamsuren & Erdelez, 2017 have variously examined.

14. Boczkowski, 2010.

15. Issues of media bias tie to matters of credibility and trust. For multiple perspectives on this, see, for instance, Choi & Kim, 2017; Kiousis, 2001; Knobloch-Westerwick et al., 2017; Livio & Cohen, 2016; and Tandoc, 2019. In recent years, these topics have been explored with particular intensity in the examination of misinformation in the news. See, for instance, Allcott & Gentzkow, 2017; Grinberg et al., 2019; Valenzuela et al., 2019; Vargo et al., 2018; Vosoughi et al., 2018; and Wagner & Boczkowski, 2019b.

16. For various perspectives about the role of emotions in the news, see, for instance, Bas & Grabe, 2015; Beckett & Deuze, 2016; Hasell & Weeks, 2016; Lecheler et al., 2015; Papacharissi, 2015; Wagner & Boczkowski, 2019a; and Wahl-Jorgensen, 2019.

17. For analyses of contemporary patterns of news avoidance, see, for instance, Edgerly, 2017; Ksiazek et al., 2010; Toff & Nielsen, 2018; Toff & Palmer, 2019; and Trilling & Schoenbach, 2012.

18. For an array of treatments of binge watching, see, for instance, Jenner, 2016; Shim & Kim, 2018; Steiner & Xu, 2020; and Turner, 2019.

19. For a more extensive treatment of this matter, see Boczkowski, Mitchelstein, & Suenzo, 2020.

Chapter 5

1. Krantz-Kent, 2018, p. 1.

2. Sistema de Información Cultural de la Argentina, 2017.

3. Krantz-Kent, 2018.

4. Sistema de Información Cultural de la Argentina, 2017.

5. Finder, 2020.

6. Rodriguez, 2019.

7. JustWatch, 2020.
8. Similar trends are relevant in the case of music content. But for space limitations, in this chapter I will address primarily audiovisual content.
9. Williams, 1974, p. 89.
10. Williams, 1974, pp. 80–81, emphasis in the original.
11. For various treatments of the contemporary relevance of the notion of flow, see, for instance, Cox, 2018; Kompare, 2006; Thibault, 2015; Tse, 2016; and Uricchio, 2009.
12. Livingstone, 2019, p. 175.
13. Gray, 2017, p. 81.
14. See, for instance, Abdel-Ghany and Sharpe, 1997; Berghman and Van Eijck, 2009; DiMaggio & Mukhtar, 2004; Savage & Gayo, 2001; Tampubolon, 2008; and Taneja & Viswanathan, 2014.
15. Lizardo & Skiles, 2015, p. 12.
16. Friedman et al., 2015, p. 3.
17. Sistema de Información Cultural de la Argentina, 2017.
18. Watson, 2019.

Chapter 6

1. Borges, 1977 (1975), p. 119.
2. Mannheim, 1952 (1927), p. 287.
3. See also van Dijck et al., 2018, for a treatment of the related notion of the "platform society."
4. van Dijck, 2013, p. 6.
5. For a discussion of the notion of the digital environment, see Boczkowski & Mitchelstein (in press).
6. Deuze, 2012, p. x.
7. Washingtonpost.com (2020, August 27).
8. See also Couldry, 2012; Jansson, 2015; Krajina et al., 2014; and Pink et al., 2017.
9. Morley, 2006, p. 200.
10. Boczkowski & Mitchelstein, 2019, p. 679.
11. Abbott, 2014, p. 7.
12. Blair, 2010.
13. Wellmon, 2015.
14. Orben, 2020, claims this is an integral part of the process she calls "the Sysyphean cycle of technology panics."
15. Vaidhyanathan, 2018, p. 203.
16. Lakoff & Johnson, 1980.
17. Terrasa, 2019.
18. Livingstone, 2019, p. 179.
19. Brady, 2020, April 23.
20. For an illuminating analysis of this matter, see Jasanoff, 2020.
21. Borges, 1977 (1975), p. 119.
22. Borges, 1977 (1975), p. 122.

References

Abbott, A. (2014). The problem of excess. *Sociological Theory, 32*, 1–26.

Abdel-Ghany, M., & Sharpe, D. L. (1997). Consumption patterns among the young-old and old-old. *Journal of Consumer Affairs, 31*, 90–112.

Akrich, M. (1998). Les utilisateurs, acteurs de l'innovation. *Éducation permanente, 134*, 78–89.

Aldoory, L., & Van Dyke, M. A. (2006). The roles of perceived "shared" involvement and information overload in understanding how audiences make meaning of news about bioterrorism. *Journalism & Mass Communication Quarterly, 83*(2), 346–361.

Allcott, H., & Gentzkow, M. (2017). Social media and fake news in the 2016 election. *Journal of Economic Perspectives, 31*, 211–236.

Andrejevic, M. (2013). *Infoglut: How too much information is changing the way we think and know.* New York: Routledge.

Ang, I. (1985). *Watching Dallas: Soap opera and the melodramatic imagination.* New York: Methuen.

Archetti, E. (1999). Masculinities: Football, polo and the tango in Argentina. Oxford: Berg.

Bas, O., & Grabe, M. E. (2015). Emotion-provoking personalization of news: Informing citizens and closing the knowledge gap? *Communication Research, 42*(2), 159–185.

Bausinger, H. (1984). Media, technology, and daily life. *Media, Culture & Society, 6*, 343–351.

Bawden, D., & Robinson, L. (1982). The dark side of information: Overload, anxiety and other paradoxes and pathologies. *Journal of Information Science, 35*(2), 180–191.

Bawden, D., Holtham, C., & Courtney, N. (1999). Perspectives on information overload. *ASLIB Proceedings, 51*(8), 249–255.

Bayer, J. B., Campbell, S. W., & Ling, R. (2015). Connection cues: Activating the norms and habits of social connectedness. *Communication Theory, 26*, 128–149.

Baym, N. (2015). *Personal connections in the digital age.* Cambridge, UK: Polity.

Beccaria, L., Feldman, S., González Bombal, I., Kessler, G., Murmis, M., & Svampa, M. (Eds.). (2002). *Sociedad y Sociabilidad en la Argentina de los 90.* Buenos Aires: Biblos.

Beckett, C., & Deuze, M. (2016). On the role of emotion in the future of journalism. *Social Media+ Society, 2*(3), 1–6.

Berger, P., & Luckmann, T. (1967). *The social construction of reality.* New York: Anchor.

Berghman, M., & Van Eijck, K. (2009). Visual arts appreciation patterns: Crossing horizontal and vertical boundaries within the cultural hierarchy. *Poetics, 37*, 348–365.

Bird, S. E. (2003). *The audience in everyday life: Living in a media world.* London: Routledge.

Blackwell, C., Birnholtz, J., & Abbott, C. (2015). Seeing and being seen: Co-situation and impression formation using Grindr, a location-aware gay dating app. *New Media & Society, 17*, 1117–1136.

Blair, A. (2010). *Too much to know: Managing scholarly information before the modern age.* New Haven, CT: Yale University Press.

Boczkowski, P. (2010). *News at work: Imitation in an age of information abundance.* Chicago: University of Chicago Press.

Boczkowski, P., & Lievrouw, L. (2007). Bridging STS and communication studies: Scholarship on media and information technologies. In O. Amsterdamska, E. Hackett, M. Lynch, & J. Wajcman (Eds.), *The handbook of science and technology studies*, 3rd ed. (949–977). Cambridge, MA: MIT Press.

Boczkowski, P., & Mitchelstein, E. (2019). The politics of contextualization in the contextualization of political communication research. *Political Communication, 36*, 676–679. DOI: 10.1080/10584609.2019.1670903.

Boczkowski, P., & Mitchelstein, E. (in press). *The digital environment: How we live, learn, work, and play now*. Cambridge, MA: MIT Press.

Boczkowski, P., & Siles, I. (2014). Steps towards cosmopolitanism in the study of media technologies: Integrating scholarship on production, consumption, materiality, and content. *Information, Communication & Society, 17*, 560–571.

Boczkowski, P., Mitchelstein, E., & Suenzo, F. (2020). The smells, sights, and pleasures of ink on paper: The consumption of print newspapers during a period marked by their crisis. *Journalism Studies, 21*, 565–581. DOI: 10.1080/1461670X.2019.1670092.

Bogart, L. (1955). Adult conversation about newspaper comics. *American Journal of Sociology, 61*, 26–30.

Bogart, L. (1989). *Press and public: Who reads what, when, where, and why in American newspapers*. Hillsdale, NJ: Lawrence Erlbaum.

Borges, J. L. (1977 [1975]). *The book of sand*. New York: Dutton.

Bourdieu, P. (1977). Outline of a theory of practice. Cambridge: Cambridge University Press.

Bourdieu, P., & Wacquant, L. J. D. (1992). An invitation to reflexive sociology. Chicago: University of Chicago Press.

boyd, d. (2014). *It's complicated: The social lives of networked teens*. New Haven, CT: Yale University Press.

Brady, J. (2020, April 23). Remarks by President Trump, Vice President Pence, and members of the Coronavirus Task Force in press briefing. https://www.whitehouse.gov/briefings-statements/remarks-president-trump-vice-president-pence-members-coronavirus-task-force-press-briefing-31/.

Bruner, J. (1990). *Acts of meaning: Four lectures on mind and culture*. Cambridge, MA: Harvard University Press.

Buckland, M. (2017). *Information and society*. Cambridge, MA: MIT Press.

Burchell, K. (2015). Tasking the everyday: Where mobile and online communication take time. *Mobile Media & Communication, 3*(1), 36–52.

Bushnell, (1996). *A culture of teaching: Early modern humanism in theory and practice*. Ithaca, NY: Cornell University Press.

Campbell, S. W. (2018). From frontier to field: Old and new theoretical directions in mobile communication studies. *Communication Theory, 29*(1), 46–65.

Carey-Simos, G. (2015, August 19). How much data is generated every minute on social media. *Wersm*. https://wersm.com/how-much-data-is-generated-every-minute-on-social-media/.

Carey, J. (1992 [1988]). *Communication as culture: Essays on media and society*. New York: Routledge.

Carr, N. (2011). *The shallows: What the internet is doing to our brains*. New York: Norton.

Chan, M. (2018). Mobile-mediated multimodal communications, relationship quality and subjective well-being: An analysis of smartphone use from a life course perspective. *Computers in Human Behavior, 87*, 254–262.

Chan, T. W., & Goldthorpe, J. H. (2007). Social status and newspaper readership. *American Journal of Sociology, 112*, 1095–1134.

Chen, Y., Shang, Y., & Kao, C. (2009). The effects of information overload on consumers' subjective state towards buying decision in the internet shopping environment. *Electronic Commerce Research and Applications, 8*, 48–58.

Cheng J., Sun, A., & Zeng, D. (2010). Information overload and viral marketing: countermeasures and strategies. *Lecture Notes in Computer Science, 6007*, 108–117.

Chewning, E., & Harrell, A. (1990). The effect of information load on decision makers' cue utilization levels and decision quality in a financial distress decision task. *Accounting, Organizations and Society, 15*, 527–542.

Choi, S., & Kim, J. (2017). Online news flow: Temporal / spatial exploitation and credibility. *Journalism, 18*, 1184–1205.

Clark, L. S. (2011). Parental mediation theory for the digital age. *Communication Theory, 21*, 323–343.

Consejo Nacional de Coordinación de Políticas Sociales. (n.d.). Monitor social: Evolución de la pobreza e indigencia (2do. Semester 2017). https://www.argentina.gob.ar/sites/default/files/pobreza-e-indigencia-2do-sem-2017_0.pdf.

Constine, J. (2016, July 27). Facebook sees 20 billion searches per day, but it's attacking Twitter not Google. *Tech Crunch*. https://techcrunch.com/2016/07/27/facebook-will-make-you-talk/.

Cook, S. (2020, July 29). 50+ Netflix statistics and facts stats that define the company's dominance [2020 version]. *Comparitech*. https://www.comparitech.com/blog/vpn-privacy/netflix-statistics-facts-figures/.

Correa, T. (2014). Bottom-up technology transmission within families: Exploring how youths influence their parents' digital media use with dyadic data. *Journal of Communication, 64*, 103–124.

Correa, T. (2015). The power of youth: How the bottom-up technology transmission from children to parents is related to digital (in)equality. *International Journal of Communication, 9*, 1163–1186.

Couldry, N. (2012). *Media, society, world: Social theory and digital media practice.* Cambridge: Polity.

Couldry, N., & Hepp, A. (2016). *The mediated construction of reality.* Cambridge: Polity.

Cox, C. (2018). Programming—Flow in the convergence of digital media platforms and television. *Critical Studies in Television, 13*, 438–454.

David-Barrett, T., Kertesz, J., Rotkirch, A., Ghosh, A., Bhattacharya, K., Monsivais, D., & Kaski, K. (2016). Communication with family and friends across the life course. *PLoS ONE, 11*(11): e0165687. https://doi.org/10.1371/journal.pone.0165687.

Dayan, D., & Katz, E. (1992). *Media events: The live broadcasting of history.* Cambridge, MA: Harvard University Press.

de Bruin, J. (2019). New Zealand migrants, polymedia and the ambivalences of staying in touch. *Convergence: The International Journal of Research into New Media Technologies, 25*, 479–495.

Debrael, M., d'Haenens, L., De Cock, R., & De Coninck, D. (2019). Media use, fear of terrorism, and attitudes towards immigrants and refugees: Young people and adults compared. *International Communication Gazette*. https://doi.org/10.1177/1748048519869476.

Depelteau, F. (2008). Relational thinking: A critique of co-deterministic theories of structure and agency. *Sociological Theory*, *26*(1), 51–73.

Deutsch, K. (1961). On social communication and the metropolis. *Daedalus*, *90*, 99–110.

Deuze, M. (2012). *Media life*. Cambridge, UK: Polity Press.

Devoto, F., & Madero, M. (1999). Introducción. In F. Devoto & Marta Madero (Eds.), *Historia de la Vida Privada en Argentina*, Tomo II, *La Argentina Plural: 1870–1930* (n.p.). Buenos Aires: Taurus.

Dewey, J. (1916). *Democracy and education*. New York: Macmillan.

DiMaggio, P., & Mukhtar, T. (2004). Arts participation as cultural capital in the United States, 1982–2002: Signs of decline? *Poetics*, *32*, 169–194.

Douglas, S. (1987). *Inventing American broadcasting, 1899–1922*. Baltimore, MD: Johns Hopkins University Press.

Duffy, B. (2017). *(Not) getting paid to do what you love: Gender, social media, and aspirational labor*. New Haven, CT: Yale University Press.

Duffy, B. E., & Chan, N. K. (2019). "You never really know who's looking": Imagined surveillance across social media platforms. *New Media & Society*, *21*(1), 119–138.

Edgerly, S. (2017). Seeking out and avoiding the news media: Young adults' proposed strategies for obtaining current events information. *Mass Communication and Society*, *20*, 358–377.

Eglash, R. (2004). Appropriating technology: An introduction. In R. Eglash, J. L. Croissant, G. Di Chiro, & R. Fouché (Eds.), *Appropriating technology: Vernacular science and social power* (pp. vii–xxi). Minneapolis: University of Minnesota Press.

Ellison, K. E. (2006). *Fatal news: Reading and information overload in early eighteenth-century literature*. New York, NY: Routledge.

Elvestad, E., & Blekesaune, A. (2008). Newspaper readers in Europe: A multilevel study of individual and national differences. *European Journal of Communication*, *23*, 425–447.

Emirbayer, M., & Mische, A. (1998). What is agency? *American Journal of Sociology*, *103*(4), 962–1023.

Eppler, M. J., & J. Mengis. 2004. The concept of information overload: A review of literature from organization science, accounting, marketing, MIS and related disciplines. *The Information Society*, *20*(5), 325–344.

Farman, J. (2018). *Delayed response: The art of waiting from the ancient to the instant world*. New Haven, CT: Yale University Press.

Feezell, J. T. (2018). Agenda setting through social media: The importance of incidental news exposure and social filtering in the digital era. *Political Research Quarterly*, *71*, 482–494.

Feng, G., Zhang, Y., & Lin, Z. (2019). A meta-analysis of the effects of sociodemographic factors on social media adoption. *International Journal of Communication*, *13*, 1996–2025.

Finder. (2020). Netflix International: What movies and TV shows can I watch, and where can I watch them? https://www.finder.com/global-netflix-library-totals.

Fischer, C. (1992). *America calling: A social history of the telephone to 1940*. Berkeley: University of California Press.

Fletcher, R., & Nielsen, R. K. (2018). Are people incidentally exposed to news on social media? A comparative analysis. *New Media & Society*, *20*, 2450–2468.

Fortunati, F. (2002). The mobile phone: Towards new categories and social relations. *Information, Communication & Society*, *5*, 513–528.

Fortunati, L., Taipale, S., & de Luca, F. (2019). Digital generations, but not as we know them. *Convergence, 25*, 95–112.

French, M., & Bazarova, N. N. (2017). Is anybody out there?: Understanding mass personal communication through expectations for response across social media platforms. *Journal of Computer-Mediated Communication, 22*, 303–319.

Friedman, S., Savage, M., Hanquinet, L., & Miles, A. (2015). Cultural sociology and new forms of distinction. *Poetics, 53*, 1–8.

Friemel, T. N. (2016). The digital divide has grown old: Determinants of a digital divide among seniors. *New Media & Society, 18*, 313–331.

Fuchs, S. (2001). Beyond agency. *Sociological Theory, 19*(1), 24–40.

García Márquez, G. (1982). *The solitude of Latin America.* Nobel Lecture. https://www.nobelprize.org/prizes/literature/1982/marquez/lecture/.

Gauntlett, D., & Hill, A. (1999). *TV living: Television, culture and everyday life.* New York: Routledge.

Gayol, S. (1999). Conversaciones y desafios en los cafes de Buenos Aires. In F. Devoto & Marta Madero (Eds.), *Historia de la Vida Privada en Argentina*, Tomo II, *La Argentina Plural: 1870-1930* (pp. 47–69). Buenos Aires: Taurus.

Gayol, S. (2000). *Sociabilidad en Buenos Aires. Hombres, honor y cafés: 1862–1910.* Buenos Aires: Signo.

Gergen, K. (1992). *The saturated self: Dilemmas of identity in contemporary life.* New York: Basic Books.

Giddens, A. (1979). *Central problems in social theory: Action, structure, and contradiction in social analysis.* London: Macmillan.

Giddens, A. (1984). *The constitution of society: Outline of the theory of structuration.* Berkeley: University of California Press.

Gil de Zúñiga, H., Weeks, B., & Ardèvol-Abreu, A. (2017). Effects of the news-finds-me perception in communication: Social media use implications for news seeking and learning about politics. *Journal of Computer-Mediated Communication, 22*(3), 105–123.

Gillespie, T. (2018). *Custodians of the internet: Platforms, content moderation, and the hidden decisions that shape social media.* New Haven, CT: Yale University Press.

Gitlin, T. (2007 [2002]). *Media unlimited: How the torrent of images and sounds overwhelms our lives.* New York: Holt.

Gleick, J. (2011). *The information: A history, a theory, a flood.* New York: Pantheon.

González Bernaldo, P. (1999). Vida privada y vínculos comunitarios: formas de sociabilidad popular en Buenos Aires, primera mitad del siglo XIX. In F. Devoto &Marta Madero (Eds.), *Historia de la Vida Privada en Argentina*, Tomo I, *País antiguo. De la colonia a 1870* (pp. 147–167). Buenos Aires: Taurus.

González Bombal, I. (2002). Sociabilidad en clases medias en descenso: Experiencias en el Trueque. In L. Beccaria, S. Feldman, I. González Bombal, G. Kessler, M. Murmis, & M. Svampa (Eds.), *Sociedad y Sociabilidad en la Argentina de los 90* (p. 97–136). Buenos Aires: Biblos.

Graber, D. (1984). *Processing the news: How people tame the information tide*, 2nd ed. White Plains, NY: Longman.

Gray, J. (2017). Reviving audience studies. *Critical Studies in Media Communication, 34*, 79–83.

Grinberg, N., Joseph, K., Friedland, L., Swire-Thompson, B., & Lazer, D. (2019). Fake news on Twitter during the 2016 US presidential election. *Science 363*, 374–378.

Gutierrez, L., & Romero, L. A. (1995). *Sectores populares, cultura y política: Buenos Aires en la entreguerra*. Buenos Aires: Sudamericana.

Halfmann, A., & Rieger, D. (2019). Permanently on call: The effects of social pressure on smartphone users' self-control, need satisfaction, and well-being. *Journal of Computer-Mediated Communication, 24*, 165–181.

Hall, A., & Walton, G. (2004). Information overload within the health care system: A literature review. *Health Information and Libraries Journal, 21*(2):102–108.

Hall, J. (2017). The experience of mobile entrapment in daily life. *Journal of Media Psychology, 29*, 148–158.

Hall, S. (1980). Encoding/decoding. In S. Hall, D. Hobson, A. Lowe, & P. Willis (Eds.), *Culture, media, language* (pp. 128–138). London: Hutchinson.

Hampton, K. N. (2016). Persistent and pervasive community: New communication technologies and the future of community. *American Behavioral Scientist, 60*, 101–124.

Hampton, Keith, & Wellman, Barry. (2003). Neighboring in Netville: How the Internet supports community and social capital in a wired suburb. *City and Community, 2*, 277–311.

Hancock, J., Birnholtz, J., Bazarova, N., Guillory, J., Perlin, J., & Amos, B. (2009, April). Butler lies: Awareness, deception and design. In *Proceedings of the SIGCHI Conference on Human Factors in Computing Systems* (ACM) (pp. 517–526).

Haraway, D. (1985 [1991]). *Simians, cyborgs and women: The reinvention of nature*. New York: Routledge.

Hargittai, E., Neuman, W. R., & Curry, O. (2012). Taming the information tide: Perceptions of information overload in the American home. *The Information Society, 28*(3), 161–173.

Hasell, A., & Weeks, B. E. (2016). Partisan provocation: The role of partisan news use and emotional responses in political information sharing in social media. *Human Communication Research, 42*(4), 641–661.

Herbig, P., & Kramer, H. (1994). The effect of information overload on the innovation choice process. *Journal of Consumer Marketing, 11*, 45–54.

Hermida, A. (2010). Twittering the news: The emergence of ambient journalism. *Journalism Practice, 4*, 297–308.

Hermida, A. (2014). *Tell everyone: Why we share and why it matters*. Toronto: Doubleday Canada.

Hiltz, S., & Turoff, M. (1985). Structuring computer-mediated communication systems to avoid information overload. *Communications of the ACM, 28*, 680–689.

Hmielowski, J., Holbert, R. L., & Lee. J. (2011). Predicting the consumption of political TV satire: Affinity for political humor, The Daily Show, and The Colbert Report. *Communication Monographs, 78*, 96–114.

Holton, A., & Chyi, H. (2012). News and the overloaded consumer: Factors influencing information overload among news consumers. *Cyberpsychology, Behavior and Social Networking, 15*(11), 619–624.

Horrigan, J. (2016, December 7). *Information overload*. Pew Research Center. https://www.pewinternet.org/2016/12/07/information-overload/.

Hu, H., & Lai, V. (2013). Cognitive-based evaluation of consumption fads: An analytical approach. *Decision Support Systems, 56*, 83–91.

Humphreys, L. (2018). *The qualified self: Social media and the accounting of everyday life*. Cambridge, MA: MIT Press.

Hunt, R., & Newman, R. (1997). Medical knowledge overload: A disturbing trend for physicians. *Health Care Management Review, 22,* 70–75.

Hutchins, E. (1995). *Cognition in the wild.* Cambridge, MA: MIT Press.

Instituto Verificador de Circulaciones. (2020). *Boletín Xpress,* Julio 2020. https://www.ivc.org.ar/boletin-xpress/2020-07.pdf.

Internet Live Stats. (2020). http://www.internetlivestats.com/one-second/#tweets-band.

Internet World Stats. (2018). Internet usage and population in South America. https://www.internetworldstats.com/stats15.htm.

Jacoby, J. (1984). Perspectives on information overload. *Journal of Consumer Research, 10,* 432–436.

Jacoby, J., Speller, D., & Berning, C. (1974). Brand choice behavior as a function of information load: Replication and extension. *Journal of Consumer Research, 1,* 33–43.

Jansson, A. (2015). The molding of mediatization: The stratified indispensability of media in close relationships. *Communications, 40,* 379–401.

Jasanoff, S. (2020, August 25). Ignorance is bliss: COVID-19 and the politics of knowledge. Presentation made at the Institute for the Arts and Humanities, University of North Carolina at Chapel Hill. https://www.youtube.com/watch?v=i3uG3JWkTOI.

Jenkins, H. (1992). *Textual poachers: Television fans and participatory culture.* New York: Routledge.

Jenkins, H. (2006). *Convergence culture: Where old and new media collide.* New York: New York University Press.

Jenner, M. (2016). Is this TVIV? On Netflix, TVIII and binge-watching. *New Media & Society, 18,* 257–273.

Jensen, K. B. (1990). The politics of polysemy: Television news, everyday consciousness and political action. *Media, Culture & Society, 12,* 57–77.

Ji, Q., Ha, L., & Sypher, U. (2014). The role of news media use and demographic characteristics in the prediction of information overload. *International Journal of Communication, 8,* 699–714.

Jones, Q., Ravid, G., & Rafaeli, S. (2004). Information overload and the message dynamics of online interaction spaces: A theoretical model and empirical exploration. *Information Systems Research, 15,* 194–210.

JustWatch. (2020). https://www.justwatch.com/us.

Karapanos, E., Teixeira, P., & Gouveia, R. (2016). Need fulfillment and experiences on social media: A case on Facebook and WhatsApp. *Computers in Human Behavior, 55,* 888–897.

Karr-Wisniewski, P., & Lu, Y. (2010). When more is too much: Operationalizing technology overload and exploring its impact on knowledge worker productivity. *Computers in Human Behavior, 26*(5), 1061–1072.

Katz, J., & Aakhus, M. (2002). *Perpetual contact: Mobile communication, private talk, public performance.* Cambridge: Cambridge University Press.

Katz, V. S. (2010). How children of immigrants use media to connect their families to the community. *Journal of Children and Media, 4,* 298–315.

Keane, J. (2013). *Democracy and media decadence.* Cambridge: Cambridge University Press.

Kemp, S. (2018). Digital 2018: Argentina. Dataportal. https://datareportal.com/reports/digital-2018-argentina?rq=Argentina.

Kim, S. (2016). A repertoire approach to cross-platform media use behavior. *New Media & Society, 18*(3), 353–372.

Kiousis, S. (2001). Public trust or mistrust? Perceptions of media credibility in the information age. *Mass Communication & Society, 4*, 381–403.

Klapp, O. (1986). *Overload and boredom: Essays on the quality of life in the information society.* New York: Greenwood Press.

Kline, R. (2000). *Consumers in the country: Technology and social change in rural America.* Baltimore, MD: Johns Hopkins University Press.

Kline, R., & Pinch, T. (1996). Users as agents of technological change: The social construction of the automobile in the rural United States. *Technology and Culture, 37*(4), 763–795.

Klingberg, T. (2008). *The overflowing brain: Information overload and the limits of working memory.* New York: Oxford University Press.

Knobloch-Westerwick, S., Mothes, C., & Polavin, N. (2017). Confirmation bias, ingroup bias, and negativity bias in selective exposure to political information. *Communication Research, 47*, 104–124.

Kobayashi, T., Boase, J., Suzuki, T., & Suzuki, T. (2015). Emerging from the cocoon? Revisiting the tele-cocooning hypothesis in the smartphone era. *Journal of Computer-Mediated Communication, 20*, 330–345.

Kompare, D. (2006). Publishing flow: DVD box sets and the reconception of television. *Television & New Media, 7*, 335–360.

Krajina, Z., Moores, S., & Morley, D. (2014). Non-media-centric media studies: A cross-generational conversation. *European Journal of Cultural Studies, 17*, 682–700.

Krantz-Kent, R. (2018). Television, capturing America's attention at prime time and beyond. *U.S. Bureau of Labor Statistics beyond the Numbers, 7*(14), 1–11.

Kraut, R., Patterson, M., Lundmark, V., Kiesler, S., Mukophadhyay, T., & Scherlis, W. (1998). Internet paradox: A social technology that reduces social involvement and psychological well-being? *American Psychologist, 53*, 1017–1031.

Ksiazek, T. B., Malthouse, E. C., & Webster, J. G. (2010). News-seekers and avoiders: Exploring patterns of total news consumption across media and the relationship to civic participation. *Journal of Broadcasting and Electronic Media, 54*, 551–568.

Lakoff, G., & Johnson, M. (1980). *Metaphors we live by.* Chicago: University of Chicago Press.

Latour, B. (1987). *Science in action: How to follow scientists and engineers through society.* Cambridge, MA: Harvard University Press.

Lauf, E. (2001). The vanishing young reader: Sociodemographic determinants of newspaper use as a source of political information in Europe, 1980–98. *European Journal of Communication, 16*, 233–243.

Lecheler, S., Bos, L., & Vliegenthart, R. (2015). The mediating role of emotions: News framing effects on opinions about immigration. *Journalism & Mass Communication Quarterly, 92*, 812–838.

Lee, A., Son, S., & Kim, K. (2016). Information and communication technology overload and social networking service fatigue: A stress perspective. *Computers in Human Behavior, 55*(A), 51–61.

Lee, B., & Lee, W. (2004). The effect of information overload on consumer choice quality in an on-line environment. *Psychology and Marketing, 21*(3), 159–183.

Lee, S., Lindsey, N., & Kim, K. (2017). The effects of news consumption via social media and news information overload on perceptions of journalistic norms and practices. *Computers in Human Behavior, 75*, 254–263.

Levitin, D. (2014). *The organized mind: Thinking straight in the age of information overload*. New York: Penguin.

Li, C.-Y. (2017). Why do online consumers experience information overload? An extension of communication theory. Journal of Information Science, 43(6), 835–851. https://doi.org/10.1177/0165551516670096

Licoppe, C. (2004). "Connected" presence: The emergence of a new repertoire for managing social relationships in a changing communication technoscape. *Environment and Planning D: Society and Space, 22*(1), 135–156.

Liebes, T., & Katz, E. (1990). *The export of meaning: Cross-cultural readings of Dallas*. Cambridge: Polity Press.

Ling, R. (2012). *Taken for grantedness: The embedding of mobile communication into society*. Cambridge, MA: MIT Press.

Ling, R. (2016). Soft coercion: Reciprocal expectations of availability in the use of mobile communication. *First Monday, 21*(9).

Litt, E. (2012). Knock, knock. Who's there? The imagined audience. *Journal of Broadcasting & Electronic Media, 56*, 330–345.

Litt, E., Spottswood, E., Birnholtz, J., Hancock, J. T., Smith, M. E., & Reynolds, L. (2014). Awkward encounters of an "other" kind: Collective self-presentation and face threat on Facebook. In *Proceedings of the 17th ACM Conference on Computer Supported Cooperative Work & Social Computing* (pp. 449–460).

Livingstone, S. (2008). Taking risky opportunities in youthful content creation: Teenagers' use of social networking sites for intimacy, privacy and self-expression. *New Media & Society, 10*(3), 393–411.

Livingstone, S. (2009). Youthful experts. In S. Livingstone (Ed.), *Children and the internet* (pp. 33–62). Malden, MA: Polity Press.

Livingstone, S. (2019). Audiences in an age of datafication: Critical questions for media research. *Television & New Media, 20*, 170–183.

Livingstone, S., Van Couvering, E., & Thumim, N. (2005). *Adult media literacy: A review of the research literature*. London: Department of Media and Communications, London School of Economics.

Livio, O., & Cohen, J. (2016). "Fool me once, shame on you": Direct personal experience and media trust. *Journalism, 19*, 684–698.

Lizardo, O., & Skiles, S. (2015). Musical taste and patterns of symbolic exclusion in the United States 1993-2012: Generational dynamics of differentiation and continuity. *Poetics, 53*, 9–21.

Lull, J. (1982). How families select television programs: A mass-observational study. *Journal of Broadcasting & Electronic Media, 26*, 801–811.

Mackay, H., & Gillespie, G. (1992). Extending the social shaping of technology approach: Ideology and appropriation. *Social Studies of Science, 22*(4), 685–716.

Madianou, M. (2014). Smartphones as polymedia. *Journal of Computer-Mediated Communication, 19*(3), 667–680.

Madianou, M., & Miller, D. (2013). Polymedia: Towards a new theory of digital media in interpersonal communication. *International Journal of Cultural Studies, 16*(2), 169–187.

Maes, P. (1994). Agents that reduce work and information overload. *Communications of the ACM, 37*(7), 30–40.

Malthouse, E., & Calder, R. (2006). Demographics of newspaper readership: Predictors and patterns of U.S. consumption. *Journal of Media Business Studies, 3*, 1–18.

Mannheim, K. (1952 [1927]). The problem of generations. In P. Kecskemeti (Ed.), *Karl Mannheim: Essays* (pp. 276–322). New York: Routledge.

Martin, V. B. (2008). Attending the news: A grounded theory about a daily regimen. *Journalism, 9,* 76–94.

Marwick, A. E., & Boyd, D. (2011). I tweet honestly, I tweet passionately: Twitter users, context collapse, and the imagined audience. *New Media & Society, 13,* 114–133.

Matsa, K. (2018, January 5). Fewer Americans rely on TV news; what type they watch varies by who they are. Pew Research Center. https://www.pewresearch.org/fact-tank/2018/01/05/fewer-americans-rely-on-tv-news-what-type-they-watch-varies-by-who-they-are/.

McPherson, M., Smith-Lovin, L., & Brashears, M. E. (2006). Social isolation in America: Changes in core discussion networks over two decades. *American Sociological Review, 71,* 353–375.

Meier, R. (1962). *A communications theory of urban growth.* Cambridge, MA: MIT Press.

Meier, R. (1963). Communications overload: Proposals from the study of a university library. *Administrative Science Quarterly, 7,* 521–544.

Mesche, J. (2018, January 28). Argentina's richest 10% control more wealth than 60% of the country. *Buenos Aires Times.* https://www.batimes.com.ar/news/argentina/argentinas-richest-10-control-more-wealth-than-60-of-the-country.phtml.

Meyrowitz, J. (1986). *No sense of place: The impact of electronic media on social behavior.* New York: Oxford University Press.

Míguez, E. (1999). Familias de clase media: la formación de un modelo. In F. Devoto & Marta Madero (Eds.), *Historia de la Vida Privada en Argentina,* Tomo II, *La Argentina Plural: 1870–1930* (pp. 21–45). Buenos Aires: Taurus.

Milgram, S. (1970). The experience of living in the cities. *Science, 167,* 1461–1468.

Miller, J. (1956). The magical number seven plus or minus two: Some limits on our capacity for processing information. *Psychological Review, 63,* 81–97.

Misra, S., & Stokols, D. (2012). Psychological and health outcomes of perceived information overload. *Environment and Behavior, 44*(6), 737–759.

Mitchelstein, E., Boczkowski, P., Hayashi, K., Tenenboim-Weinblat, K., Villi, M., & Kligler-Vilenchik, N. (2020). Intentionality as a continuum: A conceptual approach to incidental news consumption. *Journalism, 21*(8), 1136–1153.https://doi.org/10.1177/1464884920915355.

Moody, R. (2020, July 20). Netflix subscribers and revenue by country. *Comparitech.* https://www.comparitech.com/tv-streaming/netflix-subscribers/.

Morley, D. (1980). *The "nationwide" audience. Structure and decoding.* London: British Film Institute.

Morley, D. (2006). *Media, modernity and technology: The geography of the new.* New York: Routledge.

Myers, J. (1999). Una revolucion en las costumbres: Las nuevas formas de sociabilidad de la elite porteña, 1800–1860. In F. Devoto & Marta Madero (Eds.), *Historia de la Vida Privada en Argentina,* Tomo I, *País antiguo. De la colonia a 1870* (pp. 111–145). Buenos Aires: Taurus.

Navarro, G. (2020b, July 20). Number of mobile phone internet users in Argentina from 2015 to 2025. *Statista.* https://www-statista-com.turing.library.northwestern.edu/statistics/244982/number-of-mobile-internet-user-in-argentina/.

Navarro, J. (2020a, July 20). Argentina: Number of Facebook users 2017–2025. *Statista.* https://www.statista.com/statistics/282333/number-of-facebook-users-in-argentina/.

Neff, G., & Stark, D. (2004). Permanently beta: Responsive organization in the Internet era. In P. Howard & S. Jones (Eds.), *Society online: The internet in context* (pp. 173–188). Thousand Oaks, CA: Sage.

Negroponte, N. (1996). *Being digital*. New York: Alfred Knopf.

Nelissen, S., & Van den Bulck, J. (2018). When digital natives instruct digital immigrants: Active guidance of parental media use by children and conflict in the family. *Information, Communication & Society, 21*, 375–387.

Newman, N., Fletcher, R., Schulz, A., Andi, S., & Nielsen, R. (2020). *Reuters Institute Digital News Report 2020*. Oxford: Reuters Institute for the Study of Journalism, University of Oxford. https://reutersinstitute.politics.ox.ac.uk/sites/default/files/2020-06/DNR_2020_FINAL.pdf.

Newman, R., Fletcher, R., Kalogeropoulos, A., Levy, D., & Nielsen, R. (2017). *Reuters Institute Digital News Report 2017*. Reuters Institute for the Study of Journalism, University of Oxford. https://reutersinstitute.politics.ox.ac.uk/sites/default/files/Digital%20News%20Report%202017%20web_0.pdf.

O'Reilly, C. (1980). Individuals and information overload in organizations: Is more necessarily better? *Academy of Management Journal, 23*, 684–696.

OECD Economic Surveys. (2017). Argentina: Multi-dimensional economic survey. http://www.oecd.org/countries/argentina/Argentina-2017-OECD-economic-survey-overview.pdf.

Oeldorf-Hirsch, A., Birnholtz, J., & Hancock, J. T. (2017). Your post is embarrassing me: Face threats, identity, and the audience on Facebook. *Computers in Human Behavior, 73*, 92–99.

Olsen, K. A., Sochats, K., & Williams, J. (1998). Full text searching and information overload. *Intelligent Information and Library Review, 30*, 105–122.

Olsson, T., Samuelsson, U., & Viscovi, D. (2019). Resources and repertoires: Elderly online practices. *European Journal of Communication, 34*, 38–56.

Orben, A. (2020). The Sisyphean cycle of technology panics. *Perspectives on Psychological Science*, 1–15. https://doi.org/10.1177/1745691620919372.

Oudshoorn, N., & Pinch, T. (Eds.). (2003). *How users matter: The co-construction of users and technology*. Cambridge, MA: MIT Press.

Palmgreen, P., Wenner, L., & Rayburn II, J. D. (1980). Relations between gratifications sought and obtained: A study of television news. *Communication Research, 7*, 161–192.

Papacharissi, Z. (2009). The virtual geographies of social networks: A comparative analysis of Facebook, LinkedIn and ASmallWorld. *New Media & Society, 11*(1–2), 199–220.

Papacharissi, Z. (2015). *Affective publics: Sentiment, technology, and politics*. Oxford: Oxford University Press.

Papacharissi, Z., & de Fatima Oliveira, M. (2012). Affective news and networked publics: The rhythms of news storytelling on #Egypt. *Journal of Communication, 62*, 266–282.

Peng, Y. (2016). Student migration and polymedia: Mainland Chinese students' communication media use in Hong Kong. *Journal of Ethnic and Migration Studies, 42*(14), 2395–2412.

Pennington, R., & Tuttle, B. 2007. The effects of information overload on software project risk assessment. *Decision Sciences, 38*(3), 489–526.

Pink, S., Sumartojo, S., Lupton, D., & Heyes La Bond, C. (2017). Mundane data: The routines, contingencies and accomplishments of digital living. *Big Data & Society*. https://doi.org/10.1177/2053951717700924.

Pittman, M., & Reich, B. (2016). Social media and loneliness: Why an Instagram picture may be worth more than a thousand Twitter words. *Computers in Human Behavior*, *62*, 155–167.

Quan-Haase, A., & Young, A. L. (2010). Uses and gratifications of social media: A comparison of Facebook and instant messaging. *Bulletin of Science, Technology & Society*, *30*, 350–361.

Quan-Haase, A., Williams, C., Kicevski, M., Elueze, I., & Wellman, B. (2018). Dividing the grey divide: Deconstructing myths about older adults' online activities, skills, and attitudes. *American Behavioral Scientist*, *62*(9), 1207–1228.

Radway, J. (1984). *Reading the romance: Women, patriarchy, and popular literature*. Chapel Hill: University of North Carolina Press.

Rainie, L., & Wellman, B. (2012). *Networked: The new social operating system*. Cambridge, MA: MIT Press.

Renninger, B. J. (2015). "Where I can be myself... where I can speak my mind": Networked counterpublics in a polymedia environment. *New Media & Society*, *17*(9), 1513–1529.

Robinson, J. P., & Levy, M. (1986). Interpersonal communication and news comprehension. *Public Opinion Quarterly*, *50*, 160–175.

Rodriguez, A. (2019, January 1). Keeping up with Netflix originals is basically a part-time job now. *Quartz*. https://qz.com/1505030/keeping-up-with-netflix-originals-is-basically-a-part-time-job-now/.

Roetzel, P. (2018). Information overload in the information age: A review of the literature from business administration, business psychology, and related disciplines with a bibliometric approach and framework development. *Business Research*. DOI: https://doi.org/10.1007/s40685-018-0069-z.

Romero, L. A. (2002 [1994]). *A history of Argentina in the twentieth century* (translated by James Brennan). University Park: Pennsylvania State University Press.

Rudd, J., & Rudd, M. (1986). Coping with information load: User strategies and implications for librarians. *College & Research Libraries*, *47*, 315–322.

Saunders, C., Wiener, M., Klett, S., & Sprenger, S. (2017). The impact of mental representations on ICT-related overload in the use of mobile phones. *Journal of Management Information Systems*, *34*(3), 803–825.

Savage, M., & Gayo, M. (2011). Unravelling the omnivore: A field analysis of contemporary musical taste in the United Kingdom. *Poetics*, *39*, 337–357.

Savolainen, R. (2007). Filtering and withdrawing: Strategies for coping with information overload in everyday contexts. *Journal of Information Science*, *33*(5), 611–621.

Schick, A., Gordon, L., & Haka, S. (1990). Information overload: A temporal approach. *Accounting Organizations and Society*, *15*, 199–220.

Schmitt, J., Debbelt, C., & Schneider, F. (2018). Too much information? Predictors of information overload in the context of online news exposure. *Information, Communication & Society*, *21*, 1151–1167.

Schultze, U., & Vandenbosch, B. (1998). Information overload in a groupware environment: Now you see it, now you don't. *Journal of Organizational Computing and Electronic Commerce*, *8*(2), 127–148.

Schwartz, B. (2004). *The paradox of choice: Why more is less*. New York: Ecco.

Sheller, M. (2015). News now: Interface, ambience, flow, and the disruptive spatio-temporalities of mobile news media. *Journalism Studies*, *16*, 12–26.

Shenk, D. (1997). *Data smog: Surviving the information glut*. New York: Harper Collins.

Shim, H., & Kim, K. (2018). An exploration of the motivations for binge-watching and the role of individual differences. *Computers in Human Behavior, 82,* 94–100.

Silverstone, R. (1994). *Television and everyday life.* London: Routledge.

SimilarWeb. (2020). Clarin.com: October 2020 overview. https://www.similarweb.com/website/clarin.com/.

SimilarWeb. (2020a). Cnn.com Traffic Overview August 2020. https://www.similarweb.com/website/cnn.com/#overview.

SimilarWeb. (2020a). Infobae.com Traffic Overview August 2020. https://www.similarweb.com/website/infobae.com/#overview.

Simmel, G. (1903) [1950]. The metropolis and mental life. In K. Wolff (Ed.), *The sociology of Georg Simmel* (pp. 409–424). Glencoe, IL: Free Press.

Simon, H. A. 1971. Designing organizations for an information-rich world. In M. Greenberger (Ed.), *Computers, communication, and the public interest* (pp. 37–72). Baltimore, MD: Johns Hopkins University Press.

Sistema de Información Cultural de la Argentina. (2017). *Encuesta de Consumos Culturales 2017.* Ciudad Autónoma de Buenos Aires, Argentina: Ministerio de Cultura, Presidencia de la Nación.

Sistema Nacional de Información Cultural de la Argentina. (2018). Encuesta Nacional de Consumos Culturales. https://encuestadeconsumo.sinca.gob.ar/.

Smith, C. (2019, September 6). 65 amazing WhatsApp statistics and facts (2019) | By the numbers. *DMR.* https://expandedramblings.com/index.php/whatsapp-statistics/.

Statista. (2020). Global TV sales unit from 2016 to 2019 in millions. https://www.statista.com/statistics/760281/global-tv-set-unit-sales/.

Steiner, E., & Xu, K. (2020). Binge-watching motivates change: Uses and gratifications of streaming video viewers challenge traditional TV research. *Convergence, 26,* 82–101.

Suchman, L. (1987). *Plans and situated actions: The problem of human-machine communication.* Cambridge: Cambridge University Press.

Swar, B., Hameed, T., & Reychav, I. (2017). Information overload, psychological ill-being, and behavioral intention to continue online healthcare information search. *Computers in Human Behavior, 70,* 416–425.

Tampubolon, G. (2008). Revisiting omnivores in America circa 1990s: The exclusiveness of omnivores? *Poetics, 36,* 243–264.

Tandoc Jr., E. (2019). Tell me who your sources are: Perceptions of news credibility on social media. *Journalism Practice, 13,* 178–190.

Taneja, H., & Viswanathan, V. (2014). Still glued to the box? Television viewing explained in a multi-platform age integrating individual and situational predictors. *International Journal of Communication, 8,* 2134–2159.

Taneja, H., Webster, J. G., Malthouse, E. C., & Ksiazek, T. B. (2012). Media consumption across platforms: Identifying user-defined repertoires. *New Media & Society, 14*(6), 951–968.

Terrasa, R. (2019, January 6). De Bolsonaro a Vox: Cómo WhatsApp ha llegado a ser el arma más eficaz de propaganda política. *El Mundo.*

Thibault, G. (2015). Streaming: A media hydrography of televisual flows. *VIEW Journal of European Television History and Culture, 4,* 110–119.

Thomas, W., & Thomas, D. (1928). *The child in America: Behavior problems and programs.* New York: Knopf.

Thurman, N., & Fletcher, R. (2019). Has digital distribution rejuvenated readership? *Journalism Studies, 20,* 542–562.

Toff, B., & Nielsen, R. (2018). "I just Google it": Folk theories of distributed discovery. *Journal of Communication, 68*, 636–657.

Toff, B., & Palmer, R. A. (2019). Explaining the gender gap in news avoidance: "News-is-for-men" perceptions and the burdens of caretaking. *Journalism Studies, 20*, 1563–1579.

Trieu, P., Bayer, J. B., Ellison, N. B., Schoenebeck, S., & Falk, E. (2019). Who likes to be reachable? Availability preferences, weak ties, and bridging social capital. *Information, Communication & Society, 22*(8), 1096–1111.

Trilling, D., & Schoenbach, K. (2012). Skipping current affairs: The non-users of online and offline news. *European Journal of Communication, 28*, 35–51.

Tripp, L., & Herr-Stephenson, R. (2009). Making access meaningful: Latino young people using digital media at home and at school. *Journal of Computer-Mediated Communication, 14*, 1190–1207.

Trost, J. (1986). Statistically nonrepresentative stratified sampling: A sampling technique for qualitative studies. *Qualitative Sociology, 9*(1), 54–57.

Tse, Y. (2016). Television's changing role in social togetherness in the personalized online consumption of foreign TV. *New Media & Society, 18*, 1547–1562.

Tung, L. (2017, July 27). WhatsApp: Now one billion people send 55 billion messages per day. *ZDNet*. https://www.zdnet.com/article/whatsapp-now-one-billion-people-send-55-billion-messages-per-day/.

Turkle, S. (2015). *Reclaiming conversation: The power of talk in a digital age*. New York: Penguin.

Turkle, S. (2017 [2012]). *Alone together: Why we expect more from technology and less from each other*. New York: Basic Books.

Turner, G. (2019). Television studies, we need to talk about "binge-watching." *Television & New Media*, https://doi.org/10.1177/1527476419877041.

Uricchio, W. (2009). The future of a medium once known as television. In P. Snickars, & P. Vonderau (Eds.), *The youtube reader* (pp. 24–39). Stockholm: National Library of Sweden.

Vaidhyanathan, S. (2018). *Antisocial media: How Facebook disconnects us and undermines democracy*. New York: Oxford University Press.

Valenzuela, S., Halpern, D., Katz, J., & Miranda, J. (2019). The paradox of participation versus misinformation: Social media, political engagement, and the spread of misinformation. *Digital Journalism*, DOI: 10.1080/21670811.2019.1623701.

Valeriani, A., & Vaccari, C. (2016). Accidental exposure to politics on social media as online participation equalizer in Germany, Italy, and the United Kingdom. *New Media & Society, 18*, 1857–1874.

Van Dijck, J., Poell, T., & de Waal, M. (2018). *The platform society: Public values in a connective world*. New York: Oxford University Press.

van Dijck. J. (2013). *The culture of connectivity: A critical history of social media*. New York: Oxford University Press.

Van Zandt, T. (2004). Information overload in a network of targeted communication. *RAND Journal of Economics, 35*(3), 542–560.

Vargo, C., Guo, L., & Amazeen, M. (2018). The agenda-setting power of fake news: A big data analysis of the online media landscape from 2014 to 2016. *New Media & Society, 20*, 2028–2049.

Vollmann, T. (1991). Cutting the Gordian knot of misguided performance measurement. *Industrial Management & Data Systems, 1*, 24–26.

Vosoughi, S., Roy, D., & Aral, S. (2018). The spread of true and false news online. *Science, 359*, 1146–1151.

Wagner, C., & Boczkowski, P. (2019a). Angry, frustrated, and overwhelmed: Emotional responses to news about president Trump. *Journalism.* https://doi.org/10.1177/1464884919878545.

Wagner, C., & Boczkowski, P. (2019b). The reception of fake news: The interpretations and practices that shape the encounter of perceived misinformation. *Digital Journalism, 7*, 870–885.

Wahl-Jorgensen, K. (2019). *Emotions, media and politics.* Cambridge, UK: Polity Press.

Waisbord, S. (2019). *Communication: A post-discipline.* Cambridge, UK: Polity Press.

Wang, Y. (2008). Agency: The internal split of structure. *Sociological Forum, 23*(3), 481–502.

Washingtonpost.com. (2020, August 27). In 1,316 days, President Trump has made 22,247 false or misleading claims. https://www.washingtonpost.com/graphics/politics/trump-claims-database/?itid=lk_inline_manual_4.

Watson, A. (2019, August 9). Tickets sold at the North American box office from 1980 to 2018. *Statista.* https://www.statista.com/statistics/187073/tickets-sold-at-the-north-american-box-office-since-1980/.

We Are Social. (2020). *Global Digital Report 2019.* https://wearesocial.com/global-digital-report-2019.

Webster, J. (1998). The audience. *Journal of Broadcasting & Electronic Media, 42*, 190–207.

Webster, J. G. (2011). The duality of media: A structurational theory of public attention. *Communication Theory, 21*(1), 43–66.

Webster, J., & Phalen, P. (1997). *The mass audience: Rediscovering the dominant model.* Mahwah, NJ: Lawrence Erlbaum.

Weeks, B., Lane, D., Kim, D., Lee, S., & Kwak, N. (2017). Incidental exposure, selective exposure, and political information sharing: Integrating online exposure patterns and expression on social media. *Journal of Computer-Mediated Communication, 22*, 363–379.

Wellmon, C. (2015). *Organizing enlightenment: Information overload and the invention of the modern research university.* Baltimore, MD: Johns Hopkins University Press.

Wikipedia. (2020a). *List of best-selling mobile phones.* https://en.wikipedia.org/wiki/List_of_best-selling_mobile_phones.

Wikipedia. (2020b). *Market share of personal computer vendors.* https://en.wikipedia.org/wiki/Market_share_of_personal_computer_vendors.

Wikipedia. (2020c). Netflix. https://en.wikipedia.org/wiki/Netflix.

Wikipedia. (2020d). Television in Argentina. https://en.wikipedia.org/wiki/Television_in_Argentina.

Williams, R. (1974). *Television: Technology and cultural form.* Hanover, NH: Wesleyan University Press.

Winter, B. (2017, November 17). These guys were Argentina at its best. *Americas Quarterly.* https://americasquarterly.org/article/these-guys-were-argentina-at-its-best/.

Wolf, C., & Schnauber, A. (2015). News consumption in the mobile era: The role of mobile devices and traditional journalism's content within the user's information repertoire. *Digital Journalism, 3*, 759–776.

World Bank. (2020a). Inflation, GDP deflator (annual %)—Argentina, United States. https://data.worldbank.org/indicator/NY.GDP.DEFL.KD.ZG?end=2019&locations=AR-US&start=1961.

World Bank. (2020b). GDP per capita, PPP (current international $)—Argentina, United States. https://data.worldbank.org/indicator/NY.GDP.PCAP.PP.CD?end=2019&locations=AR-US&start=2016.

Wurman, R. (2001). *Information anxiety*, vol. 2. Indianapolis, IN: Macmillan.

Wyatt, S. (2003). Non-users also matter: The construction of users and non-users of the Internet. In N. Oudshoorn & T. J. Pinch (Eds.), *How users matter: The co-construction of users and technology* (pp. 67–79). Cambridge, MA: MIT Press.

Yadamsuren, B., & Erdelez, S. (2017). *Incidental exposure to online news*. Chapel Hill, NC: Morgan & Claypool.

York, C. (2013). Overloaded by the news: Effects of news exposure and enjoyment on reporting information overload. *Communication Research Reports, 30*, 282–292.

Index

For the benefit of digital users, indexed terms that span two pages (e.g., 52–53) may, on occasion, appear on only one of those pages.

Figures are indicated by *f* following the page number